The Five Principles of Middle Way Philosophy

Middle Way Philosophy

Series Editor: **Robert M. Ellis**, Middle Way Society

Middle Way Philosophy is a cross-disciplinary project developed by Robert M. Ellis over more than 20 years, to develop a consistently pragmatic approach to the justification of human judgement. It follows through the implications of the Buddha's Middle Way, rejecting absolute beliefs of a negative as well as a positive type, in the light of the developing modern understandings of uncertainty, scientific method, mindfulness, embodied meaning, neuroscience, cognitive and developmental psychology, systems theory, Jungian archetypes, and democratic political practice.

Diagnosing the central problem of absolutization that interferes with the justification of human judgement, it then seeks to identify the most effective responses to that problem. It does this through the rigorous application of pragmatic philosophy, drawing on a wide variety of evidence. Overall it thus offers a detailed normative ethical philosophy based in the conditions of psychology, and an overall framework to show the relationship of a variety of practices (from mindfulness to critical thinking) to the universal goal of improving each human judgement.

Published

Absolutization: The Source of Dogma, Repression, and Conflict
Robert M. Ellis
(Volume I)

The Five Principles of Middle Way Philosophy
Living Experientially in a World of Uncertainty

Robert M. Ellis

SHEFFIELD UK   BRISTOL CT

Published by Equinox Publishing Ltd
UK: Office 415, The Workstation, 15 Paternoster Row, Sheffield, South Yorkshire S1 2BX
USA: ISD, 70 Enterprise Drive, Bristol, CT 06010

www.equinoxpub.com

First published 2023
© Robert M. Ellis 2023
All rights reserved. No part of this publication may be reproduced or transmitted in any form or by any means, electronic or mechanical, including photocopying, recording or any information storage or retrieval system, without prior permission in writing from the publishers.

British Library Cataloguing-in-Publication Data
A catalogue record for this book is available from the British Library.

ISBN-13 978 1 80050 303 8 (hardback)
978 1 80050 304 5 (paperback)
978 1 80050 305 2 (ePDF)
978 1 80050 317 5 (ePub)

Library of Congress Cataloging-in-Publication Data

Names: Ellis, Robert M., author.
Title: The five principles of middle way philosophy : living experientially in a world of uncertainty / Robert M. Ellis.
Description: Sheffield, South Yorkshire ; Bristol, CT : Equinox Publishing Ltd, [2023] | Series: Middle way philosophy ; volume II | Includes bibliographical references and index. | Summary: "This second book in the 'Middle Way Philosophy' series develops five general principles that are distinctive to the universal Middle Way as a practical response to absolutization. These begin with the consistent acknowledgement of human uncertainty (scepticism), and follow through with openness to alternative possibilities (provisionality), the importance of judging things as a matter of degree (incrementality), the clear rejection of polarised absolute claims (agnosticism) and the cultivation of cognitive and emotional states that will help us resolve conflict (integration)"-- Provided by publisher.
Identifiers: LCCN 2022041018 (print) | LCCN 2022041019 (ebook) | ISBN 9781800503038 (hardback) | ISBN 9781800503045 (paperback) | ISBN 9781800503052 (epdf) | ISBN 9781800503175 (epub)
Subjects: LCSH: Sunyata--Doctrines. | Middle Way (Buddhism) | Buddhism--Doctrines.
Classification: LCC BQ4270 .E55 2023 (print) | LCC BQ4270 (ebook) | DDC 294.3/42--dc23/eng/20221102
LC record available at https://lccn.loc.gov/2022041018
LC ebook record available at https://lccn.loc.gov/2022041019

Typeset by S.J.I. Services, New Delhi, India

Contents

List of Figures and Tables	vii
Foreword to the Middle Way Philosophy Series *Iain McGilchrist*	viii
Acknowledgements	ix
Introduction	1

1. Scepticism — 12
   a. Uncertainty, 'Knowledge', and Sceptical Argument — 12
   b. Scepticism is not Negative — 22
   c. Scepticism is not Impractical — 29
   d. Scepticism, Embodiment, and Meaningfulness — 35
   e. Scepticism is not Selective — 42
   f. Scepticism does not Threaten Meaning — 47
   g. Scepticism Applies to Values *and* Facts — 52

2. Provisionality — 56
   a. Optionality and Adaptiveness — 56
   b. Complexity and Antifragility — 64
   c. Slowness — 68
   d. Synthesis — 73
   e. Suppression — 81
   f. Probabilizing — 86
   g. Weighing up — 93

3. Incrementality — 98
   a. Systemic Continuity — 98
   b. Tipping Points — 103
   c. Practical Discontinuity — 109
   d. Continuity of Persons — 113
   e. Continuity of Time — 117
   f. Continuity of Space — 122
   g. Continuity of Training — 126

4. Agnosticism — 130
 a. Wary as Serpents — 130
 b. Even-handedness — 135
 c. Strong, not Weak, Agnosticism — 140
 d. Awareness of Appropriation and Lumping — 144
 e. Awareness of Sceptical Slippage — 151
 f. Awareness of Unholy Alliances — 157
 g. Agnosticism and Psychological Development — 162

5. Integration — 168
 a. Recognizing Conflict — 168
 b. Reframing — 175
 c. Responses to Intractability — 180
 d. Integration of Desire, Meaning, and Belief — 185
 e. Individual and Group Integration — 194
 f. Temporary Integration — 199
 g. Asymmetrical Integration — 205

6. Practice — 212
 a. The Middle Way as a Framework of Practices — 212
 b. The Threefold Practice — 217
 c. Individual Integration of Desire Practices — 221
 d. Socio-political Integration of Desire Practices — 226
 e. Individual Integration of Meaning Practices — 237
 f. Socio-political Integration of Meaning Practices — 247
 g. Individual Integration of Belief Practices — 255
 h. Socio-political Integration of Belief Practices — 270

Appendix — 274

The Old and New Middle Way Philosophy Series — 275

Bibliography — 277

Index — 284

List of Figures and Tables

Figure 1.	The Five Principles	2
Figure 2.	Mind map of sceptical practice	21
Figure 3.	Mind map of provisionality	62
Figure 4.	The two mules	75
Figure 5.	Features of incrementality: mind map	101
Figure 6.	Agnosticism: mind map	133
Figure 7.	The process of integration: flow diagram	174
Figure 8.	Eight types of context for the integration of conflict	183
Figure 9.	Some key features of integration	192
Figure 10.	The Threefold Practice in Middle Way Philosophy	216
Figure 11.	Critical thinking	257
Table 1.	Multidisciplinary justification of the Five Principles	274

Foreword to the Middle Way Philosophy Series

Iain McGilchrist

The 'Middle Way' Ellis argues for so cogently is far from being a simple compromise between existing polarities, but a departure at right angles to typical thinking in the modern Western world, which looks to me like the path to ancient wisdom.

The perception that objectivity is neither an absolute, nor any the less real for that, is central. Ellis argues for an approach that is incremental and continuously responsive to what is given, rather than abstract and absolute. This is the difference, as he notes, between the pragmatic, provisional, nuanced, never fixed position of the right hemisphere in the face of the absolutism towards which the left hemisphere always tends.

The need for certainty must inevitably lead to illusion, whether in philosophy or in the business of living, and here too Ellis makes clear – as far as I am aware for the first time – the connections between the cognitive distortions known to psychology and the fallacies identified in the process of philosophy.

This is an important, original work, that should get the widest possible hearing.

Dr Iain McGilchrist is the author of The Master and His Emissary *and* The Matter with Things, *and is a former psychiatrist.*
This foreword was originally written for the old Middle Way Philosophy series.

Acknowledgements

I would like to thank everyone who has contributed through feedback to the development of Middle Way Philosophy, and especially here to its practical articulation in terms of the Five Principles and the Threefold Practice, which are the special focus of this book. This particularly includes, but is not limited to, members of the Middle Way Society who have given helpful feedback on retreats and in other contexts over the years. These include particularly Barry Daniel, Susan Averbach, Peter Goble, Richard Flanagan, and Lenni. I'd also like to thank my wife Viryanaya for her continuing feedback and support.

Introduction

How do we live in a world of uncertainty? The first book in this Middle Way Philosophy series, *Absolutization*, was concerned with how we often ignore uncertainty and assume that we have the whole picture when we do not. This second one, however, is concerned more positively with how we can face up to uncertainty in practical judgement and avoid absolutization. In the process of doing this, too, although we may start off focused on merely avoiding errors, we create the conditions for integration – the coming together of energies in our experience that can make our lives more positively meaningful and effective.

This book explores five interlocking principles that also indicate areas of practice (**figure 1**). These begin with the practice of facing up to uncertainty itself, and culminate with the positive fruits one can expect that to bear in our experience of the process of integration. Unlike many religious, spiritual, or psychotherapeutic approaches, I am not working top-down but bottom-up. I will not start with an inflated positive ideal and then make deductions from that: such ideals can be helpful symbols of a desirable end point, but not representations of attainable targets. Nor will I start with any claims to 'knowledge' about such an end point, or of how we can attain such 'knowledge'. Rather I will begin with a thorough exploration of our *lack* of 'knowledge', and work up from there to explain the implications of taking that limitation seriously as the basis of practice.

The central metaphor and symbol for that approach is the *Middle Way*. The Middle Way is a path in the sense of a series of judgements made by an individual (and by extension, also by groups), with each judgement offering better or worse options. It is 'Middle' in the specific sense that it lies between positive and negative forms of absolutization. I capitalize it because it is a specific concept, not just any old 'middle way' in the sense of a compromise. The capitalization is not a sign of reification or metaphysics.

2   *The Five Principles of Middle Way Philosophy*

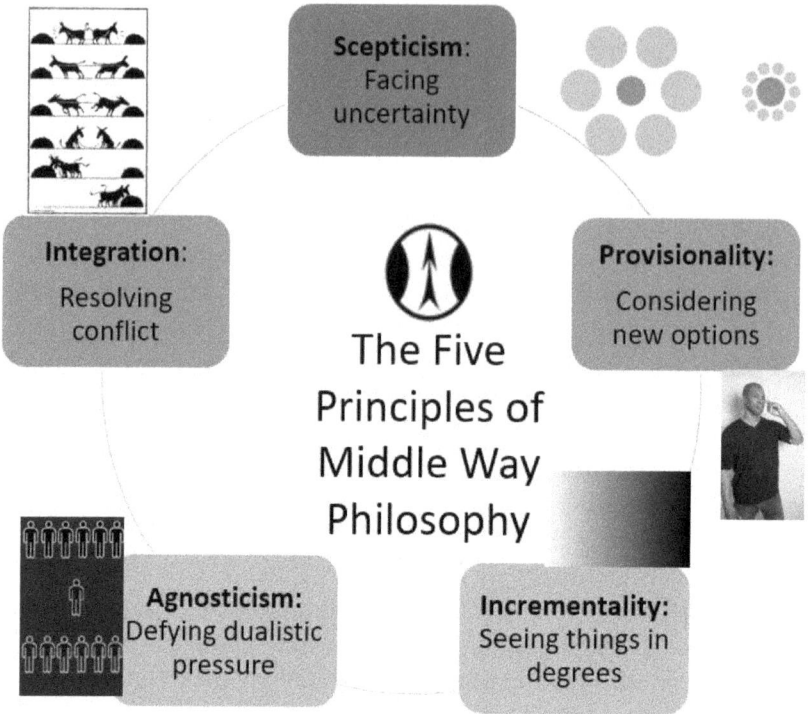

Figure 1. The Five Principles.

In *Absolutization* I explained how absolutization constrains judgement. It does this by offering only two options (the acceptance or rejection of the current belief) at a given moment of judgement, where further awareness could make us aware of many more. When we're caught up in an absolutization (for instance, the belief that that person who is talking rudely must be attacking me personally), that belief and its denial is all there is in our awareness. The positive belief absorbs all our available energy, and its opposing denial, the only possible alternative considered, is completely rejected as unthinkable. Caught up in that state, we're convinced that we 'know' the 'truth' of that situation, and anyone who contradicts us is just 'wrong'.

The Middle Way dares to remind us that this is not the only possible way of looking at things – that there is always a third alternative, if you open your mind enough to look for it. Indeed, there is not only a third alternative, but commonly a fourth, fifth, and many other alternatives. The Middle Way does not presume to tell you which of these is correct, only to point out that *there are alternatives*.

It is the Middle Way as an approach that, taken seriously, means that recognizing our lack of knowledge is not 'nihilistic' or 'relativistic'. Far from depriving us of values to live our lives by, it helps us to find them, but only *in the process of experience*, not through a shortcut substitute of adopting an absolute conceptual belief that is supposed to guarantee our values. Crucially, by recognizing that *absolute negative claims are just as absolute as positive ones*, it provides a basis for even-handedness in our treatment of absolutist and relativist positions. Absolutist positions may be associated with symbolic ideals (God, truth, etc.), but these should not be mistaken for bases of belief. On the other hand, relativist positions often offer well-justified beliefs about the conditions of our lives, but these cannot function as symbolic ideals. The Middle Way involves a navigation in which we avoid taking either the absolute or the relative as the whole story, instead building up *both* a grounded experience of motivating value *and* a realistic factual understanding of the conditions around us.

The Five Principles explored in this book build this approach from the ground up. The 'ground' here means a philosophical justification rooted in sceptical argument and brought into contact with the practical conditions of experience. The basis on which the theory that emerges needs to be tested, then, is practical. In the second half of *Absolutization*, I offered a detailed account of a set of practical criteria by which I think any response to the phenomena of absolutization need to be judged: practicality (including embodiment, responsibility, and effectiveness), universal aspiration, judgement focus, and error focus. My argument is that previous ways of addressing absolutization have not seen it as a unified phenomenon (but rather as separated phenomena like bias, metaphysics, projection, conflict, or reinforcing feedback loops). They have thus have not provided a sufficiently effective basis for addressing the interconnected conditions it creates. The Five Principles aim to fulfil those criteria for an adequate response to absolutization as a whole set of interconnected phenomena, and to demonstrate what those criteria imply in practice.

All five of the principles have developed from consideration of the questions of Western philosophy being considered in a practical context influenced by Buddhism, psychology, neuroscience, embodiment, and systems theory – the same types of sources that I drew on and synthesized in *Absolutization*. In addition, it is possible to understand these principles in terms of scientific method, or in terms of critical thinking skills. However, the principles have become so synthesized over the period in which I have developed them, that it is hard to determine any single main source for each principle. For that reason, I certainly could not present them in the same way I presented *Absolutization*, with the different kinds of sources providing starting points that help to structure the book.

However, there are some relationships with other sources that may strike the reader. The discussion of scepticism is a development of a long-standing philosophical debate – but one in which I think there have been some major misunderstandings of its implications, due to a failure to understand sceptical argument in a practical context. The discussion of provisionality will remind many of good practice in scientific method, even though it is not limited to the formal, social context in which science is practised. Incrementality connects with the philosophical discussion of vagueness – but again, given a practical context. Agnosticism will be reminiscent of discussions in the philosophy of religion, but offers a position not currently recognized in that context, and with implications that go very much further than that. Integration, finally, is very much a development of the psychotherapeutic tradition, but again, in a way that is applied far beyond the usual limits imposed on that discourse.

In all of these cases, you will misunderstand the nature and role of the principle if you approach it in a mono-disciplinary way. There is not just one discipline that determines the purpose of the principles I'm using and the way they should be assessed. Just as looking up the sources in the Buddhist Pali Canon does not give you a final account of what the 'Middle Way' is, you will not get the final word on scepticism in Sextus Empiricus or in David Hume, rich though both of these thinkers are. Nor will you get the final word on provisionality from the philosophy of science, informative though it is, nor the final word on integration from Jung, crucial though his input has been. Rather, each principle needs to be understood in the synthetic context of the Middle Way as a practical approach to human judgement, with any particular source judged in the wider context of its practical helpfulness in the widest and longest-term perspective available to us.

The fact that the principles have been developed from an array of sources also means that they can be justified from a variety of directions, since each of those directions offers overlapping insights into the same kinds of phenomena. It is the difference between wider and narrower uses of different disciplines or sources that is far more significant than which sources we use. To try to illustrate this point, I have created a table that summarizes the justification of each of the five principles in relation to a variety of different approaches, included as an appendix. Not all the points in that table are discussed in detail in the text of this book. Rather the purpose of the table is to give a wider impression of the synthesis involved, and to encourage the reader to start thinking synthetically about the five principles, rather than only in terms of whatever kinds of sources or disciplines are most familiar to him or her. A more detailed exploration of some of the points in the table may be found in subsequent volumes of this series.

The first of the principles, scepticism, refers both to a philosophical tradition of argument and to a practical basis of reflection. This tradition is typified, for instance, by the thought that you may possibly be mistaken even in what you think you see in front of your eyes at this moment. Sceptical arguments have been systematically misunderstood for millennia by not being interpreted in a practical context, and through a failure to understand that negative positions can be just as absolute as positive ones. As a result, 'scepticism' has come to be associated with negativity, is normally used selectively, and is assumed to be impractical when not used selectively. I will argue on the contrary that scepticism is an entirely practical principle, and that the very momentum of its arguments requires us to apply it even-handedly and thoroughly, without any need to feel threatened by the uncertainty that it implies. Scepticism is a *practice* of recognizing uncertainty, not just a weird view put forward by fringe philosophers. Its helpful usage needs to be thoroughly integrated with a Middle Way perspective.

The second principle, provisionality, is the capacity to make better judgements that take uncertainty into account. When we assume that we 'know' how the world is, we get locked into a binary limitation of possible ways of thinking about a given matter: there is either the 'true' view we identify with, or the unthinkable negation of that view, which is 'false'. For example, two people get locked into an argument about population in which one insists that population is the whole basis of our environmental problems, and the other insists that this is an unacceptable 'racist' view. Both of these people are making binary assumptions that are in conflict: either that population is the whole basis of environmental problems (or not), or that this is racist (or not). However, this way of thinking depends on the way that we are framing the issue, and there are in practice always alternative ways of framing it that do not leave us locked in this binary frame. In terms of the example, that there are multiple complex causes of environmental problems in which population is one possible element, and that there are many possible solutions to over-population, many of which are not racist.

Provisionality is the ability, that we can cultivate, to consider alternative possible views of things, which involves recognizing both the limitations of our current view and the possibility of alternatives. That means that it is very much a quality of the imagination, and is dependent on our mental states, rather than just formal checking procedures or a theoretical commitment to considering alternative views. Again, then, provisionality is a *practice*. The fact that most scientists would theoretically agree with the need for provisionality in their research is potentially misleading in some ways, because their acceptance of it is often superficial and depersonalized. Provisionality is rarely discussed as a wider quality dependent on psychological states. Instead, there is much more reliance on the socially-prescribed requirements of formal science, such as peer review and double-blind testing.

The third principle, incrementality, is the practice of seeing things as a matter of degree. In *Absolutization* I discussed the way that practically unnecessary discontinuity is often the most easily identifiable feature of absolutized beliefs. When we respond unreflectively to political argument in a way that is either for or against what someone is saying, for instance, we are rapidly judging whether they are part of our group or the opposing group. A discontinuous line is then drawn between that person's position and our own – for instance, that they are 'right wing' and we are 'left wing'. The complexity of the issues is rapidly obscured as we shift our priorities from addressing the issues to 'winning'. If we were able to understand those issues *as a matter of degree*, we could avoid this immediate source of conflict. Not, for instance, whether we tax the rich or give welfare to the poor, but *how much* we do either in relation to what we do already. Bargaining with figures is a much more helpful basis for disagreement than manning the barricades. If we are not *absolutely* opposed in the first place, we are in a position to assess the best response and potentially agree on it, in a way we were not before.

Incrementality is not necessarily a matter of changing our logic, but of applying it differently. Nor is it necessarily a prompt for compromise: one side may be overwhelmingly right compared to the other, but we'll only be in a position to see that when we start thinking in increments. Increments follow the contours of our experience rather than of the concepts we use to divide up that experience, and are thus a feature of organic life (and also often of non-organic processes). Cells grow incrementally, not by instantaneously changing from one state to another. By thinking incrementally, we get closer to how things are presented to us in experience, and further away from a conceptual model that's assumed to have the whole picture.

Agnosticism, the fourth principle, means taking a decisive stand in relation to the absolutized nonsense of opposing group conflict – not taking sides, not accepting the framing that tries to force you to take sides, and not believing those who tell you it's the only option you have. Agnosticism recognizes that we *don't know* the answers to metaphysical questions about ultimate realities (not just God's existence, but very many other such claims), and thus refuses to accept commitments to such positions. Note that this view of agnosticism is contrary to the popular calumny that sees it as indecisive – on the contrary, agnosticism takes constant courage. It is not those who live in the cloud-cuckoo land of thinking that their absolute conceptual beliefs must be realities who are practically facing up to conditions: instead these are the cowards who constantly take the easy option of going along with the shortcut view of things promulgated by their group. No, agnostics practise the drawing of confidence from elsewhere – from the body and from experience – so as to refuse to be drawn into absolutized conflict.

To do this, however, agnostics need not only to be courageous, but to be on their guard – as wary as serpents. They will find that absolutists on both sides of any conflict will often do almost anything to avoid the mental effort of developing a more complex incremental position. They will constantly confuse agnostic positions with negative ones, because understanding of the Middle Way is generally so poor. They will appropriate agnostic positions into their own side or lump them into the other side rather than admit that there is any third option. They will even form unholy alliances with their supposed enemies on the opposite absolute side in order to keep agnostics down, when they rightly intuit that agnosticism is a much greater long-term threat to their absolute position than their supposed enemies are (in fact they are counter-dependent on their enemies). Agnostics need to be primed to expect all these tactics, and to know how to meet them.

The final principle, integration, refers to the practice of overcoming psychological (but thus also socio-political) conflict in the long term. Given that absolutized beliefs cannot be adjusted, they are constant sources of conflict in which one belief (with associated desires) tries to repress incompatible beliefs. By judging sceptically, provisionally, incrementally, and agnostically, then, we also work to resolve conflict – whether that conflict is within ourselves in the form of cognitive dissonance, or represented in socio-political disagreement between different people holding incompatible beliefs. At the same time, by working on the overall integration of our judgement in the context of the whole mind-body system, we create the long-term conditions for the better practice of the other four principles. We are better able to be provisional, for instance, if our energies are not in conflict, but united.

Integration, then, is the main focus of long-term *practice* in following the Middle Way. That practice is just as much bodily and emotional as it is 'cognitive', and involves working with bodily, mental, and emotional states through mindfulness as well as with meaning and belief. In the process of mindfulness practice, we can allow conflicts to arise but also *contextualize* them in body awareness or other types of wider awareness. An insistent and obsessive belief that once seemed the whole story can then be seen as less important, because we are able to find alternatives *meaningful* in that larger context. The use of the imagination and the exercise of critical thinking can give us other approaches to that contextualization, where our given beliefs are just one alternative amongst many, and the framing that previously seemed completely non-negotiable is suddenly seen as dispensable.

The final section of this book, then, is concerned with practice. Here I will not so much be offering any new practices as giving a new context for old ones – such as mindfulness, the arts, and critical thinking. Often we are aware that these kinds of practices are helpful for a specific purpose (relaxation, say, or dealing with academic

Introduction

essays), but not how they are linked together in mutual support. An understanding of absolutization as a unified phenomenon, as discussed in my previous book, can also help one to understand the value of an array of practices in helping to address it as such. Bias is linked to projection, conflict, proliferation, restricting the options, and metaphysics (among other features of absolutization) I argue, not only because of the interdependence of these things in the wider phenomena of absolutization, but also because our practical response to one is a practical response to all.

The account of practices in the final section is organized in terms of what I call the *Threefold Practice* – integration of desire, meaning, and belief respectively, each of which provides different kinds of contextualization for boosting our awareness that absolute assumptions are not the whole story. In integration of desire practices such as mindfulness or bodily disciplines (like yoga or tai chi), our limited assumptions are at least temporarily placed in a wider context of embodied awareness, so that they no longer hijack our attention in emotional obsessiveness. In integration of meaning practices such as the arts, we extend our available resources for understanding, both cognitive and emotional, so that we are no longer so obsessively dependent on a limited set of symbols supposedly representing an absolutized 'reality', but are able to imagine things in a variety of possible ways. In integration of belief practices, such as critical thinking, our limited beliefs are placed in a larger conceptual and cognitive context, so that we can see how limited their justifications are, and that other possible beliefs may be better justified.

These three broad ways of practising can be found to varying degrees in a wide array of already established practices, from ordinary recreation to psychotherapy to academic study of various kinds. So it is not so much a matter of finding or developing new practical techniques as of understanding the relationships between the ones we already have in a wider context. Seeing this wider context also enables us to use them wisely rather than narrowly, not over-depending on one practice interpreted in one way, but rather drawing on an array of interdependent practices. These practices are not only focused on individual development, but also involve engaging with the wider socio-political context that is required to make integrative practice work for individuals. Each of the three types of integrative practice, I shall argue, also has socio-political elements, including friendship, care, the provision of education, the use of ritual, and political campaigning for integrative ends.

In the later part of *Absolutization*, in addition to identifying the features of absolutization, I tried to also identify four criteria for an effective response to it: practicality, universal aspiration, judgement focus, and error focus. These were not principles of practice as discussed in this book, but merely ways of identifying what is a Middle Way approach (that is, one that addresses absolutization effectively) from what is not. Obviously, the five principles advocated in this book are intended to fulfil these four criteria, but much of the time I will not need to draw explicit attention to this.

It is worth emphasizing that the five principles are all *practices* (not truth-claims), and thus take practicality very seriously. They also all aspire to universality, in the sense that I think everyone will benefit from following these principles, as far as I can judge from the evidence so far. As I argued in *Absolutization*, this is not because of a top-down assumption that the Five Principles all fulfil some cosmic requirement, but because they seem to address common features of the human experience. The lateralization of the brain is one of these, as it evidently provides the basic condition for absolutization to occur and also for remedies for it to be possible.

These principles are all also judgement-focused, because they all apply, not in relation to what we claim to be the case, but in how we go about judging it. That's why there could be much to be said for turning the principles into adverbs – we work (and play) sceptically, provisionally, incrementally, agnostically, and integratively. They should not be mistaken for more general claims about the universe, even if some provisional claims (such as ones about human functioning) play a role in our thinking about the principles.

They are also error-focused in the sense that they involve practice to overcome absolutization, rather than practice to try to reach some final positive goal (such as enlightenment) specified in advance. Of course, humans need goals, but they do not need absolute or final goals, only intermediate ones that help them to structure their activities. Rather than being united in agreement about where we are going, then, it is much more practicable to be in agreement about what we are avoiding. Any impression that this is somehow less demanding than a positive goal will soon be dispelled when we start thinking seriously about how to change the way we judge things.

Overall, then, the Five Principles provide an overview of the most important elements of the Middle Way as a universal path. They do not by any means provide a complete account of it, but my aim in this book is to provide and justify the most important elements of the structure it offers. Further details – for instance, about ethics, or about the arguments for agnostic views of a range of metaphysical dualisms – must be left to further books in this series.

1. Scepticism

1.a. Uncertainty, 'Knowledge', and Sceptical Argument

> *Summary*
>
> Scepticism is a practical recognition of uncertainty, which should not be confused with falsehood. Its arguments show formal propositional knowledge to be impossible, because we have no access to truth or complete justification. These arguments are that empirical justification is unreliable, rational justification is subject to infinite regression, and all knowledge claims depend on mistaken disembodied assumptions about meaning.

Scepticism, in the sense that I will use the term in this book, is first and foremost a practice. It is a practice of questioning what we (or sometimes others) may otherwise assume. We are led to question when we become aware of the uncertainty of what we previously believed. Sceptical arguments prompt us to become aware of that uncertainty.

Most of us are already in the habit of questioning particular sorts of information that we are aware of as being uncertain. For example, if we are asked what is going to happen next Tuesday, we'd have to admit that, although we may have some expectations and arrangements, we don't know. Similarly, if I was asked what the Australian prime minister, on the other side of the world from me, is doing right now, I might well be inclined to admit my ignorance. These are what may be called *known unknowns*, where we recognize that we don't know.

However, there is a wider class of uncertainty that we are less likely to recall at the point when we need to recall it – we could call these *unknown unknowns*.[1] If I see a bird quickly fly across the garden in a blur and identify it over-confidently as a mistle thrush, I am not taking into account my degree of uncertainty. Similarly,

---

1   The phrases 'known unknowns' and 'unknown unknowns' were most famously used by Donald Rumsfeld, US Secretary of State for Defence during the Iraq war, but are far older than him. The use of the terms should not be interpreted as indicating sympathy with Rumsfeld's political claims. See Murphy (2020).

if someone writing on social media disagrees with me, arguing for the need for authority and control on one issue, I may feel that that's because they are a Fascist, but this is an over-hasty categorization, when there could be all sorts of reasons for disagreeing with me that do not involve beliefs normally associated with Fascism. My belief that I have the whole story in these circumstances is an instance of absolutization, and to be able to change that absolute assumption, the first basic requirement is that I should become aware of uncertainty – not that I am necessarily wrong, but that I am not necessarily right.

How can I become aware of uncertainty in relation to judgements about new subjects that I may never even have considered before? Obviously, I need a *general* awareness of uncertainty. The traditional sceptical arguments used in various traditions remind us of this uncertainty in relation to any possible belief we may arrive at. These arguments have to be general to be practically helpful, because they need to be applicable to any new circumstance.

Sceptical arguments all point out reasons why we may be mistaken about things that we think we 'know'. But what do we mean by 'know'? Philosophers make a helpful distinction between propositional knowledge and knowledge by acquaintance. To say 'I know Dr Rughani' is just an example of the latter, meaning that I have lots of experience of Dr Rughani, rather than that I 'know' any particular facts about him. This sense is distinguished in French as *connaitre* (rather than *savoir*) and in German as *kennen* (rather than *wissen*). When thinking about scepticism, though, we are dealing only with *propositional knowledge* – namely knowledge consisting in claims about the universe, such as 'Dr Rughani has a pet sheep' or 'It will rain in New York tomorrow'. To test whether we are using 'know' in an acquaintance or propositional sense, try putting 'that' after 'I know' – if you can do so, it's propositional. If, on the other hand, you can substitute 'I am familiar with...' it is knowledge by acquaintance. Knowledge by acquaintance is just another way of talking about experience, and is not 'knowledge' in any other sense.

Propositional knowledge is most commonly defined in philosophy as 'justified true belief' – a definition that I have no need to object to here. The objections that have been made to it (famously by Edmund Gettier[2]) are not relevant to my purpose in this context,

---

2   Gettier (1963).

because they would not justify any substantial enough modification of the definition to make any difference to sceptical argument. If knowledge is justified true belief, then 'knowledge' is absolute, because to know something it must be true – the words of our proposition must correspond with reality. If Dr Rughani does not in fact have a pet sheep, I cannot 'know' that he has one. This absoluteness in the truth term also suggests that the justification must be absolute. I would not 'know' that Dr Rughani had a pet sheep if I did not have a good enough reason for believing it to certify my 'true' proposition. Both in the case of the 'truth' and the 'justification' of knowledge, partial fulfilment is impossible. I can't half-know, because the thing I think I know is either true or it isn't, and I either have a sufficient justification for knowing it or I don't. If I can't fulfil these absolute demands, all I can do is *believe* it. I might believe that Dr Rughani has a pet sheep when he doesn't, or when I have no evidence, but I can't *know* it.

I don't want to be diverted for too long on the definition of knowledge. It's a subject of abiding interest to analytic philosophers, but is only of practical interest because it helps us clarify the ways we *don't* know. General sceptical argument points out that we don't know *anything*. We don't know anything because we cannot have a good enough justification to know that a proposition we take to be 'knowledge' is true. Importantly, this does not mean that the proposition we take to be knowledge is *untrue* – we just don't have enough justification either way to know whether it is true or false. Nor does it mean that there is no justification for believing it – just insufficient to 'know' it. Thus, for instance, the fact that the generally honest Dr Rughani tells me about his pet sheep gives me a strong justification for believing that he has a pet sheep. However, this is not an absolute justification – he could be deceiving me, or he could just be confused or fantasizing. I thus don't *know* that he has a pet sheep.

In practice, in everyday speech, it is very common to use the term 'know' for this kind of well-justified propositional belief that is not absolute. I might say, for instance, that I 'know' Ulan Bator is the capital of Mongolia. However, there are reasons why perhaps we should try to reconsider this practice. These are all connected to the absoluteness with which we continue to treat the term 'know', even when we are using it thus casually. It remains *discontinuous* – I can't half-know something, and *representational* – I assume that my words represent reality in some way. I suggested in *Absolutization* that this use of 'know' when we mean merely 'believe with justification' is an example of the inflation of metaphysics: that is, the tendency to use absolute terms unnecessarily for things that are experiential, and thus in the process facilitate the acceptance of absolutization. I can't claim to have entirely given up this everyday use of propositional 'know' myself, and it is a difficult practice to change a lifetime's enculturated language use, but we might like to note the desirability of changing it. In the meantime, we could argue that the context usually makes it sufficiently clear that the 'know' is not meant to be absolute, but conditional on a particular set of circumstances.

Whether or not we make any headway with the everyday use of 'know', however, it is clear when we are in a more formal context that 'know' *is* deliberately intended to be absolute. That's obviously the case in philosophy, but also in a number of other contexts where people are asserting 'knowledge' against doubt, or appealing to an absolute source of some kind. For instance, if a scientist responds to anti-vaxxer conspiracizing by claiming that 'we *know* vaccines work', she is over-stating her case, even though it is a strong one. There are very good reasons for believing that most vaccines work to prevent disease, that their benefits vastly outweigh any drawbacks, and that there is no better alternative to using them – but none of this amounts to 'knowing' that vaccines work. The absolute and bald assertion that vaccines work is very likely to stimulate counter-assertions, whereas proportionate justification in relation to evidence focuses our attention, instead, on that evidence and how well it justifies the belief.

So, we need reminding that we do not 'know', for entirely practical reasons. We constantly undermine ourselves through absolute thinking that proliferates, decontextualizes, disembodies, restricts options, projects, substitutes, and creates conflicts.[3] We can identify many of those dimensions of absolutization when claims of 'knowledge' are made, however habitual these may be. As humans, our tendency is constantly to be obsessed with *what* rather than *how*, that we 'know' something to be the case rather than that we can justify it in a particular way. Claiming to 'know' is central to that absolutization process, so, however unpalatable we may find it, scepticism is needed.

---

3   I.1–5. (See 'The Old and New Middle Way Philosophy Series' listed before the bibliography in this book.)

Let me come, then, to the sceptical arguments themselves. I am not going to concern myself with the origins of these arguments, other than in references. They stand by themselves for their practical implications. They are of three kinds:

1. Arguments for the unreliability of empirical information
2. Arguments for the unreliability of rational assumptions
3. Arguments for non-representationalism

These all contribute in slightly different ways to the overall conclusion that we cannot have knowledge, because we cannot gain sufficient justification for a belief to ensure its truth. Firstly, if our senses, or our processing of them, are not reliable, we cannot sufficiently justify our beliefs that a given state of affairs in the world that we think we have sensed is true: we could be mistaken. Secondly, if our rational assumptions are unreliable, we cannot sufficiently justify our belief that we have used categorization or reasoning correctly to derive a 'true' claim, even if this is based only on reasoning. Thirdly, if our language does not have a representational relationship with the world, then our beliefs cannot be sufficiently justified, because we would be mistaken in thinking that 'truth' can even be appropriately applied to statements.

One sub-category of the first type of sceptical argument tells us about the limitations and unreliability of information from the senses. My ways of perceiving are different from those of others, especially animals: for instance, bees see in ultra-violet, but I don't. They are affected by circumstances: for instance, lighting levels or background noise. I perceive things only from one standpoint from which I may miss crucial information. I don't perceive things in a definitive final form that shows me how they are connected: for instance, just looking at flour does not tell me that it came from wheat.[4]

Another approach to the first type of argument points out that some objects of the senses are much more significant to us than others. Our attention is highly selective. Statistically, our brains only process a millionth of 1% of the input available to them from the senses.[5] In a famous experiment, subjects were asked to count the number of passes in a basketball game, and the majority were

---

4 These are some of the Ten Modes of Pyrrhonism, attributed to Anaesidimus and first recorded by Sextus Empiricus (1996).
5 Armson (2011).

so intent on doing so that they completely failed to notice a man in a gorilla suit walking into the middle of the game.[6] Our attention is driven, not by an impartial survey of sensory 'data', but a relationship with our goals or alertness to possible threats. It's thus hardly surprising that we miss crucial information about the things we think we are finding out about: rather than 'knowing' about what we see, hear, etc., we have a very limited justification for particular beliefs.

A third reason for empirical scepticism is the past record of errors. We can all probably recall perceptual errors we have made in the past. Personally, for instance, I have mistaken a mossy stump for a bear. If we have made such errors in the past, a classic sceptical argument goes, how do I know that I am not making such errors now? Such arguments can also be extended to the totality of our sensual experience in the form of what has become known as the 'dream argument'.[7] We cannot be certain that we are not dreaming at this moment, and that the sense perceptions we experience are not delusory. Note that these arguments do not involve any claim that we *are* making an error or dreaming, only that *we do not know that we are not* doing so. The argument raises a possibility – perhaps (in the case of the dream argument) one that in most circumstances is not practically relevant, but due to our limitations, we are also unable to be certain about when it is practically relevant and when it is not. In the case of the error argument, however, the immediate relevance is obvious. The recognition of, and compensation for, human error is an everyday experience for all of us. It is in the nature of error that we are not aware of it when it is happening, and thus that we may be subject to it at any moment without being aware of it.

This first type of argument, then, not only should make us aware that empirical 'knowledge' is impossible, but should greatly overdetermine that awareness, repeating its point many times over to remind us. Our beliefs can be justified to a greater or lesser extent using evidence from the senses, but at no point can those beliefs be absolutely justified in the way that 'knowledge' demands. This is still the case even if their justification is overwhelming, indicating a 99.999% confidence. We need to take the concept of absoluteness seriously here: it means what it says and is not equivalent

---

6 Chabris and Simons (2011).
7 Descartes (1968) meditation 2.

to an asymptote. For the very same reason, denying absoluteness should not be a threat. If we are not using 'knowledge' in an absolute sense, that is fair enough, but we also need to be aware of the great danger of the inflation of absolute claims through the use of the term 'knowledge', so that we start to unreflectively assume an absolute sense.

The second type of sceptical argument focuses on the unreliability of our beliefs due to the rational assumptions we are making, regardless of whether those beliefs are empirical, or whether they are *a priori* beliefs – merely abstract claims such as those of mathematics and formal logic. The key argument of this type is that of the *infinite regression of justifications*. Whenever we justify one claim by appealing to another, the supporting claim also becomes open to question, bringing in a third claim, and then a fourth, and so on *ad infinitum*. We never reach a foundational point of certainty however far we continue in such an enquiry, because we can always ask of any claim whatsoever 'why should I believe that?' and the answer to such a question can only consist of another claim. The only possible alternative to the infinite regression is circularity, which is not preferable.[8]

Another version of this argument points out the *interdependence* of our beliefs with one another. This applies equally to empirical and *a priori* types of argument. Empirically, my belief that I can hear an aeroplane outside is interdependent with my belief that aeroplanes regularly fly over this area. *A priori*, my belief that 2+2=4 is interdependent with every other correct arithmetical claim, forming an interlocking set of implications for each number in relation to all the others. The interdependence of each belief on the others is potentially limitless, and offers a strong argument for treating them in systemic rather than linear terms. Since no claim stands independently, it can claim no certainty.

These types of argument show that *a priori* claims are not immune from sceptical argument. The oft-heard claim that, for instance, we can be 'certain' that 2+2=4 neglects the impact of this argument. 2+2=4 is not 'self-evident', but dependent on the conventions and assumptions of mathematics. The lack of certainty this implies does not indicate that we cannot use our belief that 2+2=4, or any other

---

8   Absolutization employs circular and *ad hoc* argument in a vain attempt to avoid the infinite regression of justification: see I.4.c.

consistent mathematical belief, with confidence (see 2.f for more on the value of distinguishing asymptotic probability from certainty). It does not tell us that we cannot strongly justify our belief in it, only that we cannot attribute absolute truth to that belief.

The final type of sceptical argument is the linguistic one against representationalism. 'Knowledge' assumes representationalism, because for us to 'know' any given proposition we must assume that that proposition describes a state of affairs in the world. However, this is not how the meaning of language operates. Meaning is relative to persons, as we are constantly made aware by misunderstandings. The meaning of 'dog', 'Christianity', or 'purple' is different between you and me. It is also relative even to the same person over time, as I can find by re-reading something I have written in the past and failing to understand it, or finding it stupid in a way I did not when writing it initially. The boundaries of objects referred to in language are also vague, so cannot map precisely onto a state of affairs in the world. Since a linguistic proposition cannot possibly get its meaning from a state of affairs in the world, I cannot possibly 'know' any such state of affairs.

The traditional way that philosophers have responded to this is through the imposition of a false dichotomy between 'cognitive' and 'emotive' meaning. The associative meaning by which we have different understandings of the same claims is merely 'emotive', they say, but the 'cognitive' or 'semantic' sense of a claim is distinct from this, and consists only of the 'meaning' defined in the restrictive terms of, for instance, the influential truth-conditional theory of meaning.[9] This states that we 'know' the meaning of a proposition when we 'know' the hypothetical circumstances in which it would be true or false. However, there is no evidence that the meaning of the terms can be separated from associative meaning in this way. Not only does the neural processing of the syntactic relationships in propositions in Broca's area continue to depend on other parts of the brain to give meaning to the propositions, but no human experience of the meaning of a proposition is free of associative meaning – on the contrary, it depends on that associative meaning for its 'cognitive' sense. The claim that cognitive meaning can be treated distinctly depends on treating it as though it was distinct, by

---

9   Classically stated in Davidson (1967).

analysing it in abstract isolation from it being held as a belief by an embodied human being.

This third type of scepticism is more recent, and more profound, than the other two. Empirical and rational sceptical arguments should be enough by themselves to establish that we cannot have 'knowledge', but the linguistic argument makes it even clearer that the whole idea of 'knowledge' is a misconceived placing of the absolute cart in front of the embodied horse. We have adopted it as a side-effect of the shortcut to group binding offered by absolutization,[10] not because it is the best way of talking about our ways of understanding the world. Yet it continues to dominate by formatting the whole conceptual landscape, still totally dominating everyday discourse as well as that of science and education. Even embodied meaning, which gives us one of our main tools for questioning it, is referred to as 'cognitive linguistics', and even the biological systems theory of Maturana and Varela, another such important tool, refers to the practical beliefs of organisms as 'knowledge'. It's as though we couldn't even imagine using different terminology. This would not be such a big problem if the term did not maintain its implicit discontinuity at times even for these reforming thinkers.

One of the major reasons that the concept of 'knowledge' has held its unquestioned sway is the defences against sceptical argument that have been successfully operated through intellectual history. These defences primarily function by misrepresenting the *implications* of sceptical argument as those of negative assertion. The next chapter will deal with this, which is also practically relevant because it reflects the ways that we can easily misunderstand assertions of uncertainty. Sceptical argument has also been misunderstood as impractical, which is nothing short of a perverse calumny given that its whole justification is a practical one. This issue will be tackled in the following 1.c. We will then also go on to other aspects of the practice of scepticism, including its relationship to embodiment (1.d), the importance of even-handedness (1.e), the application of scepticism to issues of belief rather than matters of meaning (1.f), and the ways in which sceptical argument removes the fact-value distinction (1.g).

10 I.5.e.

Scepticism

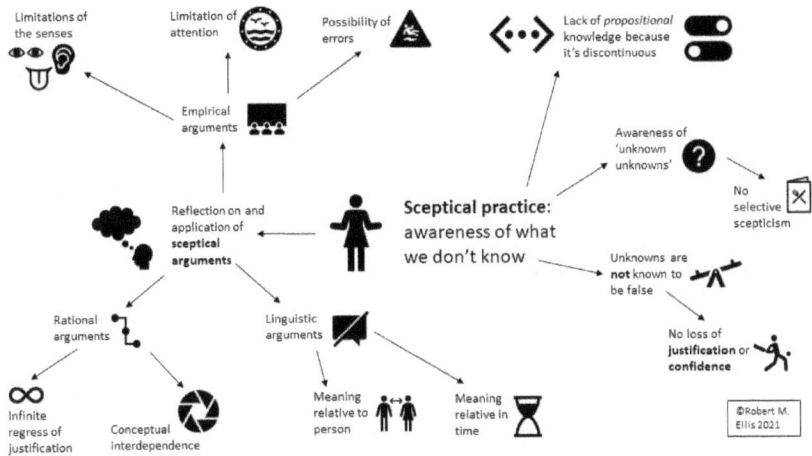

Figure 2. Mind map of sceptical practice.

As a practice, though, scepticism basically consists in the recollection and application of the arguments I have mentioned, to remind oneself of the uncertainty of the beliefs we may hold. This practice is obviously not of great efficacy by itself, but becomes increasingly powerful when combined with the other practices discussed in this book. It is summarized in the diagram here (**figure 2**).

1.b. Scepticism is not Negative

> *Summary*
>
> Scepticism is frequently misunderstood as negative in motive or application, but arguments about uncertainty in no way require falsehood. Assumptions that they do involve an appeal to ignorance, and perhaps the unhelpful application of principles from within empirical judgement (such as Ockham's Razor or Russell's Teapot) to absolute claims. We slip easily into assuming falsehood from uncertainty, because the physiologically entrenched meaning of the dualistic framework is maintained in mere negation. Challenging that framework requires the practice of agnosticism as well as provisionality and integration.

That scepticism is in some sense negative is an extremely widespread and entrenched misunderstanding. That misunderstanding is evident in the popular use of 'sceptic' to mean a denialist or someone who takes an opposing negative view against a particular belief – such as a 'climate sceptic'. It is also found in the attacks on scepticism by philosophers (most famously Wittgenstein) who criticize the position that they take to be implied by sceptical argument as supposedly involving negative assumptions that they find unacceptable.

By 'scepticism' it must be understood that I am referring to sceptical arguments (as outlined in the previous chapter) and their implications. I am not referring to any particular historical sceptical school, movement, or thinker. Some specific sceptical thinkers may have combined sceptical argument with dogmatic claims, sometimes, for instance, with the idea that scepticism could be used to clear the ground for the discovery of ultimate 'truth' (Descartes is an obvious example). Other thinkers, going back to the Pyrrhonists, have used sceptical argument to defend a recourse to conventionality, or 'going along with appearances'. However, there is nothing about sceptical arguments themselves that requires us to swallow these further assumptions along with them, whether these further assumptions are positive or negative.

Crucially, pointing out the uncertainty of any given claim does not require us to conclude that it is false, or even that it is more likely to be false than true. It just means that we have no justification for concluding that it is absolutely true or absolutely false, because the limitations of our perspective do not give us access to any such absolutes. For instance, the uncertainty attached to my judgement that I am seeing a dog in the park does not imply that I should start believing that there is no dog: the *probabilities* are still so high that my judgement is correct, that any reflection on its uncertainty is very unlikely to be practically relevant or to affect my responses. By comparison, sceptical reflections on the metaphysical belief that God exists, where there can be no such probabilities involved, justify me in withholding my judgement within the framework being used (that is, being agnostic), and seeking alternative frameworks, not in concluding that God does not exist (atheism).

I should conclude that a given belief is false only where there is a weight of evidence in that direction, not just from a lack of evidence. This is recognized in the fallacy of the *appeal to ignorance*:[1] just because there is no definite proof that the Loch Ness Monster does not exist, I cannot conclude either that it does exist or that it does not. My ignorance alone (before we get on to any probabilities shaped by the strength of evidence) tells me nothing either way.

The idea that we should assume claims about the unknown to be false is reinforced by various well-known philosophical arguments. One of these involves the use of *Ockham's Razor*, which is the principle that when all other things are equal between two available explanations, we should prefer the less complex one. Staying with a true-false dichotomy obviously seems 'simpler' than considering further alternatives. There is evidence that preferring simpler theoretical explanations provides the most efficient basis of investigation for empirical theory, because it reduces the likelihood of errors and retractions.[2] However, this point is wrongly applied to absolutizations, which draw us away from empirical investigation into an inappropriate *a priori* simplicity before we even expose ourselves to the possibility of error. Just as razors in general are better used to cut hair rather than throats, it's not a helpful use of Ockham's Razor to slash away all further options and leave us only with absolute truth vs absolute falsehood.

Another well-known argument for assuming the unknown to be false is Bertrand Russell's *teapot argument*. Russell imagines that there might be a teapot orbiting the sun in some remote and unobservable region of space. If someone were to assert the existence of

1   Locke (1824) ch. 17, §20.
2   Kelly (2007).

such a teapot, we could not prove them wrong through observation, because the object would be too small and distant to observe. However, Russell thinks that we should not take the existence of such a teapot seriously:

> Nobody can prove that there is not between the Earth and Mars a china teapot revolving in an elliptical orbit, but nobody thinks this sufficiently likely to be taken into account in practice. I think the Christian God just as unlikely.[3]

Russell is obviously correct in his assessment of the practical value of the example. We do not know about such a teapot, and we also do not care. There are many things we remain agnostic about and also never consider, because they have no practical relevance to us in our embodied situation (we do not apply them, whether explicitly or implicitly[4]). However, it is Russell's comparison of the teapot with God that is unhelpful. He does not take into account either that belief in the existence of God is an absolutization, or that people in practice care about it, and in that sense his approach is typical of the common abstraction of philosophical argument from both psychology and practice.

An absolutized belief cannot be a matter of probability, as I argued in *Absolutization*.[5] At the same time, belief in God is highly *meaningful* to many people (at least in theistic or post-theistic cultures) in a way in which the teapot is not. That means that it will be practically central to many people's consideration. Putting those two things together – that the belief is an absolutization and that people find it highly meaningful, then it is important to adopt an explicitly agnostic position about it. Firstly, then, Russell confuses something not being practically relevant with the justifiability of treating claims about it as false. Secondly he takes no account of the practical impact of denying something that people find highly meaningful. The practical effects of denying God's existence are those of creating unnecessary conflict that are most unlikely to be triggered by denying the teapot's existence. Both those with or without religious commitments can agree on an agnostic response to the 'existence' of God, and can grow into recognizing that 'existence' as irrelevant; but disagreement over the

---

3   Russell, in a personal letter (1958) cited by Garvey (2010).
4   I.4.e.
5   I.4.d.

metaphysical claim instead directs people immediately into absolutized group-identification.[6]

Given that sceptical argument only implies uncertainty, and uncertainty only implies the Middle Way, it may at first seem puzzling why there has been so much misunderstanding of it through the ages. However, the solution to this is not far to seek, once one recognizes the distinction between meaning and belief – which is most basically the distinction between possible states we experience as an organism and possible interactions as an organism.[7] Once a positive position becomes highly meaningful for us, that meaning is written into the associations of our nervous system,[8] and the negation of that position is then merely a switch of belief regarding the same meaning.

George Lakoff made a memorable catchphrase for this tendency in his book title *Don't Think of an Elephant!*[9] When told not to think of an elephant, we immediately disobey and start thinking of an elephant, because the *meaning* of 'elephant' is a basic category, far more immediate in our bodily experience than the mere belief that we should negate that thought. This illustrates how the negation of a belief merely reinforces its meaning within the framework we have given it. Another of Lakoff's examples is that by saying 'I am not a crook', President Nixon merely reinforced the idea that he was a crook. A far more effective means of not thinking of an elephant is to think about something else instead. For some reason, though, Lakoff's message doesn't seem to have reached atheists, determinists, or many other people who put a lot of emphasis on merely negating metaphysical claims that they object to.

Of course, even an even-handed reframing of an absolute claim prompted by scepticism is in danger of merely demanding that we don't think of the elephant, if we don't combine the demand for agnosticism with alternative framing. The availability of alternative framing is not just a matter of critical awareness, but of imagination. That is one reason why scepticism, even when accompanied by rigorous agnosticism, is not enough by itself. In relation to the second

---

6   I.5.e.
7   I.2.a.
8   In the term of Damasio (1996), the meaning becomes 'somatically marked' because of its possible adaptive benefit for future action.
9   Lakoff (2014).

principle, provisionality (section 2), I will say more about the role of the imagination in providing us with alternative options.

Our confusion of the two different kinds of negation – either within the frame or beyond it – also gives rise to several other phenomena that I will discuss in more detail in section 4 on agnosticism: appropriation, lumping, sceptical slippage, and unholy alliances. They are worth introducing briefly here because of the way that they also illustrate the difficulties of even-handed scepticism.

Appropriation and *lumping* are the positive and negative versions of treating a Middle Way option outside the frame as though it was inside the frame, and thus necessarily an affirmation or negation of an absolute. So the Middle Way can be *appropriated* by insisting that it is 'really' an aspect of the positive absolute view one identifies with. For instance, a Catholic monk I once met assured me that the Middle Way was all in Thomas Aquinas. *Lumping* is the negative side of this, when the Middle Way is lumped into an opposing view for rejection – as, for instance, when a reviewer of my book *The Christian Middle Way* thought that it was 'anti-absolutist, veiled subjectivism…in stark opposition to traditional Christianity and the revelation of the gospel'. See 4.d for more about appropriation and lumping.

Sceptical slippage is the tendency for beliefs that may initially be adopted with Middle Way justifications to turn into absolute negative beliefs, and increasingly be treated as such. For example, someone who rejects belief in God because of the lack of justification for supernatural claims through experience may gradually start to harden their position into atheism (in the sense of denial of God's existence). Or an employer may initially not consider an employee who lacks certain skills for promotion, but otherwise have no rigid expectations about her performance: however, after a while, he may start to view this 'lack' negatively as the 'non-existence' of skills that should be there, and eventually fail to renew her contract even in the lower position she held before. Because Middle Way thinking requires more energy and effort, we are more likely to slip into false dichotomies as a shortcut, either due to stress, or just as a matter of habit. It's simply easier to reject someone or something than it is to maintain a complex even-handed view of it over a period of time, so that even if we start off with a complex view, it may turn into a simplistic negative view. For more about sceptical slippage, see 4.e.

Unholy alliance is the tendency for those who are stuck in a dualistic frame to unite in defence of that frame, even though they may initially seem to be fiercely opposed to each other within that frame. This is a problem for centrist politics in a first-past-the-post electoral system that favours two distinctive parties that each appeal to different sections of the population, as in the UK. Here the two largest parties, Labour and Conservative, have both long had a vested interest in maintaining the existing voting system, together with the ideological and social framing favoured by it, and will readily unite to see off any challenges to that framing from the Liberal Democrat centre party. Even though the dualistic frame entrenches conflict, anyone who tries to challenge this frame will usually just get incorporated into that conflict. When the third challenge at times becomes a greater threat than the opposition within the frame, the priorities switch, and the supposedly opposed groups are likely to unite temporarily against the third party who challenges the frame. For more about unholy alliances, see 4.f.

All of these phenomena involve a failure to fully recognize the possibility of the Middle Way in the form of any kind of third option in an absolute judgement. The concept of a third option is present, but either does not maintain a distinct meaning in a consistent enough way, or (in the case of unholy alliance) is not sufficiently identified with to motivate support. Those who identify the idea of the Middle Way with an absolute belief of some kind have adopted a further defensive substitution: one where the psychological process of considering new options is suspended, and a conceptual belief about finding the 'truth' between the absolutes takes its place.

It is the difficulties created by these sorts of phenomena that create the need for the practice of agnosticism that will be more fully detailed in section 4. We have so much difficulty seeing the possibility of reframing to include third options in the first place, and then in sustaining them, that we are only likely to be able to do so in the context of a wider practice, or after a lengthy process of development. The practice of agnosticism involves the wariness of serpents, being aware of the deceptions that can lead one back into absolutizing shortcuts and resisting them. At the same time, however, there is a constant danger that such resistance to absolutization may lead one into defensive states of mind where the further options begin to get shut off. That is why agnosticism is interdependent with the practice of provisionality, in which we continue to develop the conditions for creative thought (section 2), and with integration, in which we work on maintaining the wider conditions that prevent conflict-producing, stressed, shortcut responses (section 5).

1.c. Scepticism is not Impractical

> *Summary*
>
> The idea that scepticism must be impractical results from confusing the merely meaningful possibilities raised by sceptical argument with recommendations for belief. Sceptical argument interpreted more helpfully is highly practical, supporting embodied confidence rather than certainty. To maintain that benefit we should not weaken the sense of 'certainty'. Scepticism supports the development of felt rather than absolute responsibility, and greater effectiveness due to reduced conflict.

The accusation that scepticism is impractical is well entrenched in the way that both philosophers, and wider society, have responded to sceptical argument. This well-known perspective of David Hume in the eighteenth century, discussing his personal responses to thinking about scepticism, encapsulates the issue:

> *I dine, I play a game of backgammon, I converse, and am merry with my friends; and when after three or four hours' amusement, I would return to these speculations, they appear so cold, and strained, and ridiculous, that I cannot find in my heart to enter into them any farther.*[1]

Why should scepticism be 'cold, and strained, and ridiculous'? Presumably because it draws attention to uncertainty by pointing out the *possibility* of states of affairs very different from the ones we believe in. For example, Descartes' argument that we may possibly be dreaming, or that an 'evil demon' may be controlling our experience is a well-known example of such sceptical argument. Another is the 'brain in a vat' scenario, pointing out that we do not know that we are not brains floating in vats, connected to electrodes that feed us the impression of all our current experience. However, the interpretation of these scenarios seems to be constantly subject to the 'don't think of an elephant' problem. We are being reminded that these scenarios are *possible*, but at the same time are having our attention drawn to them in a way that makes them increasingly *meaningful*. Because we keep confusing meaning with belief, we thus respond as though we are being offered a belief, even though the role and purpose of the sceptical argument has nothing to do with any claim that we should believe this scenario is true.

1   Hume (1978) p. 269.

The only function of discussing these scenarios as *possible*, however, is to remind us that our present beliefs are uncertain. We have no experience that might positively support them, and thus no basis on which to assign a probability, however small, to them. It's not just very unlikely that I am a brain in a vat, it's irrelevant even to try to calculate the chances. Considering that I *might* be one, however, is a potential tool for reflection to try to avoid absolutization of my current experience. It's a reminder of unknown unknowns of an entirely practical kind, since unknown unknowns are an aspect of our wider, more integrated experience that we are often inclined to ignore. It makes a difference to my thinking whether I assume my current beliefs to be absolute, or whether I am open to considering alternatives to even the most basic assumptions as soon as experience offers any hints of it. A process of argument with a practical purpose, then, has been systematically misinterpreted as the very opposite.

Far from requiring us to be 'cold, and strained, and ridiculous' enough to dwell excessively on possibilities, scepticism takes us back to practical experience as the best starting point we have available. It reminds us that we cannot rely on any absolute rationalized claim that takes us beyond that experience, but rather that *confidence* is our basis of judgement. I previously discussed confidence in *Absolutization*,[2] where I defined it as 'the basic ease and efficiency with which we can accomplish tasks that lead us down accustomed neural and muscular channels in interaction with a familiar and relatively predictable environment'. Confidence is fallible, but all the more reliable as a basis of practical judgement *because* it is fallible, once we have accepted that fallibility and tried to avoid absolutizing our beliefs. Scepticism, then, far from detracting from confidence, gives us a justification for relying on it, as long as we do not absolutize it. It is only *over*-confidence that pushes our beliefs beyond their embodied context, and starts to assume that they are independent or unconditional, resulting in fragility.[3]

The exploration of possibilities is a matter for the imagination. The imagination is hugely important, as we will see when I discuss provisionality, and it is the imaginative consideration of alternative possibilities that makes sceptical argument so helpful as a solvent

2   I.7.d.
3   I.2.c.

to help us break out of the rigidity of only maintaining an absolute belief and rejecting its opposite. If that leads us to imagine the *possibility* of a scenario like that in the popular film *The Matrix*, in which we are all completely mistaken about the world we think we inhabit and a completely different 'reality' operates, then up to a point this may help us to loosen our judgements and get into the habit of considering alternative beliefs. However, dwelling too much on that scenario without a clear enough distinction between meaning and belief might lead us to start taking it seriously as a practical influence on the content of our beliefs. The adoption of the terms 'red pill' and 'blue pill' from *The Matrix* by conspiracy theorists (with the red representing uncomfortable 'awakening' and the blue blissful ignorance) is a disturbing indication of the ways that sceptical argument can be abused so as to lead us to adopt sceptical scenarios too readily as a basis of belief.

The 'red pill' conspiracists, then, are quite similar to the philosophers in their misunderstanding of the implications of sceptical argument. They both 'take things literally' in the sense of assuming that something that functions helpfully as a prompt to stretch meaning should be interpreted as a basis of belief. The ways that other philosophers have phrased this offer variations on Hume's basic misunderstanding.

Burnyeat, a scholar of classical scepticism, thought that a sceptic could never in practice maintain the degree of detachment from their beliefs that scepticism demands.[4] This assumes that 'detachment' is required. I make no comment on scholarly issues of the interpretation of classical scepticism here,[5] but sceptical arguments themselves do not require us to be 'detached', particularly if 'detachment' implies a separation from, or repression of, our practical beliefs. They raise our awareness of a wider context to our beliefs, which may make us aware of their lack of justification, and thus bring conflicts to our attention of which we were not previously aware. If we practice scepticism with an attendant principle of integration (see section 5), we can work to resolve those conflicts once we become aware of them. No, of course we can't 'live our scepticism' if this implies repressing the beliefs that actually form

---

4   Burnyeat (1980).
5   I have discussed classical scepticism more specifically in Ellis (2019) 7.b and Ellis (2001) 4.b.i.

our basis of action, but it would require a 'cold, and strained, and ridiculous' interpretation of sceptical argument to take us to this.

A similar kind of argument is offered by G.E. Moore, who contended that, contrary to the sceptical argument for uncertainty, he could be 'certain' about the existence of his two hands, because any other consideration that might urge him to treat his hands' existence as uncertain was less certain in experience than his two hands.[6] This, again, assumes that scepticism offers a kind of alternative belief, and that it in some way undermines our basic bodily confidence rather than supporting it. If scepticism is only pointing out uncertainty, it offers agreement with the view that any other belief is probably even more uncertain than belief in one's two hands. However, such a comparative argument only tells us about degrees of confidence, not grounds for certainty. The 'existence' of our two hands remains uncertain, in the sense that it is possible that we could be mistaken about them, but this is very unlikely to prompt any alternative beliefs about our hands. That other things are even less certain does not establish that our hands are certain.

Moore was appealing to an 'ordinary language' sense of certainty, of a kind that Wittgenstein also invoked.[7] Objecting to the absolute philosophical sense of the term, they wanted us to use the term 'certainty' in a comparative everyday sense. For example, if someone tells me that the Queen is dead, I may respond 'Are you certain?', and the other person may reply that he heard it in a BBC news report. A BBC news report is not, of course, a basis for certainty, but on such a matter it might be held as a basis for confidence. The 'certainty' here is thus just confidence. There are important practical reasons, however, for maintaining the philosophical sense of certainty as absolute, because without such a sense I would have been unable to explain scepticism as I have done in this book so far. We need language that helps us to refer to absolutes so as to recognize that we do not possess them, and the ordinary language philosophers seem not to recognize this thoroughly practical function of philosophical language.

The relationship between scepticism and practicality depends not only on our understanding scepticism as a prompt for uncertainty, but also on us understanding practicality in terms that are

6   Moore (1962).
7   Wittgenstein (1969).

not too narrowly focused on specific judgements at specific times. In *Absolutization*[8] I discussed the concept of practicality in depth, analysing it into three components – embodiment, responsibility, and effectiveness. For scepticism to not only be not impractical but a positive aid to practicality, we need to think in these terms about long-term, integrative practicality. That scepticism has a close relationship with embodiment, and hence with root feelings and motives, is something I will discuss in the next chapter.

That scepticism helps us to be more responsible depends on the ways that it can help us understand the limitations of absolutized and imposed ideas of our responsibilities, enabling us instead to connect with our *felt* sense of responsibility and to stretch that sense. Scepticism thus has an important ethical dimension, because it helps us to see the uncertainty behind absolute moral beliefs (often socially or ideologically imposed) and rely instead on building up more genuinely justified, embodied moral beliefs. This is why scepticism, interpreted in an even-handed way rather than as negative belief, is *not* nihilistic or even relativist in implication. Far from taking away the justification for thinking one moral judgement better than another, it allows us to remove fragile absolute claims about the basis of moral judgement and substitute much more robust ones grounded in our moral experience. The widespread assumption that ethics must be absolute to avoid relativism is an entirely unnecessary one created by philosophers absolutizing the fact-value distinction (see 1.g. below), and without that assumption, the way is cleared for sceptical argument to take a morally constructive, not a destructive, role. That we can justify our values as well as our factual beliefs is a basic requirement for practicality.

That scepticism helps us to be *effective* in our actions is related to the argument about confidence that I have already mentioned above. If we make our judgements with embodied confidence rather than by adopting the brittle shortcuts forced on us through group-conformity, we can bring more unified and thus more effective energy to our actions.[9] It is conflict, hidden or otherwise, due to absolutizing beliefs and desires that prevents us from focusing our energies effectively on a particular course of action. Our relationship with groups that maintain a particular standard in a practice

8   I.7.c.
9   I.7.d.

also needs to avoid conflict in order to enable us to learn that practice and thus be more effective in actions that employ that practice. So if, for example, I am learning woodwork, and an experienced woodworker instructs me in the effective use of a plane, my scepticism will help me if it is employed even-handedly, not just to evaluate his expertise (let alone to assume that it must be false), but to examine my own resistance to learning this skill, perhaps because I don't like to admit that I didn't already know how to use a plane well. Scepticism, then, understood in the terms of the Middle Way, offers a valuable tool for boosting effectiveness rather than only an excuse for one-sided rebellion.

I hope it is thus becoming increasingly apparent that the Middle Way completely transforms our understanding of scepticism as soon as it is applied. Instead of shutting a door of learning in our faces, as some have assumed, it opens it. What may have seemed totally impractical becomes a crucial element of greater practicality, just because we have previously failed to distinguish the two sorts of negativity, agnostic and denialist. This is not, of course, to deny that sceptical arguments can be used in unhelpful ways (see 1.e below), but that can be the case for any tool or practice. The wise use of sceptical practice understands it in the context of the other principles and of the Middle Way as a whole.

1.d. Scepticism, Embodiment, and Meaningfulness

> *Summary*
>
> Sceptical arguments draw attention to our embodied limitations, and embodied awareness can also help us adapt to those limitations through the contextualization offered by mindfulness. Scepticism can cut through the dogmatic philosophies of mind that assume a separate observing mind even when they are supposedly 'physicalist'. Embodied meaningfulness, developed from infancy, is also the basis of the confidence required to stop sceptical argument being used in alienating ways.

Scepticism is an embodied approach when interpreted in terms of the Middle Way. It is embodied because it draws attention to the ways in which our beliefs are formatted and limited by our bodies, and thus that we cannot have 'knowledge', which is the construction of a mind that assumes it is independent of the body. It is embodied because embodiment can help us to make contextualized judgements that are compatible with the uncertainty that scepticism draws attention to. It is embodied because scepticism can quickly demolish the row of false dichotomies by which we try to convince ourselves that we are separate from our bodies. Finally, it is embodied because it is embodiment, as a basis of confidence, that can help us understand and hold scepticism, and heal the craving for certainty that constantly leads us away from the contextualization offered by the body.

In 1.a I have already discussed some ways in which sceptical argument merely draws attention to the limitations placed on our view by having bodies. For instance, our bodies only occupy one position in space at a time, so our sense experience always has a limited perspective: we do not see inside things or the other side of things unless we change our perspective (and in the process lose the previous perspective). Our senses are also limited to a bandwidth that is particular to humans as a species and to some extent to individuals: for instance, we cannot see ultra-violet or infra-red, and our capacity to hear high-pitched sounds (always limited) declines with age. Our attention is also limited: our bodies can pick out likely threats and opportunities, but there is much else that we miss, with our brains only processing a small fraction of what our senses pick up. In many ways, then, sceptical argument is just a corrective to our inveterate tendency to assume that we have a God's eye view, that we see everything as it is and are aware of everything we see or otherwise sense. Even when we are aided by social pooling of information and by technology, we only perceive an infinitesimal portion of one corner of the universe from one point of view.

Scepticism is also embodied because it supports the judgements that can make the most helpful use of this limited perspective. If we remain aware of these limitations, despite the ways in which absolutization constantly drags us away from that awareness, then we can compensate for it. That compensation takes the form of provisionality, in which we expect our current view to be limited and thus seek to compare it with alternatives as much as possible. Provisionality can be greatly supported through bodily awareness, where the body provides us with a context in which absolutizing views are no longer the whole story.

This is particularly the case with absolutizing judgements that are fired by the 'reptilian' brain, namely by fear or craving, and where bodily awareness enables these emotional responses to be contextualized in wider functions, rather than feeding a reinforcing feedback loop with the representational functions of the left prefrontal cortex.[1] This helps to explain how mindfulness can help us to avoid absolutization through an integrative process: a disruptive set of thoughts and emotions are not eliminated so much as put into perspective within a larger frame. The Buddha's recollection of an earlier *jhana* experience prior to finding the Middle Way can be a potent symbol of that relationship between bodily awareness and awareness that a particular belief is not the whole story.[2]

The assumption that we can have a view apart from the limitations of our bodies is maintained by a set of dichotomies that can easily be shown as false through sceptical argument. These dichotomies centre around that between mind and body, and can also take the form of the belief in a world known by the mind as opposed to one inhabited by the body. Philosophers have been criticizing the mind-body dualism of Descartes for centuries, but the alternatives they offer do not usually question the mind-body dualism assumed in the *meanings* of the terms mind and body, as opposed to our beliefs about their relationship. Many philosophers of mind suggest

1 I.1.b.
2 Ellis (2019) pp. 30–1.

monism as an alternative view (that there is one kind of thing), and that the monism is either that of body (materialism/physicalism) or of mind (idealism). However, monism continues to define itself in the terms of mind and body, even if it is believed that one of them does not 'exist'. It is the dichotomy between mind and body itself that is a discontinuous imposition of the 'mind' (well, the absolutizing representational mind) on the continuity of organic experience beyond that dichotomy. Merely changing one's philosophy of mind, then, does not address the disembodiment of an absolutizing view. This is illustrated by the absolutized abstraction in much 'physicalist' or 'eliminativist' philosophy that either assumes we can have 'knowledge' of physical 'laws', or that there is only one valid type of representation of the mind-brain.[3]

Sceptical argument, on the other hand, does not offer a particular position in philosophy of mind: rather it shows that none of the positions that might be adopted can be fully justified. This is, at root, because they are metaphysical positions beyond experience, and metaphysical positions are unavoidably absolute.[4] We do not know, for instance, that mind is separate from body, because our experiences of 'mind' may also be experiences of 'body': a thought may also be a brain event. We only experience that thought from one perspective. Nor do we know that the phenomena of mind are only body, as the perspective of causal processes in the brain is again only one perspective on those processes. The embodied nature of meaning also means that the terms we use for 'mind' and 'body' are not representations that gain their meaning by mapping reality, but associative experiences. I have yet to come across a critical argument in philosophy of mind that did not consist only in selective scepticism, pointing out the limitations of other views of the mind/body, but unable to offer any demonstration of a positive view.[5]

Nevertheless, it is very common for people to grasp at absolutes because of the conviction that they provide some kind of security or a basis of confidence. This conviction is deeply rooted in Western culture but is challenged by embodiment. Since meaning (in both emotive and cognitive senses, inextricably joined) is found in our bodily experience, we do not make our lives 'meaningful' by

3   E.g. see Churchland (1984).
4   I.4.a.
5   iv.4.e; VI.5.

adopting absolute beliefs. All we do is take a shortcut that *substitutes* for an experience of meaningfulness.[6]

For the root processes of meaning we can look to Eugene Gendlin's work as well as that of George Lakoff and Mark Johnson. To find something meaningful is to create an association for a symbol. As Gendlin puts this:

> *A symbol is something that 'stands for' something else, something other than itself. In such a view there is no inherent connection between the symbol and what it stands for. Instead, we want to understand the living body's own indicating, own implying, own way of being now or here and also being something that is not occurring now or here.*[7]

This association between what is here and what is not here is an integrative process as well as one of understanding. As we connect different objects and events *through* our bodily process we gain a capacity to recognize them and work with them, provided we experience both the symbol and its meaning through their link in our bodily experience, rather than *substituting* the symbol for its meaning. It is relating the meaning in our experience to the symbol where we might have lost those connections that is particularly the object of the practice founded by Gendlin, focusing (see 6.e). It is by creating, accepting, and recognizing the body as a bridge between symbol and meaning that we become much better able to put the symbol in its context rather than projecting it as something that must 'exist' outside that context. As symbols are also connected with each other through the body, we thus also gain a capacity for synthesis, connecting different meanings together rather than merely connecting isolated symbols with isolated meanings.

That synthesis is an emotional as well as an imaginative and intellectual one, and to some degree re-integrates the differentiating process of learning we have been involved in since infancy. In the course of this process we gradually came to associate specific experiences with other experiences, some of them symbolic in the form of speech, significant objects, or pictures that evoke other things. That past differentiation allowed us to act with increasing effectiveness to fulfil our goals in the world, as we used it to form beliefs that gave consistency to our actions. However, it also created the dangerous delusion that each symbol and its meaning can be separated

---

6   1.5.d.
7   Gendlin (2018) p. 29.

from all the other symbols and the web of neural association that connects them.

That this integration of symbolic association is the basis of our sense of meaningfulness can be readily seen through its relationship to what Mark Johnson calls 'cross-modal perception' and 'vitality affects'.[8] Cross-modal perception is the connection between what we could sense with different senses – sight, hearing, smell, etc. It's through associating our meaningful experiences through different senses with each other that we synthesize the meaning of 'objects', and indeed of ourselves. What is sometimes called the 'sense of self' connects not only different sensual experience, but also interoception, an emerging model of ourselves as agents through interaction with objects, and a 'felt sense' of the emotional tone of those objects. Vitality affects, which synthesize such meanings, consist in 'patterns of flow and development in our experience':[9] for instance, the way in which a mother's comforting stroking of an infant synthesizes with her soothing words to create an overall sense of wellbeing. The more meanings are unified in our bodies, in short, the more central they are to our sense of general meaningfulness. That meaningfulness should preferably also be based in contentment of a kind that allows greater and more sustainable integration of experience without disruptive craving or fear, but even extreme emotional states that take over our bodies temporarily are compatible with a strong sense of meaning at that moment.

Our need for a general and sustainable sense of meaningfulness can thus be best satisfied through embodied awareness, particularly mindfulness, combined with an integration process through the longer term that reverses some of the dispersal of the sense of meaning that accompanies our differentiation of meaning in different forms of language. To unite our sense of meaning, we do not have to compromise our ability to use highly differentiated, complex language, but only see that language (and its products, propositional beliefs) in a wider context. However, the shortcut method we have habitually developed to try to overcome this loss of overall meaningfulness, instead, is the adoption of absolute beliefs. Instead of connecting together all the symbols and meanings we use in bodily experience, this tries to impose a single *belief* on all our other

---

8   Johnson (2007) pp. 42–5.
9   Ibid. p. 43.

beliefs. Because of the over-dominance of the left hemisphere, we both forget and deny the role of the body in meaning and substitute a representational relationship between propositions and reality.

Sceptical argument is a potent dissolver of such beliefs, but it has to be used even-handedly to avoid association with the opposing absolute belief. It is thus scepticism *linked* to an embodied perspective, probably founded on embodied practices, that has the strongest and most sustainable long-term potential to both remove our dependence on absolute belief *and* offer an alternative. That alternative should never be mistaken for just another absolute belief, and nor does it somehow pre-suppose one.[10] Scepticism, followed through rigorously and unselectively (see next chapter) carries on offering arguments that undermine both an initial absolutization and its opposite, so as to purge us of these substitute beliefs. However, that is not enough by itself, as we can see from examples of people left in states of depression by studying philosophy that incorporates sceptical arguments without an alternative basis of confidence. Here is an example from one individual in an internet discussion who believed that 'having absolute knowledge is impossible':

> *I look at my two great friends, who are very absolutist about life, and see how great they are getting along. They are happy and well off, while I am not so as much. I feel doubt about everything and have no certainty about my life at all. Every choice I make is doubted, and nothing is done because nothing is certain to work. I feel as though, due to constant doubt, I will not do the things I wish I could do.*[11]

One can be fairly confident that a person in this state does not have sufficient bodily awareness, and there is by now a track record for mindfulness, which is rooted in body-awareness, in aiding depression.[12] Confidence is *embodied*, and embodied practice is needed to ensure that scepticism facilitates human well-being rather than undermining it.

Thus the most important connection between scepticism and embodiment is the way in which, together, they can help to provide a sustainable sense of meaningfulness. Of course, this cuts against

---

10 1.4.e.
11 https://www.reddit.com/r/askphilosophy/comments/5f32ml/skepticism_and_depression/ (accessed 2021).
12 Hofmann et al. (2010).

the long-standing absolutist tendency to portray scepticism as both disembodied and productive of meaninglessness. 'There are no atheists in foxholes', as the saying goes,[13] claiming that in situations of great stress we must turn to absolute sources of meaningfulness. Much more important than being able to find a brief shortcut to 'consolation' when you are in imminent danger of death, however, is avoiding the entrenched conflicts that produced that danger of death in the first place, by developing the confidence required to engage constructively with opposing views. Given the increasing development of both sceptical awareness and mindfulness in modern society, there is still some hope that there may yet be not just atheists, but agnostics in foxholes, or better still no need for foxholes at all.

---

13   Attributed to US military chaplain W.T. Cummings, in a sermon delivered in 1942. The 'foxholes' referred to are temporary hiding places on the battlefield.

1.e. Scepticism is not Selective

> *Summary*
>
> Scepticism must be unselective to operate as such, but the reverse assumption that it must be selective has operated in much philosophy, theology, politics, and ordinary life. Selective scepticism is the effect of confirmation bias, but this should be addressed through an expectation of even-handedness in practice rather than entrenched through institutionalized acceptance. Sceptical argument used for the Middle Way is not itself selective, and does not 'paradoxically' exempt itself from uncertainty, because it is not externalized or representational.

That scepticism should not be selective is crucial to its helpful operation. It prompts us to recognize the uncertainty of not just positive claims, but also negative ones (see 1.b); not just others' beliefs, but ours too; not just religious beliefs, but secular ones too; not just right-wing beliefs, but left-wing ones too. Nobody is exempt from uncertainty. It thus also provides a ready basis of challenge: if you challenge someone else's view by pointing out its uncertainty, you must be equally prepared to have your own view challenged in the same way. Scepticism is a great leveller.

However, the way that scepticism has been treated in most philosophical and wider cultural traditions is almost the reverse of this. Sceptical argument has been portrayed as impossible, unreasonable, and impractical at the general level, so that the only admissible uses of it are then taken to be selective ones. Throughout human discourse this attitude is regularly displayed, as we criticize other positions on the grounds of their uncertainty but, actuated by confirmation bias,[1] fail to apply the same strictures to our own position.

We see this attitude manifested in many places historically. For instance, Descartes famously used sceptical argument to argue for the unreliability of the senses, but then failed to use it against the truth of the 'clear and distinct perceptions' that form the foundations of his reconstruction of knowledge on rationalist foundations.[2] The Renaissance scholar Erasmus confessed that 'I take so little pleasure in assertions that I will gladly seek refuge in Scepticism',[3] but this Scepticism did not extend to questioning the authority of

1   I.5.c.
2   Descartes (1968).
3   Erasmus (1974).

the Catholic Church, being rather a prompt for passivity in the face of the overwhelming Christian conformity of his time. Montaigne, who was in many ways influenced by sceptical argument, had a similar view. Nor is this only a Western phenomenon: as I've argued elsewhere,[4] the attacks on the sceptic Sanjaya Bellatthaputta in the Pali Canon show an early Buddhist hypocrisy that interprets sceptics uncharitably whilst ignoring the extent to which the Buddha is himself dependent on sceptical argument.

But perhaps the most influential application of selective scepticism is found in Hume, who concludes that scepticism needs to be 'mitigated'. The 'mitigation' of scepticism can most charitably be explained as an interpretation of scepticism as a recognition of uncertainty,[5] on the false assumption that sceptical argument demanded anything more than this in the first place. In part, though, Hume also argues that we should be selective by not applying scepticism when 'nature' disinclines us to do so[6] ('nature' being our tendency to ignore sceptical doubt and continue with business as usual): this misses the point of scepticism as a practice, which is indeed constantly challenging. We are not entitled to give up a challenging practice just because we think 'nature' is opposing us (in other words, because we find it difficult), but instead we need to question our beliefs about 'nature', especially when they are implicitly deterministic.[7]

Hume also argues that scepticism should be 'mitigated' by 'the limitation of our enquiries to such subjects as are best adapted to the narrow capacity of human understanding',[8] by which he means empirical rather than rationalist forms of enquiry. However, as we have already seen, sceptical arguments apply just as much to all forms of knowledge claim, and give no basis for any such distinction. It may be that Hume's distinctions here involve a foreshadowing of the distinction between absolutized and provisional belief, but that distinction can in no way be identified with that between empirical and rationalist enquiry. Empiricists can absolutize too, by ignoring the weight of sceptical arguments that challenge evidence

---

4   Ellis (2019) 4.a.
5   Hume (1975) §129.
6   Ibid. §126.
7   See Ellis (2022) 6.a for more on the use of the term 'nature', including helpful archetypal use.
8   Ibid. §130.

drawn, selected, and interpreted from the senses, as well as the linguistic representations of empirical claims (see 1.a). Hume, like many other philosophers, then, stands convicted of selective scepticism. He was right to rage against the dogmas of 'school metaphysics', but his 'mitigated scepticism' has spawned a new metaphysics of its own, namely the 'naturalized epistemology' widely favoured in analytic philosophy. This has made analytic philosophy one of the worst examples of selective scepticism.

'Naturalized epistemology' (a term first coined by Quine) follows Hume's selective scepticism by ignoring the sceptical threat to scientific 'knowledge' and taking the 'natural' indications of science itself as the basis of an epistemology.[9] This would be fair enough if the uncertainty of scientific belief was tracked and taken into account, but instead its assumptions are then treated analytically as though they are certain, for instance by providing the basis for the fact-value distinction (see 1.g). Selective scepticism is justified through the assumption that scepticism employs an 'external' perspective (that is, a God's eye view) – which in turn depends on the confusion between pointing out uncertainty and denial. No external perspective is required to point out uncertainty, only a recognition that one's own position is *not* external, but only situated. By a strange series of moves, though, analytic philosophy has now thoroughly enculturated the idea that not only can it be 'philosophical' to selectively ignore scepticism in this way, but that 'metaphysics' consists only of the founding assumptions of an 'inside' perspective, and can thus be positively pursued as an analytic discipline. The new rationalist wolf is dressed up in empiricist sheep's clothing.

In this way, analytic philosophers continue to write absolutely about the key practical issues of justification, meaning, and value from a relative position, without having to engage with the basic issues of human experience or the problems of practical judgement as they are shown particularly in systems thinking, embodied meaning theory, psychology, and Buddhist practice.[10] Analytic philosophers are not obliged to actually justify values, consider the psychological conditions for everyday error, or address human deficits in meaningfulness, because naturalism has removed these issues from their job specification. In this way, absolutizations remain rife

9   Stroud (1984) pp. 211–12; Quine (1960).
10 As discussed in I.1–4.

in the form of unquestionable boundaries, but also immune from wider sceptical enquiry at one and the same time, and the result is a travesty of what philosophy might achieve as a discipline that might support practical human judgement: values remain unjustified (see 1.g), the human quest for meaning remains unaddressed (see 1.d), philosophy remains isolated from public awareness, and even scientific results are increasingly fragile rather than confidently accepted by the public. Philosophy needs some version of the Middle Way to address all these issues, but through a plausible naturalistic substitution for it, it is able to avoid such difficulties and thus at the same time become irrelevant. This is maintained by a system of inappropriate specialization designed for the sciences (see 2.d), and of professional standards dependent on insiders marking each others' homework.

A very similar pattern can be seen in the use and effects of selective scepticism in religion. The whole discipline of theology can be seen as selective scepticism, in the sense that theologians are allowed to ask any questions apart from those that would undermine the presuppositions of their discipline. That particularly includes the belief that the 'existence' of God and historical revelatory claims about his will are important: a belief maintained even by the radical edge who do not believe in God, but still accept the framing that his 'existence' matters. To interpret the experiences and values that actuate theology in terms familiar to psychology is unthinkable (and thus tends to trigger dualistic, absolute thinking), because this would involve a 'reduction' to someone else's discipline.

In the field of politics, selective scepticism allows politicians to attack the records of each others' parties in addressing this problem or that problem, without extending the focus either to their own or their opponents' longer-term record, or the conditions in which it was created. Because the public is used to selective scepticism and educated into it being the norm, there is no expectation that politicians will do any better than that. The rhetorical narrowing of the focus for persuasive purposes is thus effective, because it does not occur to most of the audience that there might be a wider critical context for the points being made. Where they do, that wider context may itself be constrained in other ways.

The psychological condition for selective scepticism is, of course, confirmation bias, as I have previously discussed it in *Absolutization*. There is no instantaneous solution to confirmation bias, and any claim that there is one is likely to be a further absolutization, but there are plenty of interlinked, incremental responses to it, in the form of the range of practices put forward in this book. To enable any such responses, however, the intellectual superstructure of our civilization first has to stop reinforcing absolutization by misinterpreting sceptical argument and taking its selectivity for granted. If even philosophers do not challenge selective scepticism, who else is going to do so?

The alternative to selective scepticism is at least the *expectation* of even-handedness. Even-handedness is a practice, and we will not succeed in it completely all at once, but nevertheless we can make an impression on it by changing our theoretical assumptions and thus our expectations. If we are practising even-handedness, *any* belief is open to question, but that does not imply that it is assumed to be false. We need to consider alternative beliefs alongside each other using a practical basis of judgement rather than one that merely reinforces absolutization.[11] In practice this is provisionality, which I will be considering in more detail in the next section.

Scepticism is not itself selectively sceptical. It should go without saying that the application of scepticism applies to its own strictures and makes them uncertain – but not false. They thus cannot be 'paradoxical' by being 'true' and 'false' at the same time. The uncertainty of a statement like 'everything is uncertain' is *not* a paradox, because it involves no absolute or representational claim, but rather a statement, to be understood and applied through the embodied and associative processes of human meaning, that we are justified by experience in confidently continuing to question new claims as we come across them. The conditions of that experience, which are also part of it, make it overwhelmingly unlikely as far as we can be aware that certainty could ever be attained by an embodied creature – and given the way that any belief in such certainty would create absolutization, we have every reason to avoid presuming it. As long as we are interpreting scepticism in terms of the Middle Way rather than as an absolutization, there can be no paradox.

11   I.7.

1.f. Scepticism does not Threaten Meaning

> *Summary*
>
> Scepticism is wrongly accused of threatening meaning. The accusation that it undermines the meaningfulness found in religious traditions depends on the confusion of profound religious experience with absolute beliefs that have no necessary relationship with it. Wittgenstein's accusation that scepticism is meaningless depends on the questionable assumptions that scepticism makes absolute claims, that belief precedes meaning, and that meaning is judged by communicative function rather than being an experience.

Just as absolute beliefs are widely substituted for the meaningfulness that needs to be embodied (see 1.d), scepticism is often perceived as threatening meaning, because meaning is confused with belief. As I discussed in *Absolutization*, belief is like meaning in consisting of associations that change the state of an organism, but differs because it is a potential basis of action.[1] In human terms, too, a belief is potentially propositional. Whilst our beliefs have to be meaningful, the things we find meaningful do not have to be the objects of beliefs, even if they are elaborately assembled into works of the imagination.

The domain of scepticism, however, is entirely that of belief. It reminds us that our beliefs are uncertain, acting as an antidote to representationalism.[2] Even in the domain of belief, scepticism offers no threat to *provisional* belief, because, as we shall see in section 2, provisional belief takes uncertainty into account. Scepticism is only a threat to absolute belief. Yet the unnecessary association that has developed between absolute belief and meaningful experience feeds the assumption that scepticism threatens the latter.

Two kinds of confusion seem to lead to the belief that scepticism threatens meaning. One of these is a confusion in the interpretation of religious experience that our most profoundly meaningful experiences must be experiences of 'truth' or 'reality', rather than being inspirational experiences. The other is a confusion between meaning and communication, with the claim that communication places us in a 'public' world in which scepticism is irrelevant.

1　I.2.a.
2　I.3.a.

The first of these kinds of confusion is one I have tackled in a number of other places, so I will only mention it briefly here. I think the best explanation for our association of 'reality' with religious experience is probably that truth, reality, etc. are valuable *archetypal* meanings to us, motivating us to *stretch* our identification and effort beyond our limitations at a particular moment.³ An archetypal association, like that of God or Nature, may prompt us in this way as a symbol or even just as a concept. However, the shortcut of absolutization often hijacks this valuable inspirational process and turns it into a *projection*. Instead of understanding it as a complex function, we find it easier to adopt an absolute belief in the symbol or concept as an absolute object.⁴ This is also an example of the *inflation* of metaphysics, one of the effects of absolutization whereby we attribute processes to absolute beliefs because of a wider overestimation of their importance.⁵

The second type of confusion, however, needs more discussion here. It is the product of Ludwig Wittgenstein and his influence. Wittgenstein did challenge the truth-conditional form of representationalism, but only to replace it with an account of meaning as communicative function. Although Wittgenstein showed little interest in scepticism for most of his life, he turned to it just before his death. Unlike most other philosophers, who tried to show that scepticism was impractical or contradictory, Wittgenstein tried to show that it was *meaningless*. He did this within his account of meaning as language-games: that is, that meaning is communicability within a particular social context where the relationships between symbols and their uses are shared.

Being apparently unfamiliar with the practical value of sceptical argument, Wittgenstein starts off with the claim that it makes no difference in practice.⁶ This does not take into account the possibility of provisionality – that is, that sceptical arguments may form part of a practice which helps to modify *how* one holds beliefs, namely that one is able to consider further options where relevant. This demands a psychological perspective that is not found in Wittgenstein.

His more distinctive argument, however, is that doubt presupposes a language-game, and that language-games are only

3   Ellis (2022) 6.c.
4   Ellis (2022) section 2; I.5.f.
5   I.4.f.
6   Wittgenstein (1969) §120.

meaningful because of an assumed certainty about meaning within them. Wittgenstein thus alleges that sceptical argument cannot meaningfully question the entirety of assumed knowledge in that context.[7] Wittgenstein's claims about the public, communicative nature of meaning depend on his 'private language argument', which is actually an anti-private language argument. This amounts to a criticism of the idea of a private meaning. For instance, he argues, if you were to make a note in your diary of a particular sort of private sensation you had at one time, and then again at another time, you would have no way of knowing that the two symbols referred to the same thing.[8] The connection between these two symbols would be *indefeasible*, that is, there would be no criterion for showing their identical meaning, and making the assertion that they meant the same thing *ad hoc*. In the same way, he would say that a specific doubt about one kind of thing in one context cannot simply be extended to an unknown context without the alleged similarity between the two cases becoming meaningless.

However, what Wittgenstein is doing here is trying to make meaning dependent on our beliefs about the meanings of words. In the process, he is ignoring individual experience. He is of course right that we would not *know* a recognition of uncertainty in one case to have the same sense as a recognition of uncertainty in another. However, if one pays attention to the point that sceptical argument does not show falsehood, and carefully separates uncertainty from falsehood, this turns out to be another case of confusing the two. That we cannot be *certain* of a similarity in meaning is entirely consistent with the third or linguistic type of sceptical argument discussed in 1.a, but that doesn't mean that there is no similarity, or that we cannot be reasonably confident of that similarity on the basis of experience. There is also no reason to constantly privilege public meaning over private, as both are equally uncertain, given that both are subject to variations over time. I may gradually lose my memory of a private sensation and its connection with a private symbol used to mark it in my diary, yes; but the same point applies to two people communicating, who cannot be sure that they share the meaning of what is being referred to, either at one time, or (even more) at a remove over time. Wittgenstein's claim that there

---

7   Wittgenstein (1969); Kenny (1973) ch. 11.
8   Wittgenstein (1967) §258.

is no consistency of meaning in private symbols could just as well be applied to the consistency of meaning in a conversation between two people recorded at different times.

Wittgenstein insists that the meaning itself resides not in the experience of association, but in the social conventions for the exchange of symbols within a 'language-game'. However, the experience of meaning, which is undifferentiated in infants or directly experienced in mindfulness practice, is much more than that: it is a whole set of neural associations that form our inner and outer responses to whatever we encounter, uniting 'emotive' and 'cognitive' aspects of meaning. The reason for accepting this wider understanding of meaning over Wittgenstein's narrower one is, in the end, practical: a wider view is more adequate, and enables us to link phenomena together and synthesize our response to them. Wittgenstein is correct that shared conventions are needed to enable us to communicate, but he has no grounds for insisting that the 'language-game' provides absolute boundaries of communicability, let alone meaning as we experience it. When we communicate about uncertainty, we are communicating a prompt for modification of *how* we judge things, not a specific set of propositions that always require precisely shared conventions. That this book depends upon such shared conventions I could agree, but not that every expression of scepticism calling attention to uncertainty must be so dependent. The boundaries of how we recognize uncertainty, like those of uncertainty itself, are unavoidably vague.

The work of Lakoff and Johnson has drawn attention to the ways in which meaning can be extended through metaphor or metonymy, becoming gradually more attenuated as it is extended.[9] For example, the term 'path' starts off being meaningful to us from an embodied experience of walking from one point to another, crossing space. By extension we import the meaning of that schematic term to other kinds of 'path', such as a series of decisions through time, or even the plotting of mathematical values on a graph. Our talk of uncertainty can be understood in a similar way, but this time an experience of feeling certain forms a base meaning that is attenuated through negation. The meaning of a negation is the vague shadow of the meaning of the correlative affirmation, but its vagueness does not make it meaningless. Rather, if we lose

---

9 E.g. Johnson (2007) ch. 9.

a sense of the meaning of the idea, we have to re-establish the path of its development via the positive. If we become too vague about what it means to recognize uncertainty in our judgements, we can retrace that path through the idea of certainty and what it feels like to be certain, then add the idea of negation. This process does not require a shared *belief* in certainty, but only an understanding of the *meaning* of certainty. To be able to connect that meaning with the word 'certainty' requires shared linguistic conventions, but these must not be confused with the process of finding the words, in the context of those conventions, meaningful in experience.

Wittgenstein thus follows the widespread tendency to assume that meaning in some sense depends on belief, when it is much more basic than belief. Our dependence on 'language-games' to generate linguistic conventions provides a necessary condition for us using a word effectively in communication, but not even a necessary condition for meaning itself, let alone a sufficient one. The ways in which meaning becomes attenuated when we speak more abstractly or generally about uncertainty should also not be absolutized into 'meaninglessness'. Scepticism is neither itself meaningless, nor a threat to meaning, but, as I have already argued in 1.d, can readily provide a prompt to meaningfulness through embodiment, supported by the questioning of disembodied beliefs.

1.g. Scepticism Applies to Values *and* Facts

> *Summary*
>
> Scepticism challenges the assumption of an absolute distinction between facts and values, given that both kinds of belief are not denied by sceptical argument, but incrementally justified (even if asymptotically for some obvious factual statements). Both factual and value claims depend on human goals and assumed states of affairs that depend on those goals. The particularity of values does not make them 'subjective'. Moral beliefs, like factual ones, become more justified as they are more integrated.

Sceptical argument applies equally both to factual claims (of the 'Paris is the capital of France' variety) and value ones ('Paris is a lovely city'). All of them are uncertain, and thus cannot be known to be 'true', nor justifiably be held absolutely. However, there may be a massive difference in the *degree* of justification between the claims.

However obvious we take a factual claim like 'Paris is the capital of France' to be, it is just overwhelmingly justified rather than absolute, simply because it relies on linguistic categories, as well as fallible information and communication. Even an asymptote (a graph line infinitely approaching zero) is not an absolute: a line plotting the probability of falsehood of Paris being the capital of France against the gradual accrual of confirming evidence never actually reaches zero.

Value claims, on the other hand, are often thought of either as 'subjective', or as necessary and absolute, but the absolutizing of the subjective-objective distinction masks the degree of similarity between them. Both factual judgements and value claims are justifiable to a matter of degree.

To avoid imposing a false dichotomy on our values we need to see their similarity to factual beliefs. Like factual beliefs, they consist in our responses to the conditions around us. Like factual beliefs, we make them as a result of a judgement that freezes our understanding of the conditions around us so that we are able to act in relation to them. Like factual beliefs, too, they reflect our desires and purposes in relation to the conditions around us. We lack a single widely-used term that combines them and highlights their similarity. Alfred Korzybski proposes 'semantic reaction',[1] but this

---

1   Korzybski (1993) pp. 19 ff.

could be confusing, because both terms 'semantic' and 'reaction' are often used more narrowly than is intended here. I simply use the term 'judgement' for the process of arriving at them, and 'belief' for a regular pattern of such judgements.

Let me illustrate the similarity between factual and value claims. To say that 'Paris is a lovely city' is to talk about the way that it fits our desire for aesthetic enjoyment, just as saying that 'Paris is the capital of France' reflects shared human purposes in designating one city in a country as a seat of government. The idea that there is a fundamental difference between the two statements only comes from a relentless focus on the object or state of affairs that is believed to be represented by the statement: but no discussion of a state of affairs is completely independent of the people experiencing and discussing it.

Sceptical argument, by making us aware of the impact of our embodiment in making our claims uncertain, thus places value statements in the same field as factual statements. It does not make all of these claims 'subjective', any more than it makes them all 'objective' (unless one chooses to understand these terms in an incremental rather than an absolute sense). As long as we keep applying the Middle Way, we can resist this shortcut simplification. On the other hand, an incremental term is needed to discuss the extent to which both factual and value claims are justified: I have used the term 'objective' in this sense in past writings, because there is a commonly used sense of 'objective' that is incremental ('Can't you be more objective about it?'), but one can alternatively use the terms 'adequate' or 'justified'.

Perhaps the strongest reason people have for believing that value claims are 'subjective' is their particularity: but particularity is not the same as absolute subjectivity, and should not be reduced to it. Paris is lovely for me whilst I am enjoying it, but perhaps you are depressed by the break-up of your relationship, so Paris is not lovely for you. This particularity also extends over time: I may wake up in a bad mood tomorrow and start to hate Paris, so it is no longer lovely for me. Here is the key to the extent of the justification for the claim that 'Paris is lovely': it would become more justified if you shared it, or I carried on feeling it tomorrow. Paris itself as we experience it may change too: it may be lovely in the sunshine but dreary in the rain. The more sustainably and consistently we find that value in our experience, the better justified it is. This means, in effect, that a more *integrated* value is a better justified value. There will be more about this in section 5 of this book.

An integration model for justification is entirely compatible with scepticism, because it requires no appeals to absolute facts or values to justify 'relative' ones. If I claim, for instance, that 'killing is wrong', I do not need to prove this from a metaphysical revelation from God, or from Nature. It is not known to be absolutely 'true', but it is overwhelmingly justified, even taking into account its vagueness. If, in a fit of anger, or even in the course of a war, I kill someone else, I obviously value doing so supremely at the point where I do so, but the wider the reflective context I give to that judgement, the more I am likely to experience a conflict with wider values. These wider values are not imposed abstractions, but ones that I hold and experience over time. With only a few possible exceptions, killing conflicts with my intuitive empathy with others, with order in society, and with peace in the world. Similar things can be said, perhaps to a lesser extent, about killing larger or more sentient animals. On the whole, killing is not sustainable or possible to integrate. I do not 'know' this, but I can justify my belief as a basis for refraining from killing as far as possible. This is exactly the same incremental judgement I would make about a factual claim: I do not 'know' that guns can be used to kill people, but it is overwhelmingly obvious as a justified belief from the frequency of the evidence that they are used to do so.

The particularity of my judgement means that I am making my judgement in a *particular* situation, where it is likely to have a *particular* practical impact. Any assessment of the justification of the value, then, must take that context into account rather than being unreflectively general. Moral scepticism points out, for instance, that *general* beliefs about what is good vary between different groups (for example, about one-third of cultures practise some form of 'wife lending' – adultery of a wife with the husband's permission to cement an alliance – but two-thirds forbid any such practice[2]). My judgement about value in my situation does not *necessarily* apply to another situation, and is not independent of the facts of the situation such as the cultural context.

The more different conditions I consider, though, the more my judgement aspires towards universality (without necessarily

---

2 Michalski (2016) pp. 16-17.

reaching it).³ My values can then be *normatively* justified, not by deduction from an absolute principle, nor by necessarily accepting cultural norms, but by their adequacy to the particular context. Thus the particularity required by moral scepticism, far from undermining universal morality, provides us with the key to it. In each case we need to begin with a full acceptance of the conditions we are in, including our motives and mental states, but to *stretch* those motives to take into account new moral considerations. This approach to ethics has already been outlined in *Absolutization*,⁴ and will be more fully explored later in this series.⁵

Scepticism, in ethics as elsewhere, is a great dissolver of dogma – one that helps us to recognize that what we thought were 'necessary' assumptions are merely sets of conventions creating unnecessary conflict. However, the dissolution of dogma does not involve the destruction of all our beliefs so that we can rebuild from the ground up (as Descartes thought). Rather, scepticism helps us see our existing beliefs in a bigger context. The new context is still uncertain, but it is a wider context and thus more adequate than the one we had before. In that context, the old dogmas that have made ethics an institutional failure and reduced science to fragile 'knowledge' no longer limit us, and we can synthesize our factual and value beliefs far more effectively. In this process we also begin to see value as part of a system embedded in other systems, and at the same time we do more justice to our embodied experience of motivation and responsibility.

3   I.8.a.
4   I.7.c & I.8.b.
5   VIII.

2. Provisionality

2.a. Optionality and Adaptiveness

> *Summary*
>
> Provisionality helps us positively look beyond absolutization by having alternative options available. These options may or may not be consciously considered, but are possible channels for our desires. Having greater optionality enables adaptiveness, in the sense of helping us meet a variety of needs in changing and unpredictable conditions. These further options can also be seen as a range of weak links in our neural networks. Provisionality is compatible with decisiveness, because time-framing is one of the conditions we need to address in judgement.

Provisionality refers to the ability to change our minds when we make judgements – more specifically, to be able to consider options apart from our current view and its mere negation. It is a crucial element of our response to absolutization. If absolutization is the assumption that we have the whole story, provisionality is the ability to see that we do not have the whole story. This is not achieved by adopting an opposing position to the first, but by the ability to see both our initial belief and its negation within the wider frame offered by third and further possibilities.

The practice of provisionality is interdependent with that of scepticism, but involves a more psychological and a more positive emphasis. Whilst scepticism makes us aware that our beliefs have limitations, provisionality connects this sense of limitation to the positive availability of alternatives. Without these alternatives, scepticism could not be of practical use to us. Whilst scepticism focuses on the ways that the content of our beliefs is not absolutely justified, provisionality instead focuses on the psychological capacity to entertain alternative possibilities. That capacity also depends crucially on the imagination.

Optionality is thus a vital element of provisionality. Optionality is the state of having options – that is, of having alternatives – counteracting the recognized fallacy of 'restricting the options' that is a central feature of absolutization.¹ The type of example that might spring to mind first of 'having options' is that of personal choices. If you go into a restaurant and look at the menu, at first it seems that you have the option of choosing anything on it. While your mind is still open, considering the different possible dishes you could have, your judgements about what to eat are more provisional. Once you've made your order and committed yourself to certain dishes, your options narrow.

However, optionality is a much broader phenomenon than merely that of personal choice, and it does not necessarily have to be a 'conscious' process in the way that 'conscious' and 'unconscious' are often dichotomized.² Choice presupposes desire, and a number of different routes by which that desire could be channelled. Those different channels are structured as meanings and beliefs. As discussed in *Absolutization*, our desires may be inconsistent or conflicting at different times.³ When we absolutize, our desires at different times can remain in conflict, whereas opening up options allows us to increasingly link our desires at different times and thus make their attendant meanings accessible. New meanings offer new possible beliefs and thus new possible ways of acting, whether or not we go through what we regard as a 'conscious' process of considering those new possible beliefs.

Thus we could talk of an animal 'having options' if it can easily adapt to different habitats, whether or not you think the animals have 'choices'. If the rat can no longer access a particular restaurant storeroom, it has other options, but if a giant panda's bamboo dies back, it doesn't.⁴ We could also use this language for the automatic processes of humans. If one of my kidneys ceases to function, I do have another option – the other kidney. *In extremis*, medical technology also offers further options – kidney dialysis or a transplant. The body's 'desire' to filter its blood of wastes and to regulate blood pressure and electrolyte levels can be fulfilled by one kidney or by both.

These examples show the relationship between optionality and *adaptiveness*. The more options an organism has, the better it is able to adapt to its environment. However, the sense of adaptiveness

---

1 I.1.d.
2 See Ellis (2022) 1.e.
3 I.5.a; ii.1.
4 For development of this example, see Ellis (2016) ch. 16.

here is not a narrowly evolutionary one only concerned with survival and propagation. The ability to pass on one's genes is only one possible type of adaptiveness – though one that has been taken to be reductively normative by evolutionists. We can adapt to any new condition that relates to our needs, and Maslow's well-known hierarchy of needs (including safety, belonging, esteem, and self-actualization) offers an alternative wider description of the kinds of conditions we may need to adapt to.[5] We adapt to a condition in relation to the desires that we bring to it, by considering new meanings in terms of which those desires can be fulfilled, and thus making possible their integration with other desires that may be understood in other ways. Thus we are able to fulfil more of our needs in the long term.

We can adapt to dominant desires as we experience them (e.g. recognizing homosexual feelings that we previously repressed). We can adapt to environmental conditions so as to produce a stable environment in the longer term (e.g. both limiting and adapting to climate change). We can adapt to the demands of friendship or the needs of those we are closely bonded to. All of these offer examples of conditions, and to be adequate in our response to those conditions we need to adapt to them. If that adaptation creates conflicts with our previous patterns of desire and belief (as is likely), we are faced with a task of integration in order to make that adaptation sustainable.

As in the example of our second kidney, options may take the form of facilities that make a particular channelling of desire physically possible. For example, having a swimming pool nearby gives me the option of going for regular swims. However, that option is dependent on several conditions, not just the existence of the physical facility. I may need the confidence to go to the swimming pool, the money to pay the admission fee, and the neural connections to think of doing so in the first place. At a social level one could also talk of a town having swimming as a recreational option because of the swimming pool, even though the option depends on these other conditions at the social level too.

Optionality, then, is a state of judgement that can be understood most clearly in terms of neural networks. The greater the connectivity of our neural network, the greater the options for each neuron.

5   See Ellis (2022) pp. 12 ff.

The 'choice' of an option is not a question of what one represented self does, but of the aggregate activity of millions of connected (or disconnected) neurons, each of which may be connected or disconnected in subtly different ways from previously, in response to new conditions. What we may experience as the 'choice' of a new option also consists of a complex adjustment of neural connections: some new, some established, some abandoned.

Optionality is thus not a question of having freewill to choose in a 'rational' fashion between equally weighted options. Some of those options may be much more heavily weighted, because we are in the habit of choosing them, or because they have obvious advantages. To take some of the less commonly selected options requires greater awareness, not just an abstract capacity for 'rational' choice. That awareness depends on the energy flowing through the system, and on the variety of weaker connections available to us. The greater the energy, the more likely relatively weak links are to become functionally available to us. However, that energy by itself will not increase options if the weaker links are not available.

Those weaker connections in our neural networks are those of meaning, and it is the range of weak links that offers more possible meaningful options beyond the stronger links that we have already established as cognitive models and beliefs. Every time we come to understand the possibility of a new way of acting, or of a new metaphor or a new symbol, those weak links are slightly extended, and so are our options. Neuroscientifically, these weak links are said to link *stochastic resonance* (our relationships to events with a random distribution) with *noisy internal brain states* (random firing of neurons), making the random firing more effective in responding to unforeseen events if it has more weak links to utilize.[6] A more provisional judgement about the beliefs that we should adopt, then, is generally one that maintains more options. Obviously this optionality is a matter of degree, and some options are more open to us than others.

Just as judgement that takes scepticism into account (see 1.c) is not necessarily impractical, provisional judgement is no less definite than dogmatic judgement (the neural connections involved are just as strong), but it is differentiated by the extent of weak links that surround it. When a new condition is experienced that leads

6   Teramae, Tsubo, & Fukai (2012).

us to reconsider the set of beliefs we hold (a balancing feedback loop[7]), then the energy flowing through the system forges new links beyond it amongst the weaker surrounding ones. If those links are not present, or are too weak, the energy will have nowhere to go, and will continue to reinforce the existing belief network rather than creating a new one. Imagine, by analogy, a loosely enclosed area containing a network of canals. Water normally flows freely in and out of the canal system. However, if there is a blockage in the outlet, water in the canals will rise, and the canals will become bigger and deeper (like the belief network). If, however, the boundaries of the area are open enough, and there are some smaller ditches beyond it, then the rising water will instead start to create new canals beyond the area.

If we merely recognize provisionality as a concept in the abstract, this may contribute little to actually developing it. For example, a scientist who merely claims as a matter of routine that his science is provisional, but does not respond positively to challenges, does not seem to have actually developed provisionality as a result of this assertion. However, when a recognition of fallibility leads to greater awareness of alternatives, then it creates weak links in the form of alternative cognitive models and meanings beyond current beliefs. The alternatives may not have to be very definite to provide some options: for example, the recognition that one way of fixing a faulty machine is not going to work may not itself offer alternatives, but it might lead us to look carefully for other types of fault, read manuals, etc., in an effort to strengthen our very weak hunches about what the problem might be.

A more justifiable belief or theory, then, is identifiable not only because of the coherence and strength of the beliefs that comprise it (including the links between beliefs about theory and beliefs about evidence), but also because of the options available if that belief fails us in any way. In a scientific context that may take the form of formal falsifiability: i.e. that there is a realistically strong option for recognizing a theory as wrong, which will then lead on to alternative theories.

More broadly, we can also recognize provisional theories in every area of study as more likely to be those which have been created dialectically in relation to alternatives. If we go through a critical

7   I.2.a.

process of examining alternatives, and are able to recognize both the strengths and the weaknesses of alternative theories, then this will give a larger structure to our beliefs and a lot of attendant weak links.

Provisionality involves opening the maximum number of options at the time a judgement is made. It does not consist in 'leaving one's options open', or avoiding decision-making that is needed to address conditions. Judgements about when judgement is necessary are subject to the same criteria as any other judgement – or one might say that timing is a necessary element of any judgement. Since the overall criterion for the objectivity of judgement is addressing conditions, it is the maximum optionality at the time of judgement that does this best, by allowing a greater probability that there will be an option that addresses conditions more effectively. To judge the right time to act one needs to steer the Middle Way between fixed views about the need for immediate unreflective action (likely to be accompanied by panic) and the need for endless deferment to find the ultimately right solution.

Sometimes delaying judgement will increase options: for example, 'Marry in haste, repent at leisure' is a saying that encapsulates the importance of making a life-changing decision about marriage when there are a range of options (which might include remaining single), not when one feels that there is no alternative. When saving a drowning child, in contrast, one seeks only a momentary consideration of the options before taking firm action to address the conditions. Nevertheless, having options when saving a drowning child will increase the probability of success. Is there a lifebelt nearby? Is there a stronger swimmer?

The longer we wait, though – as long as waiting is compatible with the conditions – the more likely we are to experience the range of weak links that surround our core beliefs. This is widely recognized in the importance of reflecting on important decisions, counting to ten in moments of anger, or 'sleeping on' a judgement that is either crucial or emotionally freighted. Such patience over judgement just enables a wider range of experience to come into play, and thus increases the available options that occur to us. It may also produce an intuitive decision, because in the process of allowing our full experience to emerge the strength of one option over the others becomes increasingly obvious as a distillation of our experience.

Figure 3. Mind map of provisionality.

The remaining chapters of this section will examine a number of other features of provisionality that are dependent on this basic optionality that makes it possible. The overall picture is illustrated in the mind map (**figure 3**). One aspect of this is the way that it enables us to understand and engage with complexity and respond effectively to its practical effects (2.b). Considering more options also takes more time and resources, which is why *slowness*, where compatible with a situation of judgement, is a feature of provisionality (2.c). The way in which greater optionality brings together understanding from different contexts also makes it *synthetic*, giving synthesis a key role in provisionality and relating it to the imagination – in contrast to the over-emphasis on analysis in much academic work (2.d). The moral aspects of provisionality involve maintaining awareness of desires that we don't act on for moral reasons, without simply rejecting those desires: this is suppression rather than repression (2.e). When we come to make decisions on a provisional basis, we have to consider the incremental strength of different options in relation to each other, which requires *probabilizing* so that they are comparable (2.f), then *weighing up* to make the judgement (2.g).

2.b. Complexity and Antifragility

> *Summary*
>
> Complexity cannot be an ontological feature, but rather requires provisionality, because our perspective is part of the complexity of the system. Developing optionality helps us to address the conditions of system complexity, but we need to beware merely abstract academic acknowledgements of uncertainty without it. In practice, optionality can produce antifragility by strengthening system resilience.

Complexity is something we allow ourselves to glimpse whenever we challenge our existing view of a situation, and in this sense it is simply the flip side of scepticism. Given that we don't know anything, the world *probably* has many features that go beyond our theorizations at any given point. In other words, the world is a complex system, but to say this is to say more about how we should judge it than about the world itself, given that we are also part of a wider complex system ourselves. I think there is much to learn from complexity theory, which tries to engage with these features of our experience – except on one point where I fundamentally disagree with it. Complexity theory thinks it is engaging in an *ontology* of a complex universe:[1] but have we not yet learned by now that we are not in a position to say anything about how things are? That theorization is always provisional? An articulation of provisionality (and a recognition that provisional theories cannot be ontologies) seems to be the major thing missing from complexity theory. Although some complexity theorists might say that they are using 'ontology' in a non-absolute way, failing to make any clear distinction between how things are and how we theorize them to be reduces our awareness of uncertainty.

Leading complexity theorists Boulton, Allen, and Bowman, however, do give a very useful account of various aspects of complexity.[2] The theorized complex world, they say, is systemic (formed of relationships rather than just objects) and synergistic (its elements act in relation to each other in unpredictable ways). It is multi-scalar, with different systems fitting within each other. It involves diversity, variation, and fluctuation that at first sight may seem redundant, but that confer resilience and adaptability on things through

1   Boulton, Allen, & Bowman (2015) pp. 35 & 70.
2   Ibid. pp. 35–46.

optionality. Genes throw up random variations and humans have apparently useless appendixes, but we don't know when these things may start to have a function in the system. Relatively minor changes in events can amplify in the future. Systems can seem stable (as the earth does) but then suddenly reach a tipping point of rapid change. Living systems are self-organizing and can give rise to the emergence of what seem like qualitatively different new features (as in the obvious examples of life and of reflective awareness).

All of these features constantly challenge our provisionality as we try to engage with them. Our most basic conceptual framing is often of objects (although this can vary a bit between languages), whether these refer to the actor, the object of action, the action itself, or its goals:[3] so further metaphorical extension is needed to think in terms of relationships. We tend to revert to the primary scalar level that we find most meaningful, where a particular meaning becomes a *prototype*, associating less specifically with a wider meaning at other levels.[4] We tend to fix our beliefs about our environment at a particular time, so that updating them always involves some effort, engaging a right-hemisphere response rather than the pre-set pattern created by the left.[5] It is not clear to us how significant minor events may be in future, and our tendency to normalize a particular system may lead us to underestimate how much it may rapidly change if it reaches a tipping point, as we see with the inertia that characterizes many human responses to climate change. We may understand the mechanical relationships between different components of a system, but still underestimate how the self-organizing features of living systems challenge any mechanical reduction, again due to a failure to integrate right-hemisphere operations with the conceptualizations of the left.[6]

Developing optionality at each point of judgement thus enables us to engage with all the different aspects of complexity. The limitations of our previous framing, where we assume one particular set of meanings that have solidified into a belief that is challenged only by its unthinkable negation, are challenged by new options that enable us to become aware of new features of the conditions around

---

3   Narayanan (1997) quoted in Johnson (2017) pp. 28–9.
4   Lakoff (1987) pp. 87 ff.
5   McGilchrist (2009) pp. 40–1.
6   Ibid. pp. 46 ff.

us. A brief way of referring to the advantages of provisionality is thus that it 'addresses conditions'.

Some areas of discourse that theoretically focus on complexity or uncertainty do not adequately address conditions in this way, because they focus only on the uncertainty of the object in theory, and not on the actual process of introducing new options into our judgement about objects. The discussion of quantum physics can often exemplify this, because it shows the uncertainty of our view of any particular object at the sub-atomic level given the effects of the act of viewing itself. If we take this merely as another example of complexity, then quantum physics can take a helpful place in our general understanding of conditions, but if we allow its account of objects to *substitute*[7] for the process of provisionality, we are likely to stay locked within a dichotomy of views about objects even when those objects are theoretically very uncertain. This occurs, for instance, when people draw idealist metaphysical conclusions from the uncertainty of objects in quantum physics.[8]

Provisionality as a response to complexity also has many practical effects. In *Absolutization* I argued that the more our responses address the complexity of conditions, the more effective they are, because as we consider the effectiveness of our actions in achieving goals over longer time periods, the directionality of those actions becomes more important and their intensity less important. Absolutization may give us a temporary boost of intensity, but it does not help us to maintain a sufficiently flexible response to the conditions to effectively reach our goals.[9] This applies even if we take those goals to be fixed, let alone if we take into account the need to adapt them.

It is this focus on directionality that helps to explain the phenomena of antifragility discussed by Nassim Nicholas Taleb.[10] Taleb, who coined the term 'antifragility', distinguishes it from mere robustness or resilience, which is the capacity to remain unchanged in the face of varied conditions. Antifragility goes further than this, and is the tendency for living systems to actually be strengthened by varied conditions. This occurs through incremental adaptation in which responses to a wide variety of conditions equip an organism for a

---

7   I.5.d.
8   Ellis (2011a).
9   I.7.d.
10 Taleb (2012).

wider variety of possible future conditions. For instance, exercising our muscles gives them more strength as they respond to minor stresses with growth, equipping them better for future demands. In the same way, traditional social and economic systems, such as the complex network of relationships in a *souk*, have dealt with many crises of the past, developing new capacities as they do so, whilst modern systems that have developed only in particular limited conditions (such as the stock market) may have become very complex, but are still vulnerable to 'black swans' – extreme and unexpected events that they have not yet been tested against.

Provisionality can be seen as the process that produces antifragility at the level of judgement. Each time provisional judgement allows for a new condition that would have been ignored in an absolutized judgement, we set ourselves up to cope better with that condition in the future. Even if we then start to absolutize when we get stuck in the new response, the pattern that we are absolutizing is at least slightly more adequate than the previous one. For instance, even traditionalist Western Buddhists who have got stuck on appeals to Buddhist authority may have taken a step forward by adopting mindfulness practice or other features of Buddhist thinking, which they considered more openly at the time of adopting them, as they got out of the rut of their previous ideas. That mindfulness practice may still serve them relatively well in helping to cope with new conditions, even if there are still some absolutizations in the background, because they have developed new strengths and capacities through it (this is, indeed, a way we could interpret what Buddhists traditionally refer to as 'merit', or good karmic effects from practice).

The academic response to complexity is often to develop increasingly complex models to take it into account. This is helpful as far as it goes, but is generally only comprehensible to specialists. It is also not sufficient to address complexity completely, given that it challenges our whole basis of judgement as individuals, with the mental states prior to academic formalizations. It is long-term development of our antifragile capacities as individuals that can provide a basis both for the development of complexity thinking by academics, and its effective use by others when making judgements both at individual and group levels. This in turn requires a habitual provisionality, based on practice that is also co-dependent on the other principles in this book (particularly integration).

2.c. Slowness

> *Summary*
>
> Slower and more energy-sapping processing is needed for more complex provisional judgements, when compared to faster automatized ones. Bias is maintained by fast absolutized judgements when slower ones could be used. However, sometimes speed is also required by conditions, so provisionality consists in slowing down judgement when conditions allow, to consider options and improve it later when faster judgement is needed.

Tactically speaking, provisionality takes more time. To 'go through the options', or to consider alternatives, rather than automatically maintaining a fixed positive against an unthinkable negative, requires us to explore more connections, whether you are thinking of those connections in terms of inner experience or of neural links. However, this 'slowness' is tactical, in the sense that it can be deployed when it best meets the conditions to deploy it. It thus does not prevent us from rapid responses when we need rapid responses – what it involves, instead, is slower responses when we are in an appropriate context that allows for them, because we also need slower responses to address complexity.

The idea of 'slowness' has found a place in recent cultural trends, obviously connected to the rise of mindfulness, and the recognition that body awareness can greatly facilitate not only aesthetic appreciation,[1] but also features of judgement. 'Slow television', pioneered by the Norwegian Broadcasting Corporation, shows continuous processes such as a train journey in 'real time'. 'Slow food' is a response to 'fast food', emphasizing the need both for full sensual experience of the food we eat, but also careful consideration of the ingredients and the way we prepare it. There is evidence that slower attitudes to eating lead to better judgements about food, with reduction, for instance, in eating disorders.[2] More generally, mindfulness research confirms the experience of meditators that slowing down one's attention to aesthetic processes also makes new judgements possible. Ellen Langer, for instance, describes mindfulness as creating new categories, allowing us to welcome new information,

---

1   VII.2.
2   Arthur-Cameselle (2016).

making us aware of different possible views, and allowing us to recontextualize.[3]

The biggest contribution to understanding the process of how slowness aids judgement, however, comes from the work of Daniel Kahneman and his associates in cognitive psychology.[4] Kahneman identifies two different 'systems' of thinking, the fast 'system 1' and the slow 'system 2'. System 1 provides us with a shortcut to respond rapidly to an urgent situation – for instance, enabling us to rapidly identify behaviour in someone who might be a threat, or estimate a probability of success in jumping a gap. It also allows us to save energy by doing accustomed tasks in a largely automatized way even when we are not under stress – for example, the many unreflective actions involved in driving. The fast system presents us with instantaneous, intuitive information that is unconsciously based on processing dependent on instinct and internalized previous experience. On the other hand, system 2, the slow system, is reflective and effortful, and involves deliberate concentration. We use it when we pick out one object in a complex background, when we make a calculation, or when we learn a new procedure.

Kahneman identifies the inappropriate use of the fast system 1 as the source of bias: in effect, a bias is a shortcut. As I argued in *Absolutization*, either being deceived by bias or reacting against it is absolutizing.[5] Absolutization can thus be seen as inappropriate fast thinking, defined not by its speed but rather by the assumption that the shortcut it offers is adequate. Conversely, then, provisionality is slow thinking employed to open up the options and avoid absolutization, defined not by its speed but by that function. Not all slow thinking is provisional, because of course we can sometimes think slowly but still restrict the options; nevertheless slow thinking is required to resolve absolutization. It is also possible to slow down, improve our optionality and adequacy, and then speed up again with more adequate beliefs. However, as long as we do not believe that those 'fast' beliefs, applied in a situation where speed is required, are the whole story, we are not absolutizing them (here we suppress rather than repress further reflection – see 2.e below).

Many of Kahneman's examples of biases that illustrate the distinction between fast thinking and slow thinking are based on

3   Langer (2014) ch. 5.
4   Kahneman (2011).
5   I.5.c.

probabilities. For example, he discusses the example of Linda: introduced to experimental subjects as a person with characteristics that fit stereotypes of a feminist – a politically active thirty-something philosophy graduate. Subjects were then asked whether it was more likely that Linda was a 'bank teller' or a 'feminist bank teller'.[6] The majority said the latter, because they thought of probabilities in terms of associations. However, 'feminist bank teller' is a subset of 'bank teller', so cannot possibly be more likely (it's like saying that it's more likely that a Volkswagen will pass you on the road than a vehicle). In all such cases, we routinely use association as a shortcut substitute for probability. Association is fast, being basically just a matter of how meaningful a symbol is for us, but probability requires a much slower calculation or comparison. This is an example of us failing to distinguish meaning and belief.

To respond to this example more adequately, then, we would need provisionality, recognizing other possibilities than those suggested by our immediate associations. Of course, it would help to apply scepticism to our immediate beliefs about Linda, but more important than this is a recognition of how we can justify estimations of probability, particularly beginning with the possibility that even the option that we find less meaningful may be better justified. This kind of process is also particularly crucial in voting judgements: that is, that we don't just vote on the basis of how meaningful we find a candidate's or party's symbolic self-presentation, but rather on an estimation of the probability of them achieving desirable political goals. That requires us to take the time to inform ourselves about those probabilities and think them through. I will return to the process of judging probability in 2.f below.

The slower 'thinking through' of options requires not only more time, but also more energy. Kahneman discusses the phenomenon of 'ego depletion' – the fact that what we experience as mental effort taxes our reserves of mental energy:

> *The idea of mental energy is more than a mere metaphor. The nervous system consumes more glucose than other parts of the body, and effortful mental activity appears to be particularly expensive in the currency of glucose. When you are actively involved in difficult cognitive reasoning or engaged in a task that requires self-control, your blood glucose level drops. The effect is analogous to a runner who draws down glucose stored in her muscles during a sprint.*[7]

6   Kahneman (2011) pp. 156–7.
7   Ibid. p. 43.

This explains why, in a study of parole decisions made by judges, the judges made markedly more lenient parole decisions immediately after lunch, when their blood glucose levels were high, than they did subsequently as their blood glucose levels dropped, going down from around 65% parole granted to around zero.[8] Kahneman emphasizes the ways in which a process of reasoning takes effort, but one could also apply this point to the examination of experience. Other examples of processes requiring such effort include inhibiting a strong emotional response to a film, avoiding the thought of white bears, responding kindly to a partner's bad behaviour, and (for a prejudiced individual) interacting with someone of a different race.[9] It is not reasoning as such but the relative unfamiliarity of the process that takes energy, as we are obliged to connect weak neural links more strongly, or to engage less fully utilized areas of the brain. Even for professionals as practised as judges, each new case will contain complex factual details that need to be matched up to legal criteria, and where it will be tempting to instead 'play it safe' by refusing parole, rather than making a more specific judgement about the probabilities of parole being abused.

However, such effortful processing also becomes easier and faster through practice, as will be discussed more fully in section 6. Much of the process of education could be seen as making complex judgements easier so that we can perform them more quickly and efficiently. For instance, I see this process of 'speeding up' through practice illustrated starkly in my personal experience as a classical pianist. If I start to learn a new piece (say, a Mozart sonata), at first I am working slowly and laboriously through the rendering of unfamiliar patterns of written notes using sight-reading. The reading of the notes becomes faster through practice, but at the same time, so does the pattern of movement in my fingers. Eventually, perhaps after several weeks or months of daily practice, the piece that started off as a slow, laborious, effortful experience becomes a rapid, pleasurable, and concentrated one. I will have speeded up the piece by making my rendering of it much more efficient, but if my performance of it then becomes rigid in its rapidity, it will become difficult to correct any mistakes. A preferable state for performance will be one that still combines some provisionality with

8   Danziger, Levav, & Avnaim-Pesso (2011).
9   Kahneman (2011) p. 42.

efficiency, as I maintain an overall awareness of the processes I am going through whilst I go through them, and thus leave open the possibility of modifying my performance. Where speed fails me, I must be prepared to return to slowness.

2.d. Synthesis

> *Summary*
>
> Synthesis can occur at the meaning level as imaginative connection, and at the belief level as new theorization from the dialectical integration of previously opposing beliefs. Synthesis of beliefs depends on provisionality in which new possibilities are considered, motivated by a point of frustration with conflict. Practice of the five principles is needed to prevent synthesis becoming dogmatic, but it is still required for creative thought. Analysis, by contrast, depends on and reinforces previous assumptions, and has been over-emphasized as a result of over-specialization in the modern economy and in academia.

Synthesis most basically refers to the bringing together of different elements that are combined, as opposed to *analysis* that breaks them apart. In relation to judgement, it can be understood at two different levels: the combination of ideas to make new meanings, or the combination of beliefs to make new beliefs. Either of these results in new synaptic connections, but at the belief level we are dealing with new connections that could make a difference to our responses as organisms. The synthesis of meaning is a function of the imagination, combining and recombining symbols to form new metaphors: for instance, by combining parts of different animals to make new fantastic beasts. The synthesis of beliefs, however, results in new representations of the world. Rather than simply imagining a chimera, we arrive at a view that we might or might not encounter one in a particular place, or perhaps that a story about one might entertain others. Both of these forms of synthesis are very important aspects of provisionality.

Synthesis at the meaning level is what is occurring when we consider new options. All that is required for this is to *consider* these options, to find them meaningful as alternatives to absolutization positive and negative. It is only by considering new possible meanings in an entirely hypothetical way, to begin with, that we may gradually come to identify alternative possible beliefs apart from the absolutized alternatives we have hitherto restricted ourselves to. Such imaginative synthesis is likely to be stimulated by the arts, which offer a variety of ways for others to bring new meanings into contact with the ones we have (see 6.e). By telling children fairy stories, for instance, we equip them with new possible ways of thinking.

The power of art and imagination is to continually make these alternatives possible, however much repression may be applied to try to limit the options and tell us that we're not allowed to consider any alternatives. Merely fantasizing about alternatives, telling stories about them, seems harmless enough, but it is a short step from fantasy to hypothesis, where we start elaborating our ideas *as though* they were representations of the world. That is obviously why totalitarian regimes often seek to control the arts – but even when they are purged of apparently threatening 'political' content they still provide a fund of stimulus for different ways of imagining.

It is synthesis at the belief level, though, which allows new beliefs to emerge, so that we can behave differently and transform both ourselves and the world in helpful ways. Very often it is others articulating new ways of thinking that enables new beliefs to spread, but for this the new beliefs must be brought into contact with the old beliefs and form a new adequate variant in each person who adopts them (bearing in mind that a belief never has exactly the same meaning in a different person, even if we express it in exactly the same words). We can also develop new beliefs for ourselves by combining different elements that stimulate us, and by hypothesizing and testing different beliefs against each other in a space of reflection and discussion. This is what philosophy, and indeed academic theory in general, do at their best, as long as they avoid merely spreading absolutized beliefs to others by new means (though see 6.g on why philosophy has often failed at this).

The dialectical model of synthesis, which goes back to Plato and was used in differing ways by Hegel and Marx, most simply models the process by which new beliefs can be developed in the judgement of any given person. Here I apply it without any of the accompanying absolute beliefs about reason and history that these philosophers brought to it. Like Popper, I would understand dialectic, not as a special form of logic, but as an empirical description of a process.[1] In the dialectical model, two opposing beliefs, called the *thesis* and the *antithesis*, meet. If they are to avoid merely conflicting with each other, a third element, a *synthesis* needs to be developed that addresses the conditions of each of them. For a synthesis

1 Popper (1940).

to occur, the thesis and the antithesis (as beliefs held by embodied people) have to be able to meet in a provisional space where each is meaningful to the other, without being mutually accepted as beliefs. There also needs to be both an imaginative and a critical capacity present. The critical element enables each of the opposing beliefs to be examined, and some of their assumptions to be recognized as unhelpful. However, the imaginative element also allows alternatives to the framing assumptions that keep the thesis and the antithesis apart to be considered. The thesis and the antithesis can then be synthesized or *integrated* by the compatible beliefs of each being joined together, whilst new framing is substituted for the unhelpful framing that previously placed them in opposition to each other.

Figure 4. The two mules.

The two mules pictures, originally adapted from Aesop's Fables and used on a Quaker anti-war poster, illustrate this process very directly (**figure 4**). The two mules initially have opposing desires framed by incompatible beliefs. Their beliefs are incompatible, because they assume that they must each eat their own pile of hay. However, there is an element of their beliefs – that they should eat hay – which is entirely compatible, the conflictual framing only demanding that they should eat *different* piles of hay. Once they have recognized that this framing of their beliefs is unhelpful, they can adopt different, helpful, and compatible beliefs about how to act. At the same time they need to have a *critical* understanding of the limitations of their previous view, and an *imaginative* understanding of the alternatives (though neither of these necessarily has to be explicit or linguistic).

The two mules illustrate a process of *integration* as well as one of synthesis (discussed further in 5.b).[2] Integration is more likely to be understood as a psychological process occurring over a longer time period, whereas synthesis refers to a more immediate process of meanings or beliefs being effectively combined. Nevertheless, I would see each as merely offering a particular emphasis on a spectrum of dialectical concepts. Whilst the concept of synthesis shows how provisionality allows absolutization and conflict to be overcome at the point of a particular judgement, integration can cover a wider range of phenomena, from momentary synthesis through to an increasing development of the *capacity* for such syntheses over the lifetime of an individual or a group. Integration can also cover the uniting of desires when a conflict is overcome, without necessary reference to meaning or belief, and this can be experienced more or less in isolation in the case of *jhana* or similar states (see 5.f below).

Synthesis of belief, and thus integration, cannot occur without provisionality, because two opposed beliefs have to engage with each other before they can be reframed and synthesized. The frame of provisionality that enables that engagement occurs in the fourth picture of the two mules series, where the mules are forced by *frustration* into reconsidering the framing of their behaviour. The role of frustration in creating provisional space can be seen in a wide range of ways: from antagonists finally coming to the negotiating table after a long, fruitless war, to the effect of a particular difficulty that makes an individual start to address a neglected condition, such as the difficulty of putting on a particular favourite piece of clothing precipitating action to shed excess weight. In Buddhist terms, frustration is *dukkha*, the recognition of a problem that then impels an adjustment of view[3] (and that unfortunately is often unhelpfully translated as 'suffering' and treated as a feature of the universe rather than a system prompt). In systems terms, frustration is a *tipping point* in which a reinforcing feedback loop is finally blocked

---

2   Also ii.2.b; Ellis (2022) 3.a.
3   The First Noble Truth and the first 'positive nidana' (see Sangharakshita 1988 pp. 137 ff; Ellis 2020a p. 29).

and forced to open into balancing adjustment.[4] That moment of balancing adjustment, when new influences are allowed into the system, is also a moment of provisionality. Its importance is also the reason for *error focus* in Middle Way Philosophy.[5]

Synthesis as the process of opening new potential, and then making it the basis of action, needs to be contrasted with *analysis*, which is a linear process that takes a set of meanings and beliefs for granted and reinforces them. Whilst synthesis changes the framing meaning or assumptions with which our judgements are approached, analysis merely determines the implications of existing ones, conceptually breaking down a given set of concepts or beliefs into their components or their implications. Analysis, like synthesis, can thus be analysis of meaning or analysis of belief. It is a practically necessary process for us to understand the implications of a concept or belief – to 'unpack' it. However, what is often not appreciated is that in analysing a concept or belief one also *reinforces* it in that form and with those assumptions, often making synthesis less likely in the process. As we explore it, we make it more and more meaningful in that increasingly familiar form, and harder to see other possible forms. In short, synthesis is creative, analysis merely reproductive.

Analysis has received far too much emphasis at the expense of synthesis in the context of modernity. The key force promoting this is specialization: to adopt a specialized socio-economic role one has to adopt a set of beliefs about the goals of that role and their background, and how they differ from other roles: for instance, beliefs about the goals and professional values involved in being an architect, a physicist, or a social worker. Others in the same specialism then maintain and enforce those beliefs as part of a group identity, and prevent anyone from advancing in a specialized profession without accepting those assumptions. This is reinforced through the formatting of specialized education and training, and the control of new admissions and publications in the area by expert gatekeepers. Those outside the specialism also maintain those beliefs, so as to maintain the supportive relationship between specialisms in a wider socio-economic system, and prevent encroachment on their own specialism from outside it.

4   I.2.a.
5   I.10.

For all these reasons, synthesis tends to only take place during the more basic process of education leading up to specialization, but be greatly discouraged beyond it. Lip-service may be paid to 'creativity' and 'innovation' in business and academia, but anyone who has actually tried to innovate in such contexts will probably be aware of the weight of social resistance to the synthesizing of any ideas from beyond that specialism. Instead, many advances come from analysis – that is, merely following through the implications of what a specialized group is already assuming. Once aircraft design has become a specialism, designing a jet engine is at most only partially disruptive of that profession, and once quantum physics has been established, positing the Higgs boson is not a big departure. Even in the arts, genuinely innovative approaches may have great difficulty being accepted, as genuinely creative writers struggle to get published.

It is in philosophy, though, that we can see the most baleful effects of specialization on human thought. In Ancient Greece, philosophy began as a general investigation of all phenomena, with synthesis thus a necessary core element to enable the comparison of, say, sciences and arts within the same overall frame of debate. Modernity, however, has seen the gradual advance of specialization, first on the sciences, and then on every other academic study in imitation of the sciences. Whilst specialization works well for the study of relatively discrete phenomena such as mosses or beetles, when applied to complex, multifaceted systems such as the human mind-brain it results instead in lots of blind men all feeling different parts of the elephant and each insisting that they have the whole picture.[6] Philosophers think it acceptable to ignore psychologists and vice-versa. Sociologists and anthropologists define their work only at the social level and ignore the individual, whilst psychologists may ignore the social level. Systems theorists think they are doing science rather than philosophy, whilst philosophers ignore systems theory. Scholars of religion think it's acceptable to investigate only the texts or other phenomena of religion and take their authority for granted without exploring the function of religion in human experience. Neuroscientists engage with the complexity of the human brain whilst making little connection with the huge implications of those brain events in human experience. Linguists and linguistic

---

6   See Ellis (2019) 3.f.

philosophers take the meaning of language for granted without considering its relationship to the psychology and neuroscience of the processes that make language meaningful. All of them, in effect, are busy analysing the implications of the principles of investigation passed on in their respective disciplines, and the extent of their synthesis often only goes as far as the making of new observations formatted according to those assumptions.

Philosophy, which once offered a synthetic overview, now has to offer itself as a 'specialism' in order to maintain its socio-economic position in academic culture. In the case of analytic philosophy, this effectively means that it has abandoned the most vital role that philosophy has historically had – that of taking an overview – by taking the role of philosophy to be primarily analytic. In the continental tradition, rather more synthesis continues, but that does not necessarily mean that philosophers there are not also pressured by specialization into other kinds of dogmatic assumptions.

Of course, synthesis taken *beyond* the realm of provisional discussion can become dogmatic. The realm of 'big theory' is full of failures because its attempts at synthesis have not also been accompanied by even-handed scepticism. For instance, if we look at Hegelianism,[7] or at Ken Wilber's integrative 'Philosophy of Everything', there are many insights that arise from the synthetic processes that have produced these philosophies, but unfortunately also metaphysical assumptions that undermine their perspective as a whole. Where big theory adopts metaphysical premises, its ability to synthesize different elements misfires because it is simultaneously erecting new sources of conflict in the form of absolutizations. The speculative dogmatism of big theory then invites dismissal, in the form of selective scepticism without practically helpful alternatives being offered.

I suggest that the way to keep synthetic theory reliably provisional is to keep it in the context of the practice of the five principles in this book. Not only do we need to maintain a sense of the uncertainty of our synthetic constructions, but also to maintain awareness of alternatives, think of their advance on previous beliefs as a matter of degree, avoid metaphysically-based appropriation or dismissal of them, and maintain a sense of our own integrative practice and mental states as a context for maintaining provisionality.

---

7   For detailed discussion of Hegel see Ellis (2001) 3.h.

Whatever the possible pitfalls that accompany its use, though, synthesis remains a vital element of human thought, both allowing and depending on provisionality. Philosophy completely loses its way without it, and wider academia is also in danger of doing so. Such synthesis occurs primarily at each moment of judgement where we bring two different elements together to form new meaning and consider new beliefs. Only in this way can we respond to new conditions and maintain a relevant engagement with the world of experience.

2.e. Suppression

> *Summary*
>
> Suppression is highly necessary to provisionality, because without the ability to temporarily direct our attention away from absolutizing distractions, we would remain stuck in them. Suppression allows awareness to continue, in contrast to repression which tries to eliminate an object of conflict. Suppression is recognized in psychology as a 'mature defence', which may also take the form of sublimation, altruism, anticipation, or humour.

How do we deal with unhelpful desires at the wrong moment, such as a wholly inappropriate sexual attraction, or sudden anger? Suppression is the diversion of attention away from particular desires that are dominating that attention, and is a practically necessary process for provisionality. Without the ability to suppress, we would be unable to direct our attention, to concentrate, or to make ethical judgements, because our attention would be constantly hijacked by loud desires attached to insistent absolute beliefs. Suppression enables social institutions to function – for example, allowing straight male teachers to focus on the job when teaching pretty teenage girls – but beyond that, it also enables us to shape our responses to things.

This suppression is not itself an absolutizing process that seeks to deny or eliminate the unwanted desire – that would be *repression*, discussed in *Absolutization* as a basic psychological feature of it and the source of conflict.[1] The distinction between suppression and repression, which many people neglect, is thus crucial. This distinction goes back to Freud and early psychoanalysis, and is basically one of awareness. When we repress, we lose awareness of what we are repressing, whilst when we suppress, we maintain it.

This leads to a common rough and ready distinction between repression and suppression as being that the former is unconscious and the latter conscious. However, the distinction between conscious and unconscious is itself an absolutization of an incremental and permeable boundary.[2] As Simon Boag puts it, 'problems arise from confusing consciousness or unconsciousness with properties

---

1 I.5.a.
2 See Ellis (2022) 1.e.

or qualities of mental processes'.³ Of course, when we suppress, we don't have to keep the object of suppression constantly in mind: the practical criterion is that it should be accessible to us, with those channels sufficiently available. Likewise, when we repress, we may not be unconscious of what we are repressing, but we will decisively reject it and may try to eliminate it. The concept of absolutization thus offers the basis of a clearer distinction between repression and suppression than does that of consciousness: repression occurs on the assumption that we have the whole story and that alternatives to it must be eliminated, whereas suppression is an aspect of provisionality.

Another perspective from which we may be able to distinguish between suppression and repression is neuroscientific. Suppression as we experience it seems to be a right-hemisphere function, with the right frontal cortex being the locus both of emotional awareness and of its inhibition.⁴ However, repression seems in contrast to probably be a left-hemisphere function, the result of absolutized beliefs inhibiting that right-hemisphere awareness.⁵ The two processes are thus qualitatively different neurally in a way that is reflected experientially. In suppression we shift our focus away from a particular desire *because* we are emotionally aware of a wider context, but in repression we tell ourselves a supposedly complete story in which the repressed desire is excluded.

Suppression is not just *compatible* with provisionality, but actively required for it, as we can see if we consider its relationship with absolutization. If we were unable to suppress, we would not be able to maintain a sceptical perspective on absolutized beliefs, which could take over and dominate our awareness, to the exclusion of other options. If we *repress* absolute beliefs, we get more opposing absolute beliefs, but if we suppress whilst leaving the suppressed ideas accessible, we can *put aside* absolute beliefs without either accepting or repressing them. It is this that makes agnosticism not only possible, but distinctive and practically necessary. Balanced scepticism is not negative, as I argued in 1.b above, because by failing to affirm an absolute claim and focusing elsewhere one suppresses rather than represses it.

3   Boag (2010).
4   McGilchrist (2021) p. 223; Kinsbourne & Bemporad (1984).
5   I.5.a.

Suppression can also be seen as delaying an intuitive fast-thinking response and allowing us to become aware of alternative responses before judging. It slows us down and thus enables integration of alternative responses over time. This has been demonstrated in empirical psychology by the imposition of a two-minute delay on experimental subjects who were asked to make a judgement on a harmless but intuitively 'yucky' action (a case of brother-sister incest with reliable contraception). The two-minute delay contributed towards a greater degree of tolerance for actions of this kind.[6]

The role of suppression in provisional judgement, and its contrast with repression, will become clearer if we think about the effects of the alternatives on judgement. If we repress inconvenient feelings, they may distort our judgement directly in the form of what psychologists in the psychoanalytic tradition have called 'immature defences'. For example, we might project repressed feelings onto another person – say, being uncritical of them because of an unconscious repressed sexual attraction. Or we might confuse the repressed feeling with ourselves as a whole and create passive aggression based on self-hatred, for instance blaming ourselves but in a way that tries to make someone else feel bad. The displacement of the repressed feelings might result in 'acting out' – bouts of violent behaviour, or withdrawal into fantasy.[7] However, the opposite fault of not suppressing at all may just result in daydreaming; not neurotic but merely ineffectual. If we do not bring our attention to bear on a situation, we will not make any judgements about it, but merely drift passively or go along with socially dominant suggestions.

In between, then, suppression can enable us to make balanced judgements that do focus energy, but not in a way that is disruptive to our judgement in the long term. This necessary suppression can be identified with mature defences as recognized by George Vaillant on the basis of long-term empirical surveys. He lists five mature defences: sublimation, altruism, suppression, anticipation, and humour;[8] although this includes suppression explicitly as one of five mature defences, one could also identify suppression as an aspect of each of the other four. Mature 'defences' are also integrations incorporating suppression.

6   Paxton, Unger, & Greene (2011).
7   Vaillant (1993) pp. 45–59.
8   Ibid. pp. 66–73.

Sublimation, the first of these, involves the refinement of difficult feelings into more subtle forms, such as the arts. To do this, clearly, we need to suppress any grosser expression of these feelings at the time we become aware of them, but be able to maintain awareness of them over time until artistic expression can be achieved. Since works of art of any kind always take time to create, sublimation requires a sustained integration of suppressed feelings that are kept alive and channelled into the sublimated form, throughout the time of creation. Vaillant movingly discusses the example of the dramatist Eugene O'Neill here, sublimating his traumatic childhood experiences into his play *A Long Day's Journey into Night*.[9] Through this process O'Neill was able to gradually gain a more adequate view of his childhood experiences, including a sympathetic understanding of the pain undergone by his mother.

Altruism similarly involves the suppression of one's own feelings in order to direct them into activity that is concerned with others. Someone who is bereaved, for instance, but who has to keep going with caring for their children, might either use those demands to repress their grief, or alternatively use them as a means of working through that grief. The difficult feelings need to be maintained in awareness in order to be channelled empathetically. This kind of altruism, as Vaillant defines it, needs to be distinguished from 'reaction formation' that involves self-hatred in contrast to one's feelings for others. Instead, altruists can integrate their own responses in relation to others, entering a balancing feedback loop in which the impact of the new situation helps to make them aware of all the conditions around all their relationships. By doing this, again, they are able to make increasingly adequate judgements about others, recognizing their range of assumptions and motives.

Anticipation involves the suppression of present feelings in order to plan how to manage them in the future. This obviously requires an integration of one's beliefs over time in relation to a range of conditions. Someone who suppresses their feelings at a particular time by deciding to think about them later is anticipating in this way.

Humour also involves the suppression of unacceptable feelings, but continuing awareness of these feelings in the guise of playful expressions of them. Humour obviously puts difficult feelings in a provisional framework that is no longer subject to 'serious' reactions

9   Ibid. ch. 11.

because framed by playfulness, as illustrated by the way that our humour often focuses on topics that could create strong emotional reactions, such as death, sex, or group identity. In this framework one can continue to acknowledge those feelings without being dominated by them. Humour as a practice is also discussed in 6.e below. However, judgements made humorously may not address conditions well in the longer term because they do not involve a 'serious' engagement with conditions, and thus humour can also be used as a form of evasion, 'laughing it off', that slides from suppression into repression.

In this way, then, sublimation, altruism, anticipation, and humour can all become potential aspects of a provisional judgement. They all continue to leave options open that might otherwise be closed and create absolutization, and they all slow down our responses in a way that allows us to address wider conditions in the long run. They all also enable synthesis between different ideas that might otherwise be separated by a narrower analytic framework of thinking: sublimation by bringing subtler or more creative ideas together with a grosser one, altruism by bringing together concerns of different people, anticipation by bringing together concerns over time, and humour by bringing together apparently contradictory ideas in a manageable framework. None of these integrative processes, however, would be possible if we could not first sideline the absolutizations that may threaten to take over the whole context.

2.f. Probabilizing

> *Summary*
>
> Estimating probability, even if it cannot be very precisely determined, is an important aspect of provisionality practice. It is an estimate of justification rather than of a relationship to 'reality', and the process of making that estimation is more important than the results, because it helps us avoid absolutizing. We need to take very small and very large probabilities seriously, and even recognizing the distinction between asymptotic probability and certainty is still of general practical value. We can also probabilize value claims by considering the probability of the prescribed desires being fulfilled in an integrated form.

To think in terms of probability is to take into account uncertainty from the beginning, when making judgements about events. 'Probabilizing' is a term that turns the estimation of probabilities into a verb, the process being more important than the precision of the probability itself. Recent research shows that framing judgements in probabilistic terms helps people to avoid disinformation, when compared to framing things in binary terms.[1] However, it is the ability to recognize and signal uncertainty that is shown to make the difference in this research, rather than the precision of the probability itself. I want to suggest that thinking in terms of rough probabilities, rather than in terms of certainties one way or the other, is another crucial feature of provisionality.

It's helpful to consider from the outset what relationship probability tries to capture. Conventionally this is seen as the relationship between a description of an event and the reality of that description (the two being identical making a 100% probability), but since our embodied situation (and basic sceptical argument) makes it unjustifiable to assume any such representational relationship, I propose that probability should instead be seen as the relationship between a description and the weight of experiential justification for it in practice. Probability is usually applied to factual claims, but this pragmatic interpretation of its meaning also allows it to be applied to value claims (a point I will come back to below).

Probabilizing also overlaps with incrementality (tackled more fully in the next section), because probabilities are a matter of degree rather than of discontinuous absolute belief. Probability

1   Guilbeault, Woolley, & Becker (2021).

does not involve claiming that a particular statement is 'true' or 'false', but rather considering how far we are justified in believing in it. Commonly this is applied to future events – for example, a 30% chance that it will rain tomorrow. However, it could also be applied to past events, especially where we have limited justification for our beliefs – for example, how likely is it that the Duke of Edinburgh had secret extra-marital affairs? – or to ongoing events through the present – how likely is it that recent trends in African population growth are being maintained? We can even estimate the likelihood that what appears to be an offensive statement in an email was intended to be so.

Probabilizing is valuable because it opens up new options for our judgement. Rather than the absolutizing alternatives (for instance, that either it will rain tomorrow or it won't, or either the person meant to be offensive or they didn't), forming our beliefs as a probability forces us to consider a range of possibilities and face up to more complex conditions. It also forces us to make ourselves part of the picture and take into account the limitations of our information concerning a particular event, such as the unpredictable complexity of the weather or the limitations in understanding someone else's mental state based only on a few words. To form a probability we also have to slow down and synthesize a range of relevant information. We have to think *conditionally*, taking into account the relationships between different events rather than thinking about them in isolation.

Clearly these helpful processes are most strongly present when scientists work through a precise and formal mechanism for generating a probability, by considering a range of evidence about the conditions at work, and perhaps even measuring or otherwise quantifying what they find. However, not every condition can be easily or appropriately measured so as to form such relatively precise probabilities. This is of course the reason why much research, especially in the humanities and social sciences, is qualitative rather than quantitative. If you are concerned, for instance, with people's sensations or feelings, you cannot measure these directly, but only substitute very approximate proxies such as changes in physiological processes (like heart rate) or reported feelings on a notional scale. The likelihood that someone will be made to feel jealous by seeing their partner speaking at length to someone else, for instance, could only be very roughly measured, if at all. Nevertheless, it is worth *probabilizing* such an event when we think about it as an aspect of making our beliefs provisional. We could do this by considering whether it is 'very likely', 'somewhat likely', 'somewhat unlikely', or 'very unlikely', using deliberately vague language that reflects the vagueness of our justification. Alternatively, we could compare the likelihood of one event with that of another (for instance, considering whether it is more likely that someone will feel jealous than not).

So, vague probabilizing has considerable value in the process of judgement in practice, when compared with absolutization. The evident precision of scientific probability, in contrast to vague probabilizing, can be false, as it sometimes conceals the uncertainty of the assumptions and the vagueness of the evidence on which it is based. The *attempt* at precision can be valuable because of the process that went into considering the conditions as precisely as possible, but the outcome can then potentially be interpreted absolutely, particularly by others who are unaware of the complexity of the process by which a probability is reached, and adopt only the idea of it being precisely justified. A good example of this is the probabilities used to express the effectiveness of vaccines, which are based on tests conducted with a particular group at a particular moment of the evolution of the disease to be prevented by the vaccine. This inexactness can to some extent be addressed by margins of error, which add further layers of probability by estimating the probability that a probability will be wrong. Sophisticated Bayesian processes of modifying one set of probabilities in the light of further evidence can also help to refine and complexify probability. However, offering further complexity of this kind, whilst helpful, cannot prevent the abuse of probabilities by those who absolutize them, often filtering out accompanying complexity in the process.

The research of Daniel Kahneman and his associates has cast light on the way we actually judge probabilities, by showing the discrepancy between formally stated probabilities and the ways that they weight decisions in practice. This discrepancy is especially evident at the extremes of the scale, showing our tendency to distort increments by interpreting them in absolute terms. A 1% probability, for instance, is in practice treated as a 5.5% probability, as we over-react to a small probability, whilst a 99% probability is treated as 91.2%, as we over-react to the lack of total certainty in a particular event.[2] Our responses here are shaped by whether we are likely to gain or lose by the probable event, so Kahneman distinguishes two kinds: a 'certainty effect' for high probabilities and a 'possibility effect' for low probabilities. When there is a large probability of gain that is not quite a certainty, we become risk-averse (treating 99% as 91.2%), but when there is a slight chance of gain we become risk-seeking (treating 1% as 5.5%). On the other hand, when there is a large danger of loss we become risk-seeking (treating 99% as 91.2%) and when there is a small possibility of loss we become risk-averse (treating 1% as 5.5%).[3] At the same time, then, these results show that we could respond more adequately to what strike us as near-certainties by taking small probabilities seriously. This is perhaps one of the key aspects of probabilizing as an aspect of provisionality – making the reflective effort to treat small probabilities as just that, not as effective certainties.

This point applies particularly to asymptotes – that is to probabilities that infinitely approach the line of certainty when plotted on a graph, but never actually get there. As I argued in 1.c above, sceptical arguments that raise *possibilities* are still helpful because they are effectively telling us about the difference between an extremely small probability and a certainty. For example, it is *possible* that there is an aardvark hiding somewhere in my house, though it is not in the least likely, I have no positive reasons for believing it, and the consideration is not practically relevant. The only value in raising the possibility is to help make me aware of the impact of unknown unknowns – which do have an effect. I do not *know* that there is no aardvark hiding in my house because I do not *know* the falsehood of many other possibilities, most of which I may never even have imagined. Such events are subject to the limitations of the ways we classify, interpret, and describe our experience as well as to the unpredictability of the events themselves (What is an aardvark? Would I know it if I saw it?). By reflecting on this, I increase the general adequacy of my response to conditions by taking into account the limitations of my beliefs about them. A similar function can be played by probabilizing assumed certainty at the other end

---

2   Kahneman (2011) pp. 314–16.
3   Ibid. pp. 316–19.

of the scale, for instance noting that it is *possible* that the sun may not rise tomorrow.

If we follow through the implications of scepticism as explored in the first section of this book, an asymptotic probability is indeed the nearest we can get to certainty *whatever* statements we may make. Oft-cited claims of *a priori* certainty, such as that 2+2=4 is absolutely certain, rely entirely on representationalism, and take no account of the possibility of both unknown unknowns and interpretative errors in the relationship we assume between our *a priori* system as a whole and reality. That the symbols used in mathematics have not descended from the Platonic heavens, but gain their meaning from a relationship with our bodies, and gain coherence because of the construction of cognitive models, has been demonstrated by Lakoff and Nuñez in a book that should be required reading for all Platonically-minded mathematicians.[4] There is no doubt about the totally coherent relationship between the signs used in mathematics: 2+2=4 is consistent with the laws of arithmetic, geometry, logic, etc. What is in doubt is the relationship between that extensive system of signs and reality, which is at best asymptotic. So there is a very high probability that universally accepted mathematical or other *a priori* 'laws' are correct in relation to reality, but no certainty.

The recognition that probability is basically a *practical* judgement about a claim being the best one available in a particular situation also leaves it open for us to apply it to values. Just as the probability that a factual claim like 'the cat is pregnant' or 'Ulan Bator is the capital of Mongolia' is the best fit can be given a more or (often) less precise quantification, so could the claim that 'we should look after the cat' or 'Mongolia is a beautiful country'. An understanding of values and of ethical and aesthetic justification in terms of Middle Way Philosophy requires a much more extended discussion than I can provide here.[5] However, the crucial point is that they can be probabilized. The probability we ascribe to a value claim is the likelihood of it being correct, in the sense of being the best value claim we can apply in the specific circumstances of its application.

The treatment of value claims is often given a false, absolute distinction from factual claims. In *Absolutization*, I explained how any effective response to absolutization requires us to take the claims

---

4   Lakoff & Nuñez (2000).
5   See VII and VIII for full discussion.

we assess as *normative* as well as descriptive, because recognizing that normative element is a prompt to provisionality.[6] Absolutized ethics encourages us to think of ethical judgement as necessarily absolute, only because this is seen as the only alternative to relativism, but instead we can think of normativity as *stretching* our motivated judgement (often in response to an archetypal symbol of an absolute position that reminds us of the possibility of going further). The best available normative claims will be the ones that, in practice, stretch our identifications most effectively without breaking them – the ones that *work* by stimulating us to extend our desires in a way that takes more of the conditions into account. The probability of a value claim being the best one is the probability of it doing this, rather than merely offering an idealization or a signal of social conformity.

To probabilize a value claim, then, takes investigative work parallel to that undertaken by scientists investigating a theoretical factual claim. We need to become aware of the value claim (typically that something 'should' be done, or that a type of belief or action is 'good') in relation to our desire to fulfil it, and assess the *integration* of that desire. More will be said about this in section 5, but the integration of a desire marks how well it is actually capable of being fulfilled (even in a modified form) in a variety of conditions. For example, I may desire to give up drinking alcohol, but the integration of that desire depends on how well it is coherent with my other desires over time, and how well it fits with the environment created by my relationships with others who might encourage or discourage this goal. There is a high probability of my desire to give up alcohol being the right desire for the circumstances (and thus of a precept I might adopt to give it up being the right precept) if it is sufficiently in harmony with my other habitual desires and sufficiently in tune with my environment to be successful. If, on the other hand, my valuing of giving up alcohol is just an idealization of what I think it 'right' to do 'in theory', based only on more limited abstract considerations (such as the rules of a religion I pay lip-service to for mainly social reasons), it has a much lower chance of success.

In such cases, the assessment of probability is thus increasingly hard to separate from an overall judgement about how to act, which I will consider in the next chapter. The two are especially

6   I.8.b.

interdependent where value claims are concerned, compared to what we normally see as factual claims. A factual claim has a limited probability of being correct, but at least we can try to ascertain this in a way that is largely independent of our judgement as a whole. It is this relative independence that we often mistake for a factual claim being 'obviously true': people are likely to agree that Ulan Bator is the capital of Mongolia (at least if they look it up), and that flying in a commercial airliner is a relatively safe mode of travel (at least if they're not in the grip of a fear of flying), regardless of the specifics of a particular trip to Mongolia. These claims have a high probability of being pragmatically correct. Whether it is likely to be right for me to fly to Mongolia next week, though, is very difficult to differentiate from the justification of a wider decision process about whether to actually do so.

In some cases, though, value claims can be of a very general kind that seem obviously correct, because they accord with most people's experience. That it is wrong to tell lies or to commit murder is generally correct because in most cases such actions would probably produce conflicts in the longer term – perhaps extremely acute and dangerous ones. We could not integrate the justification of such actions in most situations, although we also cannot rule out the possibility of exceptions, which are the stock-in-trade of ethicists. For example, if a murderer comes to your house with the clear intention of killing your friend, it seems ethically right to lie to him. Nevertheless, we can attribute quite a high *probability* to 'lying is wrong' being correct in most cases.

Probabilizing, then, is not merely a specific scientific or mathematical process, but on the contrary a much more widespread and basic way of making every kind of judgement provisional, and thus of taking the implications of scepticism into account. The use of numbers to denote probability quite often gives a false impression of precision to it (though not always – it depends what these figures are based on). What is far more important is that we are making every judgement on the basis of an attempt to assess the adequacy of the way we understand the circumstances of that judgement. This applies in both general and specific factual terms, and also in terms of the values we may be inclined to apply to it.

2.g. Weighing up

> *Summary*
>
> Weighing up is the final process of making practical judgements when these are required, a process that can be contrasted with that of merely deducing our conclusion. The process of weighing up involves determining comparative justification through both 'positive' elements that do involve reasoning (comparing options with criteria and with evidence) and 'negative' elements that determine the range of conditions considered by contextualizing beyond absolute assumptions. Deductions are often less important, because they are only about distinctions we identify with rather than practical outcomes.

Provisionality is not only about the general mental conditions in which we make our judgements, because it is also about the decision-making process itself. Decision-making is a practically necessary aspect of being an embodied organism. We act in the world, and thus we must judge. To make a provisional rather than an absolutized judgement, though, we *weigh up* rather than *deduce*. Provisionality thus does not imply indecisiveness, but rather a modified process of decision.

An absolutized judgement in which there are only two opposed options is not a process of weighing up, only a process of deducing one's judgement from a prior absolute belief. *Deducing* applies a specific abstract commitment to a case. It could also be seen as a process of *matching*, associating one case with another. Deduction or matching is used for absolutized judgement when our desires are oriented primarily towards a quick solution that will maintain the basic self-esteem that we have, still dependent on group approval. To do that we have learnt to apply the absolute rule we have learnt from the group, in the process rejecting the negative opposite that is associated with the outgroup.[1]

The presence of further options in a provisional judgement, however, makes a different kind of process necessary – one that involves comparison of different possible beliefs about the same issue and estimation of their degree of justification, prior to selecting the one that is most justified. This better fits the metaphor of 'weighing up' – seeing which of the options 'carries the most weight'. In terms of the brain, this process is one that takes place in the right prefrontal

1   I.5.e.

cortex, which maintains awareness of relationships between different views, and then mediates any conflicts between them.[2] This process can be distinguished from the mere application of one proposition or categorization to a new case, which takes place in the left hemisphere.[3]

Although there may be some deduction involved here (to recognize the consistency or inconsistency of different beliefs, and to check each option against a possible criterion of adequacy), this is far less important to the outcome than maintaining awareness of the different options at the same time, and identifying appropriate criteria from a synthesis of those options. If we imagine more options, say, but make a mistake when working out whether they are consistent, this makes little difference to the practical outcome, only to the labels we apply to it. It only matters whether one position is consistent or inconsistent with another when there is a conflict of some kind. For instance, if I turn out to have made a mistake of comparative reasoning and Middle Way Philosophy is actually identical to a position I have criticized as absolutizing, then that position will still in practice be the best available one, whatever we call it. Whether it is or is not really Buddhism, Marxism, Naturalism, or any other ism is largely a matter of group identification, pride, and narrowly focused scholarly energy (all very much dependent on deductive reasoning that merely categorizes and applies propositions) – but what matters is how we understand the position we do end up identifying in relation to practice.

In contrast, the dominant academic language tends to identify many of the features of provisionality with 'rationality'. This is a term I deliberately avoid, because at best it is likely to model the synthetic process of weighing up within an assumed framework of analysis, or at worst to ignore the synthesis altogether.[4] As I argued in *Absolutization*, the inflation of logic to make it apparently apply to many things it does not apply to is an aspect of absolutization,[5] and discussions of 'rationality', especially in analytic philosophy, tend to just be exercises in appropriating all judgement to a framework dominated by an association with logic.

---

2   McGilchrist (2021) p. 170; Stolstorff, Vartanian, & Goel (2012).
3   McGilchrist (2021) p. 176.
4   For a critique of one recent analytic account of 'rationality' see Ellis (2017).
5   I.4.f.

Rather than provisional, allegedly 'rational' judgements modelling reasoning, it is in absolute judgement that non-relational deductive reasoning is most obvious, as it commonly involves a relatively clear belief and a reasoning of the implications of that belief. The reasoning of fundamentalists, for instance, is impeccable in its deduction of practical rules from absolutized texts of which only one interpretation is allowed. In provisional thinking, however, it is the assumptions we start with (which are just as much 'emotional' as 'rational') that make the difference between absolute and provisional judgement, and it is a combination of integrative practices (see section 6) that can most effectively help us to modify those assumptions by contextualizing them.

Instead of reasoning, I suggest that the emphasis in provisional judgement needs to be on *how justified* each of a set of available options is. *Justification* includes both 'positive' and 'negative' (or agnostic) forms. The positive element of justification does involve reasoning in the sense of identifying and resolving a relationship: for instance, judging whether an option accords with the evidence that we have encountered, the testimony of sources we trust, or other beliefs we already hold. Our assumptions about these things, however, depend in turn on the assumptions we have made further back, including how we have interpreted the evidence we are using, and whether this has been considered in a wider context. Positive justification is required for practical judgement, but it is constantly subject to confirmation bias. It thus needs to be supplemented by a 'negative' or 'agnostic' awareness of the limitations of its own basis. Perhaps counter-intuitively, a belief is *better* justified when we are aware of the limitations of its justification due to a wider context. These 'positive' and 'negative' elements can be mixed in complex ways at different stages of our thinking. What is crucial is that they fertilize each other as much as possible. The final process of 'weighing up' has to involve both: a positive judgement along with expanding awareness of what is being considered.

To compare the differing weights (or justifications) of different possible beliefs, we must have some basis for comparing them. This does not necessarily mean precise quantification, but it must offer some basis of differentiation in experience. Absolutized claims do not do this: for instance, God cannot be judged more or less likely to exist,[6] but is assumed either to exist or not exist metaphysically. Even if an absolute claim were to take an apparently incremental or comparative form (for example, a dogmatically held claim that cheetahs always run faster than lions), the psychological conditions of that claim would prevent it from being weighed up, with the claim being infinitely rationalized[7] rather than examined in relation to alternatives (for example, 'that slow cheetah you recorded must have been injured – it doesn't count').

In some cases, absolutization is relatively easy to identify, whilst in others, its presence may be much more debatable.[8] For example, if someone directly claims to have an infallible perspective, the presence of absolutization becomes so obvious that our judgement about it, though still fallible, is asymptotically near-certain. We thus need to probabilize our judgements about the *presence* of absolutization (not to be confused with the absolutization itself, which cannot be probabilized). Such judgements about the likely presence of absolutization need to be taken into account alongside our positive judgements about the content of what is being said.

Weighing up, then, is the comparison of justifications of the different possible beliefs we could arrive at, based initially on a check for the likelihood of absolutization for each belief, and then on the positive probability of the belief being correct. If there is a very high chance of absolutization (as evidenced, for instance, by the presence of some common biases and fallacies[9]) then we may well discount a particular possible belief as not acceptable because it is not justifiable in experience at all as far as we can tell. If, however, the belief is fairly clearly not absolutized, or there is more reasonable doubt about whether it is, we can then go ahead to weigh up the positive justifications and choose the one with the strongest justification.

Let's take an example from very ordinary experience. Supposing I have an area of grass on my property. If I just assume that the grass needs to be cut, there would simply be a practical judgement to be made about the best sort of lawn-mower to use. Petrol-driven? Electric? Manual? A scythe? Sheep? Guinea pigs? However, it's also possible that my view that the grass needs to be cut contains an absolute assumption based on cultural norms: perhaps I should also

6   I.4.d.
7   I.4.d.
8   I.3.d.
9   iv.3; V.

consider the ecological advantages of simply letting it gradually grow into forest (a consideration that group norms might well have excluded!). If I have checked for absolutizations of this kind to start with and concluded that they are not likely to be present, then I just need to consider the comparative advantages and disadvantages of the different possible approaches to the task.

That weighing up is an aspect of provisionality can be readily seen from its close relationship to all the other features of provisionality. We can only weigh up different *options* if we recognize them initially. To do so takes into account more *complexity* through the recognition that a variety of models may explain our experience in ways that are more or less adequate. Weighing up takes longer than merely selecting an absolute option, so involves *slow* thinking. It brings together different options in a way that requires *synthesis*. The initial process of recognizing and discounting absolutized options is one of *suppression* (but not repression), and the basis for comparative judgement is created by *probabilizing*.

Weighing up also connects closely with all the other principles. We are able to weigh up because we do not immediately accept one belief as 'true', due to basic *scepticism*. We are able to compare different options because each one is understood *incrementally*. We discount absolutized options because of an awareness of absolutization and its effects, which is dependent on the practice of *agnosticism*. The conclusions we reach by weighing up are also compatible with each other in a way that absolutized ones are not, creating *integration*. In some ways, the process of weighing up also depends on integration that prevents premature judgement due to conflict.

Weighing up is the final element of the picture of provisionality that makes it an entirely practical approach. In some cases, it results in a decision to act in one way or another. In other cases, it results in a judgement that is itself incremental and feeds into a wider and more long-term process of weighing up over the longer term. At every level, the making of judgements that accord with the structure of systems reflects systems themselves, interacting at many levels.

3. Incrementality

3.a. Systemic Continuity

> *Summary*
>
> Incrementality is the practice of conceptualizing the qualities of all objects and events as a matter of degree rather than as discontinuous absolutes, aiding our continuing attention rather than shortcut absolutization. This gets us closer to a systemic view of objects that is not just left-hemisphere formatted. In practice this needs to be done in moments of reflection.

The term *incrementality* (from the Latin *crescere*, to grow) suggests gradual growth as opposed to instantaneous change. I use it interchangeably with *continuity*, and particularly to mean the principle that we should try to conceptualize the qualities of all objects and events (in space, time, and conceptual space) as a matter of degree, rather than as absolutes. In *Absolutization* I explained the way in which absolutizing creates discontinuity, particularly through the over-dominance of left-hemisphere sequencing of discrete representations over the sustained attention of the right hemisphere through time.[1] If we are to appreciate anything gradually changing, either for itself or because we are focusing on changing parts of it, we need to maintain the continuity of our attention between the different parts, seeing them as both the same in some respects and different in others. If we absolutize, on the other hand, we apply a verbal description to an object or event that makes it uniform and permanent. Incrementality is the practice that helps us to avoid absolutization by working against this tendency.

Incrementality is an obvious development of embodiment, aiding our capacity to adapt our understanding of both the world and ourselves. That world appears to show continuity as a basic feature, whenever we get beyond our imposition of conceptual discontinuity. It is a *systemic* feature of things, because it is through the interrelationships of a system that continuity becomes

[1] I.3.c.

unavoidable. Any system can potentially be analysed into sub-systems that interact with each other, and it is the relationship between these sub-systems that make the system: for instance, the cells make an animal or plant, and the planets or other bodies make the solar system. It is the relationships between these sub-systems that can help us visualize why systems always involve continuity. For that system to change, its sub-systems need to change, either by entering or leaving the larger system or by re-organizing themselves within it, and that change requires some period of time. Entering or leaving, however, is just re-organization within the terms of a wider system. For the elements of a system to re-organize means they need to move around relative to each other. Think of a group of people asked to exchange places: they can't do this instantaneously, but each has to move to their new place relative to the others. An instantaneous change is impossible because it would require one sub-system to occupy the same niche as another simultaneously.

We may be especially reminded of that continuity when we think of the growth, decay, movement, and interaction of living systems. Living systems are cells, each of which is in turn a living system, for which each change involves a gradual mutual adjustment. Not only the conditions out there, but the processes of our body-minds are continuous, so to think of things as continuous also gets us closer to understanding our own conditions. Even when a change seems 'purely mental', it involves a development of our neural connections that is subject to the same systemic incrementality.

However, the main reason why it's important to recognize continuity is the negative one of the discontinuity of absolutizations. Our right-hemisphere mediated, empirical understanding will obviously understand things as they are experienced, incrementally, but absolutization instead imposes a conceptual abstraction that overrules that continuous experience. Since the discontinuous sequencing of time in the left hemisphere makes these conceptual abstractions unavoidably discontinuous (see 3.e below), their discontinuity becomes one of the clearest indications of potential absolutization. When absolutization is occurring, one of the easiest ways to introduce new options into our framing of the situation is thus to incrementalize our concepts.

In practice, we incrementalize by reflecting on the concepts we are using at points when we have the opportunity to do so. We are unlikely to be able to introduce new incrementality in the midst of practical activity, but whenever we reflect, we can examine our assumptions about the absolute nature of the objects or events we consider. For example, when we're interacting with someone this is often on the basis of fixed and discontinuous categories – 'businessman', 'Japanese', etc. – but reflection can make us recognize that the influence of business and of Japanese nationality or culture are both matters of degree and interact with other influences (see 3.d for more on continuity of persons). This reflection can be made effective by prior awareness of incrementality as an alternative, and might be prompted by a symbol that is archetypally associated for us with the experience of awareness of such wider alternatives. This could be the Middle Way in general as a symbol, or perhaps a specific symbol of incrementality such as steps.

Incrementality needs clarification in a number of other respects, that will be the subject of the remaining chapters in this section. One initial question is that of the speed of change, as although all systemic change is incremental, systems can sometimes change very rapidly. In systems terminology such rapid changes are known as *tipping points*, at which instability in the system causes it to break down and reassemble in a radically different form. In 3.b I will go into more detail about how we can distinguish tipping points from instantaneous change, and why it is important to do so. Another area that will need considerable discussion is the way in which we are obliged to assume discontinuity for practical judgement, which may seem in conflict with the principle of incrementality. How can we navigate this need to switch between continuity and discontinuity? That will be the focus of 3.c. Some of the key points about the nature of incrementality covered in these three chapters (3.a–c) are summarized in the mind map here (**figure 5**).

To explore the implications of incrementality, it will also be helpful to look at some of the different ways it can be applied. Our view of persons, whether ourselves or others, is an obvious starting point, where discontinuity can also be seen in what are readily identifiable as biased or prejudiced judgements. This can apply to our view of others (especially those in other groups, such as other races and other political tribes), but also to ourselves. This is the subject of 3.d.

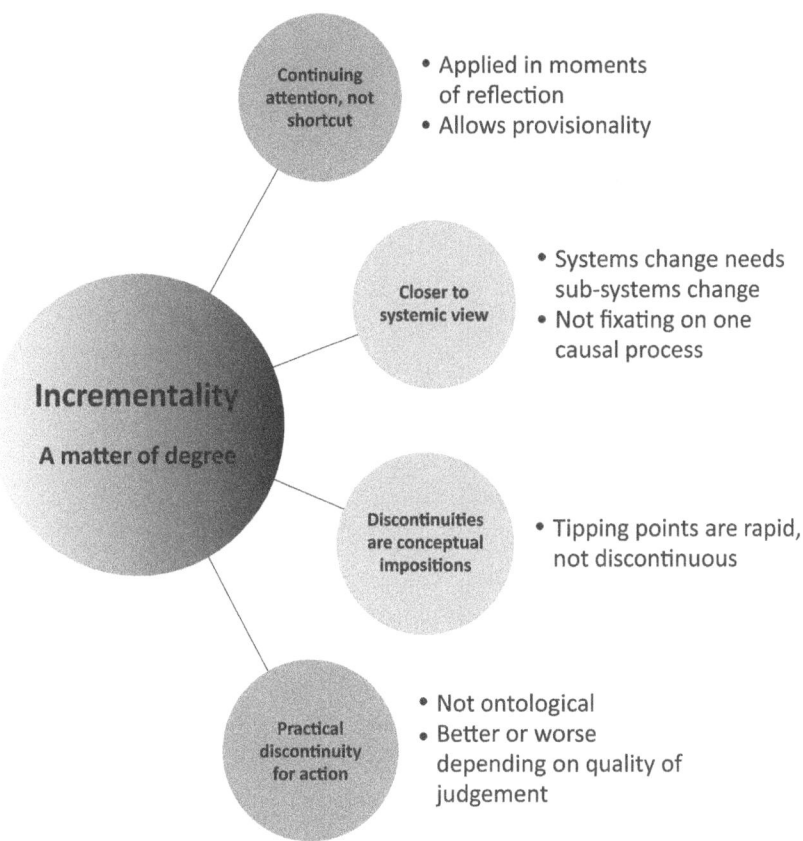

Figure 5. Features of incrementality: mind map.

More broadly, also, recognizing the continuity of time prevents us from absolutizing our perspective at one time, in the process neither denying the sequencing of time nor taking the phenomena we observe at one time to be fixed. Incrementality applied to time, then, can capture many of the insights offered in the Buddhist doctrine of impermanence (*anatta*), without us needing to interpret it into a metaphysical claim about the universe. I will discuss this further in 3.e.

The continuity of space follows from the way in which our observation of space changes with the movements of our attention and embodied perspective over time: so if we start to treat time as continuous, we must treat space in the same way. There are thus no absolute boundaries between objects to be assumed in the phenomenal world we inhabit. This point also extends to conceptual spaces developed from more directly experienced ones through metaphor. This is the topic of 3.f.

Finally, the incrementality in the way we develop also needs to be reflected in what we might call the continuity of training. This means moving from the kind of paradigm of learning in which we are expected to 'not know' something and then 'know' it, to one in which we extend the neural connections of meaning further whilst they adjust in relation to each other. This is the most directly recognized form of incrementality in Buddhist sources, but is also interrelated with the other applications of the principle. I'll discuss this in 3.g.

3.b. Tipping Points

> *Summary*
>
> Tipping points are rapid changes in systems that should not be confused with conceptually imposed discontinuity. Changes in systems take time, which is why attempts to force a conceptual vision without addressing all the conditions backfire. Genuine change in systems requires change in all the sub-systems, but we often fallaciously attribute a change only to its most immediate and evident cause. We adopt discontinuous social conventions and substitute these for gradual processes, or assume total change has occurred when previous conditions still have an influence.

A tipping point is a rapid change in a system, in which instability accelerates to the point where key features break down. Academic attempts to describe this rapid change tend to use the term 'discontinuity',[1] which is somewhat unfortunate given that one of my key arguments is that tipping points are *not* discontinuous! The difference is explained by the fact that I am using the term 'discontinuity' in an absolute sense to discuss the role of absolutization and how we can avoid it, whilst systems theorists are only discussing discontinuity in a relative sense. However, relative discontinuity is simply rapid change. Absolute discontinuity is, instead, instantaneous change of a kind that we never observe in practice, only in our conceptual idealizations.

A tipping point is also only relatively rapid compared to the change seen before it. An obvious example is the tipping point with which we are currently threatened in global climate change. The loss of reflective capacity from melting ice, the release of methane from thawing permafrost, and a number of other phenomena, all contribute to reinforcing feedback loops that threaten to accelerate global warming uncontrollably and take it beyond a point where we could possibly halt it. Compared to the relative stability of the climate beforehand, these changes are rapid. In the context of the earth's long history through geological time, they may seem almost instantaneous. However, from our short-lived point of view they still seem to take quite a while, and it is partly the slow-motion nature of the impending disaster that seems to make it difficult for

---

1   Lamberson & Page (2012).

us to grasp it and respond adequately to it. A tipping point may accelerate towards a climax of rapid change, and yet still seem relatively slow from other points of view.

The practice of incrementality in relation to tipping points is to continue to frame even rapid changes as incremental ones. That does not imply that we should not act as rapidly as possible in response to them in cases such as climate change (incrementality is not an excuse for inaction). However, the expectation of instantaneous change is one of the major forms that absolutization can take, distorting our understanding of conditions and seriously detracting from the adequacy of our responses. For instance, an impatient expectation of learning (whether of oneself or others) fails to take into account the time required to change the conditions in a human system. The belief in absolutized freewill is accompanied by the assumption that we can instantaneously change our habits or views through the acceptance of a proposition. At a social level, the expectation of instantaneous change through revolution has been very damaging – and of course always backfired. Revolutions cannot succeed in creating instantaneous change, because systems do not change instantaneously: instead, the attempt to force rapid change to correspond with conceptual belief is followed by a recursion of previous conditions entrenched in the system, and these are rationalized either in terms of the revolution or as against it. This is the insight of Edmund Burke in relation to the French Revolution:[2] even if he had questionable assumptions of his own, Burke was one of the forerunners in recognizing the fruitlessness of trying to force instantaneous change on a complex system when a wide range of other supporting conditions had not been addressed.

However, there are of course tipping points of psychological and social change in which change happens relatively quickly: for instance, dramatic religious conversions and coups d'etat. Rapid psychological change seems to depend on the release of previous repression, causing a surge of energy, ecstatic emotion, and a sense of new insight as previously separated neural connections are unified. The more integrated psychic system is then able to adopt new meaning more deeply, throughout the whole of it, than it did before. Social change, on the other hand, seems to occur rapidly at times when the conditions in many of our individual systems

---

2   Burke (1910/1790).

respond similarly, so that a particular new condition applied to a whole lot of people causes them all to respond rapidly in similar ways. This is the pattern in an epidemic, when the same vulnerabilities in a lot of people cause the rapid spread of a virus, and Malcolm Gladwell points out the ways in which many other social tipping points follow the same pattern.[3] It only requires a few particularly influential people to adopt a new product, for instance, that also fits a particular niche in the desires of humans ('stickiness'), for the new product to be rapidly adopted.[4]

In general, then, a tipping point in a wider system is caused by similar (and often connected) changes in the smaller systems that comprise it. If you can find the similarity of pattern in all the sub-systems, you can change the wider system quickly by changing all the sub-systems simultaneously, but only if the conditions in all the sub-systems are similar enough or interdependent enough. Of course, the sub-systems still take some time to change, and they may not all change exactly simultaneously. If there is sufficient warming of a wide area of tundra, permafrost will melt and methane be released in many different places simultaneously. If a map and clear instructions are provided on where and how to get a tetanus vaccination, a larger number of people who appreciate the dangers of tetanus will actually move to get vaccinated, and you will get a surge rather than a steady trickle of them.[5] If I learn a new word in a foreign language, I am more likely to remember it a month later if I have associated it with meaning in more different contexts at different times (following the general 'spacing effect'[6]), so that the new sub-systems of verbal memory are interdependent. I will then apparently pass from 'not knowing' the word to 'knowing' the word.

Even when tipping points are understood as processes, they can't be precisely separated from the time before they began or after they finished, because to do this would be another form of absolute discontinuity. The beginnings and ends of tipping points are thus asymptotes, as already discussed in 2.f. We cannot say for sure when we began or finished learning a foreign language, or when the

---

3 Gladwell (2000) p. 9.
4 Ibid. ch. 1.
5 Ibid. pp. 97–8.
6 Woźniak & Gorzelańczyk (1994).

tundra is either completely melted or not melted at all. The conditions are too subject to uncertainty.

Gestalt psychology involves another sort of tipping point. *Gestalt* recognition, say of a pattern, depends on grasping it as a whole rather than as a set of parts. We may ponder the parts of a picture but still not 'get it', until we reach the 'aha moment' of suddenly grasping the pattern of the whole thing. In neural or psychological terms, though, this is still a relatively rapid tipping point event, not an instantaneous event, as has been shown in studies of animate face recognition.[7] The making of a final connection allows a whole set of other neural connections to be rapidly integrated, but the previous connections were still important to the process, and even the making of the final connection is still a process.

The temptation to absolutize tipping points is associated with various forms of fallacious thinking. One of these is the fallacy of the single cause, in which the most immediate and obvious contribution to a given new event is assumed to be its sole cause. In this way, the 'straw that broke the camel's back' is taken to be the cause, rather than all the other weights that are loaded on the camel's back. Another is the fallacy of composition, in which we mistake a part for a whole: we may think that an apparently instantaneous turning point is the whole of the process of a decisive change. Causes of death are a good example of this, when we assume that 'Covid-19 killed John', even though he was already in a vulnerable position and could have been readily carried off by some other disease. We also tend to absolutize the contributions of people for decisive but complex changes, by failing to think about responsibility in incremental terms – for example, we may assume that Gandhi achieved Indian independence single-handed.

Of course, even the breaking of camels' backs or death take time. We may assign a precise moment at which we say they occurred, but in doing so not only are we turning a tipping point into an instantaneous change, but probably also condensing a longer process of change into a tipping point. Indian independence, however, is a slightly different kind of example. India gained independence from the British Empire at the stroke of midnight on 15 August 1947, an instantaneous moment that was defined conventionally by the British government that granted independence and the new Indian

---

7 Looser & Wheatley (2010).

government that accepted it. Some kinds of events are instantaneous because they are defined as such by us, and we have no experience of them beyond the framing provided by that conceptual definition. However, independence in that precisely defined sense was not an event in a system taking into account the complexity of relationships. Independence could also be described as a process taking place in a system – the political system of the Indian subcontinent – but that process of course occurred over time. The two senses of 'independence' – the one that is defined into precision by our conventions and the one that is unavoidably vague – should not be confused with each other, and it is often by confusing them that we absolutize events.

We may also want to treat tipping points as instantaneous in order to repress and deny that the state before the tipping point continues to have any influence. That's particularly the case with psychological changes like dramatic religious conversion. Someone who has converted from Hindu to Christian in response to an experience of Jesus, for instance, may claim to now be entirely Christian and not Hindu at all, even though Hindu assumptions are likely to recur – for instance, the Hindu caste system persists amongst Indian Christian communities.[8] However, when people identify with the absolute beliefs of their new group, they are also likely to assume that they are 'essentially' different in this new group identity, and to project this onto every aspect of their experience, in the process treating an incremental change with asymptotic boundaries either as an instantaneous change, or as a gradual change that nevertheless has absolute boundaries.

Instantaneous and absolute interpretations of tipping points also become the basis of appeals to authority. When someone gains a qualification, is ordained, or assumes an office, for instance, it's possible that their preparation for their new status is intensive and it carries a big weight in their view of themselves. Even so, they are not wholly different from how they were before. Social absolutization, however, gives people in such positions a new position of power that they did not have before, based on other people's discontinuous view of their role. The student is suddenly a teacher, the trainee suddenly a manager, the pregnant woman suddenly a mother. In some ways, the social rules around these new forms of

---

8 Fuller (1976).

status are necessary for the functioning of society, but in other ways we absolutize them unnecessarily, perhaps being unhelpfully dismayed when a person newly elevated to a position of trust makes mistakes.

3.c. Practical Discontinuity

> *Summary*
>
> Practical discontinuity is a requirement for acting in the world, which is necessary to our embodiment. This also means there are necessary social discontinuities such as the law. These practical discontinuities need to be carefully distinguished from ontological discontinuities. Practical discontinuities can be judged better or worse according to how far absolutizations were avoided up to the point of judgement, and this creates the basis of Middle Way ethics.

Practical discontinuity is the discontinuity we need to assume at a moment of judgement in order to create the conditions for action. Such discontinuity is required, because we can only act against a background of assumed beliefs. For example, if I want to pick up a stick from the ground, I have to assume that the stick is graspable, that I can bend down to pick it up, and that it will suit the purposes I want to use it for. Once I've committed myself to those assumptions, I've committed myself to completing the action. Incrementality in the action itself would make little sense: there's no value in half bending down and then changing my mind, or in picking up half the stick. There's discontinuity there, because I either complete the action on the basis of the assumptions I've made, or I don't.

We could not live without practical discontinuity. To eat something, I need to assume that it's edible and digestible. To act co-operatively with someone else, I have to make positive assumptions about how they will behave. Even to meditate, I have to make a discontinuous decision to start meditating rather than doing something else. Practical discontinuity is an aspect of embodiment.

Other kinds of discontinuity in the social realm are developments of practical discontinuity. Linguistic discontinuity means that I use nouns in my speech, forming propositions about identifiable things so as to develop appropriate shared beliefs with others, and so that we can act in a compatible way. Conventional social morality requires practical discontinuity so that I can judge, in practice, whether someone is suited to cooperate with: if they break basic social rules I may have to rule out cooperation with them of the kind that requires trust. The law requires discontinuity, so that socially agreed rules can be enforced. Whatever the incremental complexity of someone's behaviour, there are entirely practical reasons why they should be judged guilty of a crime, if they break agreed rules that are the basis of cooperation. They are either guilty of a crime, in terms of the conventions we apply for practical purposes, or they are not.

Unfortunately, however, people often confuse practical discontinuity with ontological discontinuity: that is, they take what we need to assume for practical purposes to be an aspect of the universe itself – to be 'how things are'. However, when we investigate more closely, the trend always seems to be for the universe as we understand it to display incrementality instead: for instance, when we look into his background more fully, the criminal was only responsible to some extent; when we examine its coat more carefully, the dog is black only to some extent; when we examine the complexity of the evidence, religion is violent only to some extent. Whenever we get beyond our previous understanding of a situation to view it more adequately, we find that a more integrated view is also a more incremental view. Although we can't be certain that practical discontinuities are a result of our needs rather than how things are, all the indications from the evidence available suggests that they come from our needs projected onto the world.

Ambiguity is thus unavoidable. We can easily choose to apply practical discontinuity in an entirely opposite way from others in a particular case. Viewed from one point of view, the criminal is responsible, but from another, he is not. Recognizing our discontinuity as merely practical is an important aspect of the practice of incrementality, because it gives a further context to our judgement rather than absolutizing it. Our practical judgement can be the best one available to us without being absolutely the right one.

It's also often assumed that practical discontinuity is logical, and that there are thus 'true dichotomies' in a rational framework that we have to use to understand the world. The more basic statement of this is the Aristotelian law of the excluded middle: that a given thing is either *a* or *not a*. A given animal is either a kangaroo or not a kangaroo. A given country is either in the United Nations or not in the United Nations. This is correct within the terms of the logical framework being used, but tells us nothing about the necessity for that logical framework. Logic is only ever as good as its premises. We can classify animals in all sorts of ways – the term 'kangaroo' actually refers collectively to several species, but we could classify animals by sex, by health, by size, by diet, or in all sorts of other ways rather than only by species. Whether an animal is or is not ultimately a kangaroo may thus be either irrelevant or impossible to determine. The basis on which species are differentiated is in any case a matter of convention, and may be based on morphology (identifiable features), genetic similarity, or phylogeny (shared ancestry). If we are interacting with kangaroos, however, we are likely to adopt a practical basis of discontinuity for identifying what is a kangaroo and what is not, which we will only need to question if it creates practical confusion of some kind. We can do this on a provisional basis without having to believe either that kangaroos are 'really' like that, or that our logical structures necessarily oblige us to think about them in a particular way.

The difficulties that people have had with practical discontinuity are reflected in what philosophers call the *Sorites Paradox*, 'sorites' being the Greek word for 'heap'. Supposing we are dealing with a heap of sand and we remove it one grain at a time: at what point does it cease to be a heap? All numerical boundaries for the vague term 'heap' seem to be arbitrary. The idea that there is a *real* boundary to what is a heap or what isn't, even if we can't 'know' it, depends on representationalism, either in the form of the belief that meaning consists of truth conditions, or that meaning consists of use within a particular group.[1] However, if we face up to embodiment, including the embodied nature of our experience of meaning, vagueness has to be accepted as unavoidable in the conditions we deal with, and discontinuity determined in each instance of practical judgement.

If each practical discontinuity is determined uniquely, however, this does not imply that there are no criteria by which to distinguish whether one judgement of discontinuity is preferable to another. Practical discontinuity is not arbitrary, but can be justified according to the extent that it avoids the error of absolutization. This also tells us the extent that it enables the effective use of experience to inform judgement.[2] We need to freeze our judgement at the best possible point, after considering the maximum amount of experience possible beforehand that is compatible with the practical situation.

The basis on which practical discontinuity should be judged is the central question of ethics, and thus one that demands future detailed discussion.[3] I will only give a brief outline of it here. To

1   E.g. Williamson (1994).
2   I.9.a.
3   i.7; VIII.

begin with, ethical judgement should not be entirely separated and made subsidiary to 'factual' judgement, as is done in more established Western philosophy: *all* of our judgement influencing behaviour is ethical as well as factual. Matters like the interpretation of experience and choice of language are also ethical ones, in which values are applied. The Middle Way in relation to our judgement applies our values without taking them absolutely. Thus, when explicit or implicit moral claims are made about the importance of fulfilling certain goals, obeying certain principles or developing certain virtues, it is vital *not* to take these values absolutely, but rather weigh them up provisionally in relation to other values. Values are just as much part of the experiences we have to work with as sense experiences, apparent factual states of affairs, and cultural contexts.

We judge when to apply practical discontinuities on the basis of a total embodied experience at a particular point – an embodied experience that includes values. All we can do then is to try to avoid absolutizing those values or any other assumptions we are making, and make a provisional judgement in the light of as wide a range of possibilities as we can consider. We then may need to make our judgement, and make it decisively to address the situation. In some cases, that judgement may need to decisively apply social rules or laws. However, that judgement is justified, not by its decisiveness, or by the 'truths' we may assume it is based on, but by the extent to which we have stretched the limitations of our perspective in making it. In that way, we become more morally justified than we might have been otherwise. In the process, we apply practical discontinuity in a thoroughly practical way, but continue to justify our position in terms that maximize incrementality.

3.d. Continuity of Persons

> *Summary*
>
> Applying incrementality to persons means that we need to treat our descriptors of the qualities or categorizations of persons as a matter of degree rather than as absolute or essential, aiding provisionality. This applies to ourselves as well, offering a helpful interpretation of the Buddhist doctrine of 'no self'. It can be applied in an array of ethical issues, for instance incrementalizing the absolute boundaries of personhood used in the abortion debate. This does not threaten *respect* for persons, which is dependent on *how* we judge our responses to others rather than essentialist beliefs about them.

I now come to focus on four areas of application of the principle of incrementality. Persons are perhaps the first and most obvious context to apply it. To understand persons as a matter of degree, we understand both ourselves and others as sets of incremental qualities interrelated with each other. These incremental qualities also change their extent incrementally through time.

Such a way of seeing persons operates in the teeth of the entrenched metaphysics of persons as it has developed both formally in Western philosophy and informally in popular thought. As with all metaphysical claims, the problem is not a particular metaphysical position, but rather the expectation that metaphysics offers an appropriate way to talk about persons at all. Metaphysical views of persons are discontinuous, insisting that a person is *essentially* the possessor of a particular descriptor – whether that descriptor is a categorization or a quality ('male', 'thoughtful'), whether it is assumed to be intrinsic to their character or acquired instantaneously due to some event ('she's always helpful', 'she lost her mind after the accident'). The metaphysical view may apply to an individual person uniquely, or to a whole class of persons ('conservatives are untrustworthy'). There is an important distinction between making such statements provisionally, and making them absolutely or essentially – a distinction that the thoughtful application of incrementality can help with.

That any such descriptors are inadequate can be readily seen if we avoid the assumption that we can 'know' the final 'reality' of a person, but rather recognize our increasing understanding of them as penetrating successive layers of complexity in their appearance.

A categorization that seems clear, like race, turns out to be much more complex when we ask how we identify it (genes), and then recognize that genetic variation is a matter of degree – so people are blacker or whiter, not black or white. An individual quality, such as intelligence or strength, is obviously a matter of degree, and to describe someone as 'strong' is effectively to compare them to other humans of our acquaintance and find them relatively strong (whereas others may find them relatively weak). Some qualities may also be variable over time, or dependent on conditions: courage, for instance, only being evident in situations that demand it.

The practice of incrementality in relation to persons becomes of obvious ethical and political relevance when we consider some negative absolutized categories applied to people. 'Terrorist' is an obvious example of a term that may reflect a degree of violence used or threatened violence in pursuit of a cause, and may also indicate a degree of conflict with ruling authorities: but how far these characteristics have to go to justify the labelling of someone as a 'terrorist' is far from clear. At one end of the scale there are people who engage in mass killing of civilians in pursuit of goals that are obviously in conflict with most other people's, like the activities of Al Qaida in destroying the World Trade Center in 2001 or bombing the London Underground in 2005. At the other end of the scale, in 2021, President Lukashenko of Belarus accused Raman Pratasevich of 'terrorism' simply for being an opposition blogger and journalist, to justify the enforced grounding of an international flight that was passing over Belarus, in order to arrest him.[1] A judgement of practical discontinuity is required to apply the term 'terrorist' in a way that reduces conflict and associated absolutization in the long term, but in order to apply it most appropriately, we have to first recognize that the context of usage of the term in the group we may be embedded in does not identify a discontinuous category.

Considering our own case creates even greater difficulty: Who am I? What categories am I in and what attributes do I have? Whatever answers I give to that question carry a particular danger of absolutization if I don't understand them incrementally, because of the obvious emotive weight of our self-view in our entire embodied experience. If I adopt a positive self-view, it can easily become

---

1   https://www.theguardian.com/world/2021/may/25/hes-always-taking-risks-how-raman-pratasevich-lives-life-on-the-frontline (accessed 2021).

arrogance or over-confidence, but if I adopt a negative one it can impact the basic self-confidence I need for balanced judgement. If, however, I adopt both positive and negative views of myself as a matter of degree, a wider context of alternatives is always available to me. The insights of this position are perhaps reflected in the Buddhist doctrine of *anatta* or no-self, but this is too often presented as a metaphysical truth, and also as a negative claim about the 'non-existence' of the self. Understood as an avoidance of *discontinuous* views of oneself (and combined with agnosticism about the 'existence' of the self), it may become much more consistently helpful.

The continuity of persons in general over time also resolves ethical questions that are a major source of unnecessary conflict. The polarized 'debate' about abortion is a good example of this. The development of a fertilized ovum into a baby is obviously an incremental process, yet everyone who stakes a position on abortion insists on imposing discontinuity on it. The underlying assumption that personhood must start to 'exist' at a particular moment creates immediate conflict with those who choose a different moment, with each assuming that their point must have an absolute justification. It is no more obvious that personhood 'begins' at fertilization as a discontinuous point than that its 'beginning' must be deferred until birth so that we consider the foetus 'only a part of the mother's body' until it is physically separated from it. Nor is a discontinuous judgement at any other point obviously correct, given the incrementality of whatever developing qualities one may choose to highlight: personhood does not suddenly flash into 'existence' at six weeks of gestation, or at twenty weeks, or at any other point. There may of course be a point where we have to impose a practical discontinuity for the purposes of deciding whether or not a specific abortion should take place, or what the law should determine – but this discontinuity can only be at best a conscious imposition on an increment imposed for entirely pragmatic reasons.

The same issues of discontinuity affect the end of individual lives, our attitude to bodily boundaries, our judgements about those who are genetically human but lack many normal human capacities, and our understanding of the phylogenetic origins of persons in evolutionary history. In the last of these kinds of cases, Richard Dawkins visualized a line of ancestors:[2] imagine your mother alongside her

---

2   Dawkins (1995).

mother and her mother's mother, and so on. If you followed this line of ancestors back far enough, at what point would it cease to be a line of persons? The distinction between humans and animals is obviously another one that involves an imposition of discontinuity onto incremental sets of qualities, with, again, the inadequacy of our moral judgements often due to the absolutization of practical discontinuities. If the cow is your cousin, why is it 'natural' or 'necessary' for you to eat her?

It may be felt that a failure to apply discontinuity to persons is in some way a failure to respect them, or involves some kind of reductivism that reduces persons to their supposed component parts. This is far from being the case. *Respect* for persons is a very basic moral motivation, arising from our instinctive recognition of others as worthy in themselves and distinct from manipulable objects. Iain McGilchrist examines the distinction between respectful recognition of others and manipulative attitudes to them in relation to the right and left brain hemispheres, as reflecting a mode of operation we are liable to move in and out of according to hemispheric dominance.[3] The recognition of others through the right hemisphere is a *gestalt* process, which happens quickly and as a whole, but in order to make moral decisions in dependence on that recognition of others we nevertheless need to place them in a wider assumed representation of the situation using our left-hemisphere capacities. It is then vital that we use the more complex capacities applied in incrementality rather than the shortcut ones involved in discontinuity.

There are thus a whole set of ethical issues associated with the continuity of persons alone, concerning not only the boundaries of personhood in general, but also our categorization of others and the rigidity of our self-view. None of these issues should be understood in complete isolation from each other, as a consistent practice in one respect needs to be extended to the others. Fuller discussion of the ethical issues, however, will need to wait till volume VIII of this series, when incrementality with regard to persons will be brought further into contact with agnosticism about absolute values, to show how a coherent Middle Way ethics can be developed that is more adequate to the whole breadth of conditions than the more partial ethical approaches that clash in current debate.

---

3 McGilchrist (2009) pp. 54–8.

3.e. Continuity of Time

> *Summary*
>
> The discontinuity of time depends on the differing way that our left hemisphere merely sequences, whilst the right experiences time passing. Applying incrementality to time prevents us fixating on one of the three times to the exclusion of others, and thus enables us to identify with our desires at different times. Temporal biases show the differing forms that this absolutization of time can take, with any view of an object having a temporal dimension. We need to shift from abstract beliefs *about* time to focusing on how we make judgements *in* time.

As I discussed in *Absolutization*, the way we experience time as discontinuous can be readily understood in terms of differences between the two brain hemispheres, each of which we also experience directly as a mode for experiencing time.[1] When the left hemisphere is over-dominant, we experience time only as sequencing: a series of discontinuous jumps. These jumps may be in a temporal order, but are dominated by impatience in relation to the process of time passing. For instance, as we are waiting for a bus, our attention jumps ahead to focus on the arrival of the bus as the next event in the expected sequence, rather than recognizing and accepting our intervening experience before the bus arrives. In this mode, the sequence of events is merely conceptual, and their temporal relationships are just further concepts. We need, instead, to be in touch with our right-hemisphere experience to actually experience time passing. It is only by engaging with that experience that we can find *patience*, or the acceptance of time passing.

Experiencing that continuity of time is vital for us to be able to identify with desires and beliefs that we can only otherwise recall or anticipate in abstraction. A procrastinator, for instance, is not really experiencing the future goals that she feels she 'should' be working on – they are just abstractions in a future sequence, of little interest compared to current desires. To really engage in those future goals they need to be integrated with current desires, and accompanied by an experience of the intervening time before their fulfilment, as part of a living process. Rather than only being based in the present and absolutizing its desires and beliefs, the practitioner seeking to

---

[1] I.3.c. Also McGilchrist (2009) p. 76.

overcome procrastination needs to start identifying with desires at different times simultaneously. Rather than thinking of a past commitment as a merely abstract event in a past sequence, we need to be able to think of it as a living extension of the present. Rather than thinking of our current resolves as decontextualized events that are merely projected into the future, we need to be able to imagine them *in the context of* the future, where our goals may have changed, but will still have a living link with the present.

The overcoming of absolutization is central to this process, because when we absolutize we decontextualize temporally as well as in other respects. Temporal absolutization can be based in past, present, or future, because all it requires is that we identify with a particular time, but it then means that we repress alternative times in relation to the time we identify with. Absolutization limits our consideration to two alternatives – the currently accepted one and its unacceptable negation – and to see the temporal aspect of this we only have to recognize that all the alternatives we may consider or not consider have implied times. Every time we absolutize, then, we fixate on one time in which we maintain particular beliefs and reject others, but as we repress alternative beliefs we also repress alternative times that might offer awareness of those alternative beliefs.

If we identify with the future, for instance, it might be in the form of an unquestioned belief in the value of new electronic devices – a form of *neomania*. Supposing we're waiting in an all-night queue to purchase the latest release of the Apple iphone as soon as it comes out, because we believe in its capacity to benefit us in the future. The idea that this is a waste of time and money becomes unthinkable as we absolutize this belief. Alternative possible beliefs about the future, including the possibility that a new iphone might have very marginal advantages over the previous one, and that we may or may not actually use these advantages, and that they will be quickly superseded anyway, are simply not on the agenda. Also not on the agenda are reflections on the past (a context where we may all have lived happily without even having heard of an iphone), or the present (where I have lots of experiences that may lie beyond my iphone desire – such as breathing, love for my children, etc.).

It is often too much to simply demand that we 'snap out' of our temporally-situated obsessions, and such a demand at best may only result in a flip to an opposing identification. However, the extension of our current identifications towards greater awareness of the continuity of time is less demanding and more realistic. When obsessing over the specifications of the new iphone, for instance, I might think about its battery life, and then imagine a situation where the battery proves insufficient and runs out – say, during a camping trip with no charging facilities available, thus confronting the possibility of frustration rather than merely projected fulfilment of my desires. That imagined scenario begins to extend a living experience of actually using the iphone as an embodied being, to replace the entirely abstracted fixation on its positive features. When I imagine, my whole body takes part – for instance, my pulse may change and muscles may tense – whereas my abstracted obsession merely consists of a dopamine-fuelled loop between the representing and motivating parts of the brain. Merely connecting with more of that embodied experience may connect us with a wider temporal experience: childhood memories of simple enjoyment without any concern at all with electronic devices, for instance.

The crucial advantage of stretching or extending our identification over time is that we continue to be aware of the time we begin with, in addition to the one we are stretching into. We then develop a wider context of awareness, with a wider range of possibilities to consider. Rather than darting from one position along a timeline to another, we extend a searchlight along an increasingly longer section of that timeline. In the process, rather than fixating on specific states of subject or object at specific times, we see those subjects or objects as continuous, changing, and interacting rather than isolated.

A recognition of the continuity of persons, as discussed in the previous chapter, is a result of this, and the same sort of awareness can be applied to impersonal objects over time, recognizing them as gradually changing through the extension of our awareness of their characteristics from one time to another. For instance, a ripe bowl of strawberries left in a warm room for 24 hours will already start to decay in that time, so my intention to enjoy them the next day may be slightly marred by a decline in their taste. It is not the same, fixed, bowl of strawberries, but rather part of a system of relationships with the surrounding environment.

The value of the Buddhist teaching of impermanence (*anicca*) is captured in practice, not by 'believing' in impermanence, but by the value of us extending our awareness of objects through time, and thus adjusting our identifications to adapt better to our environment. If we think of impermanence instead as a 'truth' about the universe, there is a danger that we will identify with this 'truth', rather than extending our identification in a practical way. We do not know whether or not every object always changes, but we can readily experience the way in which developing our *judgements* about those objects so that we are more aware of changes over time is helpful to us.[2]

The temporal biases recognized by cognitive psychology are also helpful for developing awareness of incrementality. These take the form of identification with the past over the present, the present over the past, the present over the future, or the future over the present. For example, the sunk cost fallacy involves absolutizing a past effort over present awareness of conditions, failing to give up a doomed project because one has worked so hard on it in the past. Survivorship bias, in which we focus on limited present evidence of the past without sufficient awareness of the wider past conditions from which it has been selected (for instance, all the archaeological evidence we might *not* have found), absolutizes the present over the past. Procrastination, already mentioned above, absolutizes the present over the future, and neomania, also mentioned above, absolutizes an idea of the future over the present. These common identifiable forms of absolutization all involve discontinuity, as we fail to connect one isolated point in time with the rest of the timeline. Being aware of these temporal fallacies can be very helpful both to help us notice when ourselves and others may be caught up in them, and to try to compensate for them by extending our awareness over time. Temporal biases and fallacies deserve a much more detailed discussion, which I have made and will make elsewhere.[3]

However, the most crucial point about temporal continuity is not to understand it in isolation from the other principles, and not to treat time abstractly in a way that is abstracted from *judgements* in time. Much philosophical discussion about whether time 'exists', 'subjectively' or 'objectively', from St Augustine to Heidegger, is just so much unhelpful metaphysical speculation when it is disconnected from our *experience* of identifying and making judgements in time, and thus our experience of practising in relation to it. An application of the principles of agnosticism may, as in other areas,

2   See Ellis (2019) pp. 203–4.
3   iv.3.j & k; V.5.

be required to help us let go of this absurd preoccupation with whether time is 'real' or not, and help us instead to focus on our attitudes to the specific 'things' and 'events' that we interact with in our assumed framework of time.

3.f. Continuity of Space

> *Summary*
>
> Our sense of the continuity of space is dependent on that of time, and also interacts with conceptual models of lines in space. We can recognize the incrementality of a boundary in physical space dependent on concepts, and also of conceptual boundaries modelled on physical space. We need provisional boundaries in practice, but these can be optimized by contextualizing our spatial assumptions. The Middle Way itself is also modelled in spatial terms, but has no absolute defined boundaries.

Our awareness of the continuity of space is dependent on our awareness of the continuity of time, since it takes time for us to move through or survey space. Even to construct a model of our surroundings based on what we see, we need to spend time looking around us, not only in different directions, but also focusing on different objects to different degrees of detail. To get a sense of space beyond the immediate range of our senses, too, we need to move through space, which takes more time. The metaphorical relationships by which we connect a path through space to one through time help to show the degree of interdependence between them. For instance, we talk of time 'coming' and 'going', of 'the weeks ahead', and of 'the arrival of Christmas',[1] which map time metaphorically onto space. However, we also use our temporal experience to describe our traversing of space, as in 'a tedious journey', or 'a twelve hour flight'.

Our sense of the continuity between locations in space is thus largely a sense of the experience of gradually moving between them, or at least of moving our attention from one to the other. Discontinuity, on the other hand, is the spatial correlate of the binary restriction of options created by absolutization. Dualism may take the form of a proposition being true or false, but it can also take the form of a line in space which defines and constricts our spatial attention in a particular way.[2] Examples of this may be borders, imprisonment areas, or forbidden zones: in all of these it becomes the sole framing of the situation that one can either cross a particular defined line in space or not do so.

1   Lakoff & Johnson (1980) pp. 41–3.
2   I.1.d.

One cannot get beyond the importance of that line in space or think about it in a wider context, as long as one is in the grip of that absolutization. Finding spatial continuity, then, involves returning to embodied awareness and recognizing that in experience we actually have a great many options for our bodily and attentional movement in space. Even a line in space itself, when examined more closely, turns out not to be so absolute – in practice it often has a thickness, or a degree of ambiguity, or other limitations: for instance, borders often have a no man's land in the middle of them. Even a line drawn in pencil has a thickness, and within that thickness one is not on one 'side' of the line or the other. These ambiguities help to make us aware that the spatial lines we set so much store by are not entirely under our definition and control, and there are always wider contexts we can see them in.

Perhaps Shakespeare's Hamlet conveys an insight into these when he says 'I could be bounded in a nutshell, and yet count myself a king of infinite space, were it not that I have bad dreams.'[3] One could read this as a recognition that if it were not for absolutization, we could simply choose to free ourselves of bodily constraints by taking our attention elsewhere. The repressive effect of constraints, after all, depends not only on the outward conditions preventing us from acting as we wish, but also on our absolutization of those constraints. In theory, even the prisoner in chains can be as free as she wishes, by freeing her mind – but this is a very demanding practice, not to be made into a social expectation or a rationalization for the chains.

These points about experienced phenomenal space also extend into what we can only call 'conceptual space'. Conceptual space can be modelled in diagrams, such as mind maps, tables, or flow charts, which express relationships such as conceptual similarity, causality, or inference in spatial terms. In this modelled space, too, absolutization can readily appear in the form of discontinuity, and that discontinuity can be dissolved into continuity. If the relationship is one of conceptual similarity, we draw a line asserting absolute dissimilarity, typically through *a priori* assumptions about the 'essential' meaning of the term: for instance, we disconnect values from desires. If the relationship is one of causality, we draw a line asserting an absence of causality, a barrier to interaction. If the relationship

---

3   Shakespeare *Hamlet* II.ii.

is one of inference, we draw a line denying any implication between two things. Nations have their borders in phenomenal space, but religions and ideologies have their borders in conceptual space. The boundaries of 'Christianity' for instance, are constantly being drawn and redrawn by its theology, with discontinuities insisted on whenever it is asserted that one view is 'Christian' whilst another is not. Incrementality, on the other hand, involves the recognition that there are degrees of Christianity.

As already discussed in 3.c, there are practical justifications for *provisional* discontinuities in space. In a conceptual world without any boundaries we would probably be totally lost. Boundaries, in spatial terms, are orientations that help us to reach our goals, whether they are located in phenomenal or conceptual space. It is the absolutization of those boundaries in the form of total discontinuities that is problematic. When we recognize continuity in space, we do so within embodied limits by recognizing alternative options for movement that are not defined in terms of the absolutized spatial lines. Those alternative options are still finite, because we cannot practically engage with a non-finite number of options, but our movement beyond spatial limitations may still be inspired by an associative concept or symbol of infinity.

We develop an awareness of the continuity of space, not by leaping discontinuously to an infinite position, but by a process of *contextualization*. Each recognition of new options beyond the terms of an absolutized boundary is, spatially speaking, a contextualization. Even if we only contextualize slightly, to focus not just on an isolated object but on its immediate surroundings, we then begin to think in terms of a set of systemic relationships rather than an isolated object. For instance, when contextualizing a tree we realize its interdependence with all the other trees in its vicinity. When contextualizing a person who has offended us, we realize all the conditions that helped to create their behaviour, and that their responsibility is thus not negated but incrementalized.

All the practices I will discuss in section 6 for reducing absolutization are also practices for contextualization. Mindfulness, for instance, enables us to put any experience in a wider contextual space, so that a pain, say, is diluted by a wider embodied context without being denied or removed. The arts enable us to put any set of ideas that have become the object of obsession in a wider context of the imagination – so that paranoia about my neighbour as a threat, say, is not denied but diluted by awareness of many other qualities or experiences of my neighbour, playing on the beach with his children or completing his carpentry. Critical thinking also puts our beliefs in the wider context of comparative justification so that the way our confirmation bias makes us focus on particular beliefs is challenged by the lack of total justification for that belief, and the potential justification for other possible beliefs. In all of these kinds of practices, we are placed in a conceptual (or emotional, or imaginative) space and asked to widen our awareness within that space.

As we contextualize, at each point we also incrementalize, because we find that the space we were imagining no longer has the external boundaries that we took it to have. Our development as individuals and as a race also follows this process of incrementalization of space, as we 'broaden our horizons'. We gradually extend our focus from a cot, to a room, to a house, to a neighbourhood, to a town, to a country, to a world, to a universe. At each stage of this development our previous boundaries melt and are pushed out further, whilst at the same time our psychological capacities develop in a way that depends on the recognition of that new context.[4]

The continuity of space, then, is not only an application of the principle of incrementality to a particular kind of context, but also a way of thinking about the principle of the Middle Way in general as it can be understood metaphorically. Indeed, the Middle Way is itself a spatial metaphor, and one that demands continuity. In conceptual space, I proceed along the Middle Way, avoiding absolutizations on either side, but the way itself is not a single defined line, nor is it a band of space like a road with clearly defined edges. I can be confident about the need to avoid absolutizations whilst maintaining a provisional sense of how the way is defined, its boundaries, and its destination. As I move along that way in conceptual space, I also move along it in time and, as we will see in the next chapter, in terms of training.

4 III.2.

3.g. Continuity of Training

> *Summary*
>
> Training and learning are subject to tipping points (which create psychological stages) but are nevertheless continuous, and consistently recognizing this is a crucial practice. This means avoiding the expectation of instantaneous change, and cultivating a growth mindset in which failure is incrementalized and contextualized. On the other hand, specific achievements in learning in a given field also do not confer absolute authority in it.

The final aspect of incrementality I want to look at is the continuity of training or of individual development. By this I mean the recognition that our process of development, and the practices that can help support it, do not proceed in discontinuous ways, but rather incrementally. This point is compatible with there being tipping points (as discussed in 3.b) in learning and training: that is, sudden breakthroughs that we may all have experienced. Incrementality does not rule out rapid change in training as elsewhere, but it does rule out *instantaneous* change of the kind that we are likely to try to impose on ourselves and others when we are absolutizing in our understanding of learning and training. Since persons only go through gradual adjustments (as discussed in 3.d), it is obvious that learning and training is also a process of gradual adjustment.

Discontinuous assumptions about training tend to be linked to absolutized assumptions about freewill. If a person is engaging in anti-social behaviour, for instance, we assume that all they have to do is to decide to stop that behaviour – to 'get a grip', or to 'pull themselves together'. From the fact that we do sometimes experience relatively rapid changes in behaviour, it does not follow that we could change our behaviour 'at will'. Nor does the opposite follow, that our behaviour is absolutely predetermined and we could not decide to change it in any way. Rather, the process of learning requires an adjustment in response to conditions – an adjustment that we normally refer to as learning.

The recognition that learning and training are incremental also does not conflict with the identification of stages of psychological and moral development. Such stages, as identified by Jean Piaget and Robert Kegan, will be discussed further in the next volume of this series.¹ Developmental psychology does identify tipping points in psychological development, in which periods of stability are punctuated by periods of rapid change. For example, the transition between a developmental stage dominated by a self-identity formed in relation to peers can change quite rapidly into one in which a rationalized ideological basis of judgement becomes dominant.² This might be externally reinforced, or prompted by the experience of leaving the parental home, prompting a developing sense of adult responsibility for one's beliefs as an individual. There might even be a specific moment of recognition, at which a young person consciously notices that a turning point has been reached. Nevertheless, this process of adjustment happens organically over a period of time, and is not instantaneous. A parent or teacher who expected the change to be prompted instantaneously in an 'act of will' would be likely to be disappointed. A failure to recognize the incrementality of training can create a good deal of conflict, either within an individual or between individuals, as we try to impose premature expectations of growth on ourselves or others. Robert Kegan writes extensively about such damaging expectations in our educational and social systems in *In Over Our Heads*, the title of which vividly conveys the experience of being subject to damaging premature expectations.³

The incrementality of training is valuably recognized at times in the Buddhist tradition, and can be particularly strongly symbolized by the image of the beach leading down into the ocean, as used in the *Udana*:

> *Just as the great ocean, bhikkhus, gradually shelves, slopes and inclines, and there is no sudden precipice, so also in this Dhamma and discipline there is a gradual training, a gradual course, a gradual progression, and there is no sudden penetration to final knowledge.*⁴

What's especially valuable about this image is that it makes it clear that change does occur, and there are boundaries in our experience (being in the sea is different from being on land). Nevertheless, entering the sea is a process for us in our embodied context. In another place, the Buddha compares his 'gradual training' to that of

---

1   III.3.
2   Kegan (1982) ch. 7.
3   Kegan (1994).
4   *Udana* 5.5: Ireland (1990) p. 76.

an archer, an accountant, or a horse.[5] One cannot just jump onto an 'unbroken' young horse and expect it to immediately accept a rider, and instead a process of training is required to gradually adjust the animal to being ridden.

The continuity of training is also reflected in the work of Carol Dweck on the 'growth mindset' as the basic requirement for learning.[6] The growth mindset involves an ability to contextualize failure as part of a learning process, rather than absolutizing it: so, for example, if I am a student who does badly on a test and I have a growth mindset, I will work harder in response so as to do better on the next one. If the student had the opposite fixed mindset, however, she would take the poor result as an indicator of her essential identity as a failure. She would thus be demotivated and perhaps enter a spiral of doing worse and worse on all such tests. The importance of *contextualization* in this concept is also accompanied by that of seeing learning as a *process*, rather than as an attribute or accomplishment that one should already possess. In a study, Dweck found that students with a fixed mindset all assumed that a test would measure their abilities forever, whilst those with a growth mindset assumed only that it would measure their abilities at that time.[7]

The continuity of training is thus a crucial application of the principle of incrementality to avoid absolutization both in general education and in the more specific context of spiritual training. It implies primarily that we should see our own or others' development of desirable attributes as acquired incrementally over time rather than instantaneously. A further application of it, however, also leads us to see those desirable qualities at a given time as a matter of degree rather than discontinuously. There can thus be no completely discontinuous markers of status, such as those of expertise or authority, even though we are also justified in giving fair weight to such markers when we interpret them incrementally. If someone has a PhD, for instance, they have attained a socially recognized discontinuous marker of expertise in a particular area, but they are not thus infallible in their judgements in that area. Similarly, someone who is thought to be 'enlightened' may have high levels of certain incremental qualities, such as wisdom or awareness, but cannot be

---

5   *Majjhima Nikaya* 107.2 ff.: Ñanamoli and Bodhi (1995) p. 874.
6   Dweck (2017).
7   Ibid. pp. 26–7.

assumed to have crossed a discontinuity into infallible wisdom or awareness.

In this way, continuity of training also implies agnosticism with regard to the kinds of absolute claims that are often made on the basis of assumptions of discontinuous authority. It is easy to theoretically disavow such absolute assumptions of authority, but far harder to consistently avoid making them in practice. In the next section, I will explore much more thoroughly the implications of treating expertise or authority as incremental in the active practice we need to adopt to avoid absolute beliefs.

4. Agnosticism

4.a. Wary as Serpents

> *Summary*
>
> We can find both non-absolutizing and absolutizing views in unexpected places, but the latter particularly require us to be on our guard. Agnosticism is the practically necessary defensiveness involved in refusing to yield to pressure on both sides from polarized absolutizing groups. It also involves wariness to a whole set of absolutist dirty tricks against agnosticism, that try to make absolutism seem unavoidable. These include weakened accounts of agnosticism, appropriation of it, lumping into the opposing view, slipping even-handed positions into negative ones, and creating unholy alliances against it.

'Be wary as serpents, innocent as doves'[1] says Jesus to his disciples, in one of his most insightful pieces of advice. I interpret this as suggesting two contrasting aspects of our practice in avoiding absolutization. 'Innocence' probably here involves a continuing provisionality whenever we encounter anything that might pose a threat, not only directly but by influencing us towards absolutized judgement. We can find wisdom in the most unexpected places, in the midst of highly dogmatic groups. For instance, James Ault's open-minded study of attitudes in a fundamentalist church community records a practical flexibility (such as in attitudes to divorce) likely to surprise outsiders who take all the dogmatic group-binding pronouncements at face value.[2] At the same time, however, we can also find absolutization in equally unexpected places, including those that may have explicitly set out to apply the Middle Way or some roughly equivalent principle. Buddhist organizations offer plenty of instances of dogmatic flaws to illustrate this point, which I have tried to illustrate in depth myself through my study of the thinking of the influential Western Buddhist thinker Sangharakshita.[3] We thus need to be provisional in our acceptance as well as our rejection

---

1   Matthew 10:16 ('wary' is also often translated as 'wise').
2   Ault (2004) pp. 196–7.
3   Ellis (2020a).

of ideologies and group positions, maintaining a critical awareness even as we welcome the overall practical benefit of approaches that invoke the Middle Way. We need to be wary as serpents as well as innocent as doves.

The principle of agnosticism is the one that I would see as applying this wariness in our approach to belief, whether those beliefs are philosophical, religious, political, scientific, artistic, or otherwise. In many ways this is an application of the principles of scepticism and provisionality that I have already discussed in sections 1 and 2. It begins with a recognition of uncertainty, and an attempt to maintain awareness of alternative possibilities even as we make practical judgements. However, there are some specific defensive applications of scepticism and provisionality that are required in many situations to realistically prevent us from being overwhelmed by the power of absolute group beliefs and their accompanying false certainties. Though we need to be selective in our use of such defensive thinking, it is unfortunately also necessary if the practice of the Middle Way is to stand any chance. We need to be prepared, at times, to be confident and tough-minded in our *refusal to accept absolute ways of thinking*, despite the pressure from both sides of a polarized discourse to do so. That tough-mindedness needs to be even-handed in avoiding *both* positive absolute claims and their equally absolute rejection, along with the opposing groups who together maintain both sets of opposing absolutes and their supporting framework of assumptions.

The term 'agnosticism', coined by Thomas Henry Huxley in 1869 in reference to beliefs about God, is derived from the Greek terms for 'not-knowing'. As a position regarding God, it has been subject to huge misunderstandings, but at the same time it does show the development of an approach that navigates between two absolute positions. In the way I am using the term here, it applies to the avoidance of both sides of any pair of opposing absolute beliefs. As detailed in *Absolutization*, absolute beliefs are not entirely defined by their verbal content, but by the way in which they are held. It is thus the absoluteness of holding a particular belief that is roughly indicated by its content rather than vice-versa, and the goal of agnosticism is to avoid that absoluteness.

Nevertheless, there are various sets of explicit, philosophically articulated, pairs of opposing beliefs that are almost impossible not to interpret absolutely because of their metaphysical nature, making claims that go beyond human experience.[4] Some of the most common and influential of these, beyond theism and atheism, include freewill and determinism, realism and idealism, mind (or soul) and body, and moral absolutism and relativism. In the realm of political thought they include the absolutization of any one particular political value (such as justice or freedom) at the expense of others, and as opposed to the total dismissal of that value. Agnosticism, in the broad sense in which I am using it, thus means the resolute avoidance of both sets of absolute beliefs in any of these polarized pairs, as well as many others, so as to enable the development of more adequate provisional beliefs in relation to the conditions that these absolute beliefs seek to fix. Such absolute beliefs often come in associated interdependent clusters (for example, those who believe in God's existence also often believe in the soul and in cosmic justice), but absolutizations cannot be defined in terms of such clusters, which remain contingent. In *The Buddha's Middle Way*, I have argued the case that we cannot base our understanding of the Middle Way on such assumed clusters of absolutes (normally called 'eternalism' and 'nihilism' in Buddhist tradition).[5] We need to recognize absolutes more flexibly than this to be able to respond to them effectively.

In the remainder of this section, I will not be exploring specific pairs of absolute beliefs and how to mediate them in any detail: that is a task for a later book in this series.[6] Instead, I will be looking at some general structural features of absolutized pairs of beliefs. The careful agnostic responses to these, demanded from Middle Way practitioners, help us to identify different aspects of the practice of agnosticism. These are illustrated in the mind map here (**figure 6**). In many ways, the common misunderstandings to which agnosticism in relation to the existence of God has been subjected can help to alert us to these structural features.

The difficulty of maintaining even-handedness is at the centre of this, and arises from the ways in which absolutization operates as a tool of repression and power. In order to maintain that power, absolutists (or the absolutizing parts of ourselves) use every possible technique to deceive us into the assumption that absolute ways of thinking are the only possible ways. This is done primarily by

4   I.4.a.
5   Ellis (2019) 4.d.
6   VI; iv.4.

denying the very possibility of the Middle Way, because this would challenge the absolute framing on which both sides rely, even as they conflict with each other. It can also be done by maintaining an expectation of absolute solutions even in the context of provisional ones, or of presenting Middle Way solutions as implicitly favouring one side or the other.

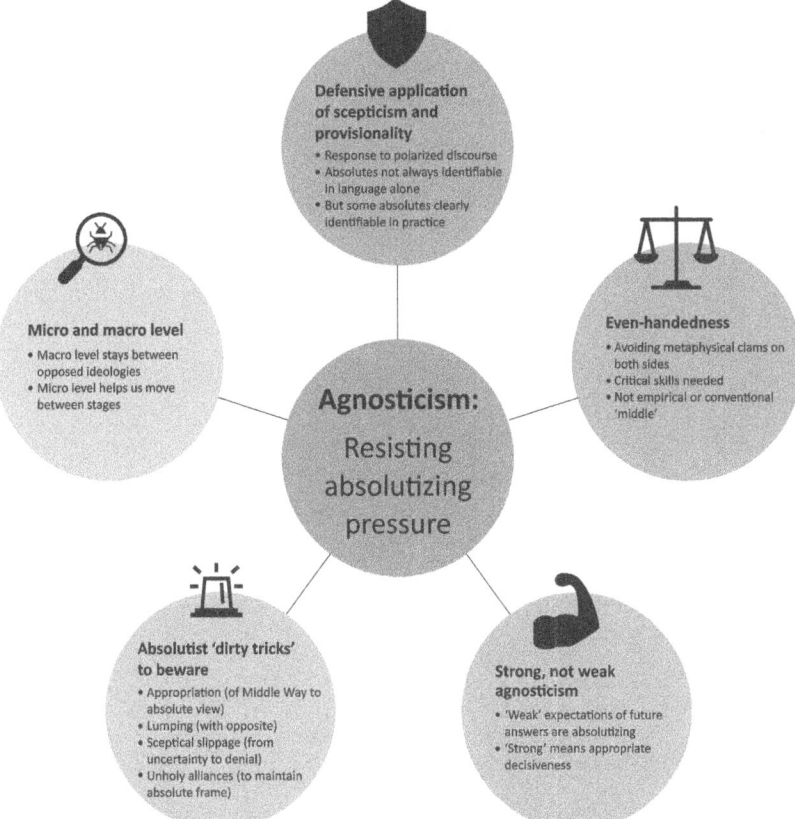

Figure 6. Agnosticism: mind map.

As we will see, the history of agnosticism in relation to God's existence can illustrate this whole spectrum of absolutist dirty tricks. Agnosticism has been 'weakened' so that it appears to be a mere temporary expedient whilst waiting for an absolute solution. Agnosticism has been both appropriated and lumped – that is, treated as part of the absolute position on one side, or rejected as part of the absolute position on the opposite side. The criticism of absolute positions that is needed for agnosticism has been constantly misinterpreted as supporting negative absolute positions (sceptical slippage). Pairs of normally opposed absolutists have even been known to gang up against agnostics, forming unholy alliances to maintain their absolute frameworks. The transitional psychological value of absolute concepts as meanings in certain conditions has also been misinterpreted in absolute philosophical terms, as vindicating the value of absolute beliefs. To become sufficiently versed in the practice of agnosticism, we will need to become aware of all these absolutist tricks, be prepared for them, and be able to avoid their deceptions through wider critical awareness.

4.b. Even-handedness

> *Summary*
>
> Agnosticism is the practice of critical metaphysics, which needs to be even-handed in ways that previous criticism has often not been. This means an even-handed avoidance of absolutizations prior to any empirical investigation, not necessarily a 'middle' position in other respects. Views presented as 'middle' can still be metaphysically framed, or wrongly present moderation as necessarily correct. An even-handed assessment of empirical evidence can still incline us strongly to one side, but we still need to avoid even a leaning towards one side of a metaphysical debate, as this validates the metaphysical framework.

Agnosticism could alternatively be described as the practice of critical metaphysics: that is, not the practice of 'metaphysics' as holding or defending metaphysical beliefs, but that of *maintaining a critical awareness of the reasons for avoiding any such beliefs, both positive and negative*. In *Absolutization* I worked through the grounds for that avoidance. I explained why metaphysical beliefs are unavoidably absolute, because they involve speculation beyond experience.[1] I showed why their philosophical justifications either involve a dogmatic foundationalism or are circular.[2] I explained how the role of infinite rationalization helps to maintain metaphysical beliefs, which are identifiable by their infinite scope (for a classic example, think of the way that any amount of evil can be reconciled with God's existence).[3] I also showed how metaphysical belief is not inevitable, and should not be confused with basic assumption, since practically relevant assumptions can be held provisionally, however basic we may consider them, as long as we are willing to consider alternatives.[4]

I also discussed the past failures in critical metaphysics, for instance of logical positivism and postmodernism.[5] Central to those failures is one-sidedness, including the assumption that to overcome metaphysics we merely have to criticize and negate metaphysical beliefs. This assumption fails to take into account the way

1 I.4.a.
2 I.4.c.
3 I.4.d.
4 I.4.e.
5 I.4.a.

that metaphysical framing is shared both by positive metaphysical claims and by their negations. Time and time again, then, as a result, we see reformers attacking metaphysical assumptions, only to get caught up in dogmas of their own that lead to further conflict, not only with the original metaphysical beliefs that were rejected, but also often with other reformers. Martin Luther, who rejected the absolute authority of the Pope but not that of the Bible as interpreted by an individual, provides a well-known example of this, sparking not only massive conflict between Catholics and Protestants in Europe, but also intractable conflicts between different Protestant groups.[6]

The story of the Buddha's early life instead offers a far more effective model for transcending metaphysics. After going forth from one context of absolute assumption (the Palace) into an opposed one (the Forest), the Buddha in turn recognizes that the Forest also does not have the whole story, and discovers the Middle Way. The overcoming of metaphysics has to be a *two-stage* process, first rejecting the 'positive' absolute and then the 'negative' (although they may only be 'positive' and 'negative' in relation to each other). In relation to the polarized interaction between the 'extremes', the Middle Way approach thus remains agnostic, not claiming to know either that the positive claim is true, or that it is false and that the contrary is true. Central to this agnosticism is its *even-handedness*, as the slightest concession to absolute beliefs on either side is likely to re-engage one in argument at the level of the extremes being rejected.

Unfortunately, agnostic or Middle Way stances are rarely understood as even-handed, whether by their critics or even by their advocates. In 4.d below I will discuss *appropriation* and *lumping*, which are ways that absolutizers continue to impose their model on agnosticism by categorizing agnostics as necessarily in one camp or the other. Even those who adopt agnostic positions may do so apologetically, as though they were temporarily defying some deep law that they should really take sides only because of a personal inadequacy – we will see this in the phenomenon of 'weak agnosticism' in 4.c. It's also common to be superficially agnostic but with a bias towards one side or another. The preference in Buddhist teaching for eternalism over nihilism, favouring one 'extreme' on one side of the Middle Way over the other, follows this pattern. For instance,

---

6   See Ellis (2001) 3.f.viii for fuller discussion.

one commentary says of eternalism that 'its faults are not grave' in contrast to the grave faults of nihilism.[7] This favouring of eternalism provides ideological support for the monastic-lay division in tradition Buddhism, as lay eternalism in practice is deemed acceptable even if not ideal. The Middle Way in traditional Buddhism thus tends to collapse into a hierarchy of options.

Even-handedness is a balanced avoidance of absolutization, rather than a positive preference for 'middle' positions considered in isolation from that balanced avoidance. Both 'extremes' are recognized as having similarly unhelpful structural features, regardless of the precise content of the beliefs they absolutize. The structural features are those of a lack of wider contextuality rather than those of specific verbal expression that enables one to identify deluded beliefs, so we navigate between opposed decontextualized views rather than seeking a 'true' middle view.

The avoidance of absolutization needs to be continued even when the contents of a belief are framed as 'middle' in one respect or another, as it is quite possible to absolutize the 'middle'. All one has to do to absolutize the 'middle' is to insist that a 'middle' solution is the whole story, and cease to apply provisionality in holding it. This is the drawback with any kind of 'middle way' position that is treated metaphysically, from Aristotle's Golden Mean to Lou Marinoff's modern book on the Middle Way.[8] The latter presents 'the Middle Way' as a kind of natural law, and ignores almost all critical or epistemological questions, to concentrate only on dogmatic exposition of 'the Middle Way' as an eternal truth.[9] The fallacy of the appeal to moderation,[10] which consists in the assumption that a conventionally middling position must be right, is a further indication of the absolutization of middles. Since conventionally middling positions are compromises between 'extremes' that are dependent only on contingent anchor points, there is clearly nothing necessarily correct about a position that is defined as moderate in isolation from the dialectic of absolutes.

Nevertheless, the absoluteness of the opposition between opposed views can offer an obvious signal of the need for agnosticism in a

---

7   Pesala (2013); Ellis (2019) 4.e.
8   Marinoff (2007).
9   For more details see my review at https://www.middlewaysociety.org/books/philosophy-books/the-middle-way-by-lou-marinoff/
10 E.g. Lambdin (2006).

particular case. Whether two people are arguing about the existence of God, or the merits of Liverpool Football Club, the intransigence of the opposition can immediately show the Middle Way practitioner the value of resisting the whole framing of both polarized positions. In empirical matters that are being absolutized, the balance of evidence may well *not* lie equidistantly between the extremes, yet one still starts by disassociating oneself equally from both extremes, in order to adopt a position in which one can better assess that unevenness free from absolutization.

The even-handedness ceases as soon as we are able to start finding an incremental solution. This point is perhaps most obvious with sceptical argument: one needs to be even-handed initially in rejecting the absolute presupposition either that there is or is not an aardvark hiding in a room in which there is no positive sign of one, but as soon as one has moved beyond absolute presuppositions, one can readily acknowledge an asymptotic 99.999% probability that there is no aardvark present. The step from certainty to asymptosis is still important in such cases (see 2.f), because of its wider support for the principle of provisionality, even in cases of practical obviousness. It is our sense of the importance of that step that prevents metaphysics from being inevitable, as I argued in *Absolutization*. Whenever an empirical matter is practically called into question, we need to be ready to assess it even-handedly according to the evidence, even if the evidence falls overwhelmingly on one side rather than the other. Without that even-handedness, our claims to have justified our beliefs on the basis of experience turn out to be hollow, because we will merely have pre-judged them. We do not know in advance which beliefs that seem obvious now will turn out to be questionable later, and thus agnosticism remains a valuable stance whenever there is a danger of taking any belief absolutely.

However, the most obvious applications of agnosticism remain those that are more generally recognized as matters of metaphysical belief, even though agnosticism is rarely considered as an option for many of them. Agnosticism may be recognized, at least by some, as an alternative to theism and atheism. However, it is less common to recognize agnosticism as an alternative to the assumptions of free-will and determinism, of absolutist and relativist ethics, of idealism and materialism, of mind and body, or of opposing political values such as justice and freedom. Merely establishing agnosticism as an option in such discussions, and showing its value for resolving what would otherwise seem like intractable conceptual conflicts, is an exercise worth engaging in detail – which is why I will be devoting volume VI of this series to that task. For the moment, though, it is worth noting how central even-handedness is to such arguments. We cannot be agnostic about freewill and determinism if we actually lean, even subtly, towards determinism, for instance. Nor can we resolve conceptual conflicts between mind and body by leaning towards mind and against body. As far as we can manage, our philosophical approach needs to offer no trace of any such bias. Even-handedness needs to be rigorously applied both in theory and practice to enable the practice of agnosticism.

4.c. Strong, not Weak, Agnosticism

> *Summary*
>
> Contrary to the philosophical assumptions that dominate, 'strong' agnosticism (facing up to the state of not knowing) is far more provisional than 'weak' agnosticism (not knowing yet, perhaps in future). If the 'knowing' of weak agnosticism were to actually occur, it would require massive absolute assumptions that the strong agnostic avoids through greater decisiveness. An analogy with addiction may make this clearer. This topsy-turvy cultural attitude to agnosticism results from a widespread obsession with discontinuous 'knowledge', and has so far prevented agnosticism being applied to all the other issues (beyond God's existence) where it needs to be applied.

It is normal to think of a 'weak' version of some position as one that is more provisional, open to change, whilst a 'strong' version is more inflexible and dogmatic. However, in the case of agnosticism about God's existence (the main variety of agnosticism discussed so far by philosophers), absolutized thinking has become entrenched through the use of terms. Perversely, the routine use of absolutized assumptions comes to appear more moderate than the recognition that we can have no access to absolute perspectives, because a version of agnosticism that maintains absolute assumptions has been labelled 'weak' (or 'soft'), whilst the version that faces up to human embodied limitations has been labelled 'strong' (or 'hard'). In this chapter I want to set this assumption on its head: it is weak agnosticism that is dogmatic in its implications, not strong agnosticism.

Perhaps the most straightforward definition of strong agnosticism is the view 'that we cannot know whether or not God exists', as Robin Le Poidevin puts it, in contrast with weak agnosticism as 'a confession that we do not know whether God exists'.[1] This is sometimes supplemented with the idea that the weak agnostic is open to further evidence. Being open to further evidence sounds open-minded enough, until we examine what this further evidence would consist in if it were to arrive – that is, a supposed revelation

---

1   Le Poidevin (2010). Using these simplified definitions avoids a lot of the diversionary clarifications that would be required if we took the definitions offered by Graham Oppy (2006, 1.3), the philosopher who is best known for his contributions on the subject. These involve terms like 'obligatory' and 'reasonable' that assume a certain conventional context.

Agnosticism 141

that would somehow allow us to justify an affirmation that a proposition absolutely represents a reality, regardless of our position of embodiment and all the ways that this prevents the meaning of language being representational.[2] To accept such further evidence, and to 'know' that God either exists or does not exist, would require us to adopt a dogmatic assumption equivalent to assuming that we are God ourselves, beyond the limitations of embodiment and the uncertainty this implies for us.

Counter-intuitively for some, then, 'strong' agnosticism is far less 'strong' than the 'weak' version, in the sense that it allows us to adopt a consistently provisional perspective. We can only consider any question provisionally if we are able to consider alternative views on it, and that openness to alternative views is immediately undermined by the imposition of an absolute framework of assumptions that forces our responses to a given topic into a binary polarity. The tendency to think of our beliefs about particular metaphysical topics only in terms of such a binary polarity is inseparable from the assumption that we can have 'knowledge' of them (see 1.a above). The discontinuity of 'knowledge' can be readily replaced by incremental justification, preventing our recognition of our lack of knowledge turning into an absolute negative position. There is a need to be clear and decisive in our agnosticism in order to avoid the seductions of 'knowledge' claims, but leaving the door open to them in future merely sends us back round cycles of circular justification,[3] endlessly seeking absolute justification from an incremental experience, rather than engaging ourselves in finding an appropriately incremental interpretation of that experience.

Perhaps a helpful analogy here would be to see weak agnostics, not as 'open-minded' investigators, but as recovering addicts hooked on absolutization. We do not recover from addiction by continually going back to check whether the drugs we were previously hooked on are still addictive, and whether we could find the complete solution we once sought from them this time. Instead, we can recover from addiction by remaining aware of the wider needs of our body rather than rationalizing our craving for final solutions. To be able to maintain such awareness sustainably, we need to be decisive in our judgement not to return to the substance

2   See I.3.a.
3   I.4.c.

we are addicted to, as if we do so, it will continually reshape our thinking in its terms. Such decisiveness is not easy either to initiate or to sustain, so we need all the help we can get – from new ways of imagining and thinking, and from social support. We will also need to be wary as serpents, to be aware of the wiles of addictive thinking whenever they arise. In this case, though, many of our influential institutions are still run by addicts who continually try to lure or pressure us back.

A popular view of agnosticism as indecisive is obviously related to a widespread tendency for agnosticism in general to be defined in its weak form – a form that merely suggests a practical person's puzzlement in the face of polarized absolutization, rather than a full recognition that we *cannot* have linguistic propositions that are certified to represent reality due to basic features of the human condition. A failure to face up to those basic features of the human condition is constantly reinforced by our routine and socialized use of the discontinuous term 'to know' in a propositional sense, reinforced by educational systems that still see their goal as providing 'knowledge'. When the dominant ideology is so deeply *gnostic* (in the widest sense of taking knowledge as our goal), but this constantly conflicts with the agnosticism of bodily experience, it is no wonder we become puzzled. Characterizing agnosticism as mere ineffectual puzzlement, however, is part of the defence mechanism that keeps absolutization institutionalized. Further training may well be required to help a merely puzzled, weakly agnostic person to become more effectively and consistently agnostic – to learn and apply agnosticism as a practice.

At least strong agnosticism is recognized as an option in philosophy in relation to the debate about God's existence. However, in the many other debates dominated by binary metaphysical polarization, it is very unusual for the possibility of agnosticism to even be mentioned. Instead, the insistence on a particular binary framing means that nascent agnostic positions are usually quickly appropriated or lumped (see next chapter). In the case of freewill and determinism, for instance, the practically-oriented puzzlement of those who experience a degree of freedom in their actions will often be succeeded by an adoption of one absolute position or another once the freewill-determinism debate is understood. There may then be an attempt to interpret one's practical position in terms of the absolute positions one has adopted as framing the discussion. If you understand, for instance, that metaphysical freewill is literally a matter of choices made free of causation, and then identify with that position for moral, social, or other reasons, freewill may begin to seem necessary for any attribution of responsibility or morality. Any weakly agnostic recognition that we do not know whether such choices occur will then probably be undermined by the conviction that we experience that absolute freedom when we choose. One needs to develop a strong agnostic position, recognizing that we *cannot* know whether such absolutely free choices occur or not, to be justified in moving beyond the absolute framework of thinking on these issues that the philosophical debate and its ideological popularizers have insisted on.

The debate about God's existence, turgid and entrenched as it often is, nevertheless offers us a model of what strong agnosticism looks like that it seems has hardly been considered elsewhere. Once we unite that strong agnostic position with an even-handed scepticism, and a recognition of its enormous practical value in freeing us from absolutization, there is no limit to the range of issues we can helpfully apply it to. As in any entrenched conflict, we do not start by taking the positions of each side at face value, but rather apply a balanced critical awareness that will enable us to work with them. As we will see in the last two sections of this book, strong agnosticism can also play a helpful supportive role in practice to support integrative development, in the wide range of cases where absolutization threatens to derail that development.

4.d. Awareness of Appropriation and Lumping

> *Summary*
>
> Appropriation defends against the Middle Way by assuming it to be part of a favoured absolutized belief, whilst lumping rejects the Middle Way by assuming it is part of a rejected absolutized belief. This can be done in either case by defining the Middle Way in absolutized terms, by applying the Middle Way in an absolutized way, by seeing the Middle Way as an aspect of an absolutized view, by substituting an absolutized view for a Middle Way view, or by seeing an absolutized view as an aspect of the Middle Way. This is problematic and requires wariness only because it obscures the Middle Way and results in further absolutization. Appropriation and lumping can also be used in service of the Middle Way.

This chapter, and the following two, are concerned with the challenges that the practice of agnosticism requires us to be wary of. If agnosticism merely consisted in the avoidance of opposing absolutes that were always clearly identifiable as such, it would still involve difficulties, but would be a markedly easier practice than it is. Much of the time, however, issues of interpretation make the Middle Way far harder to find and follow. Beliefs are presented as Middle Way beliefs that on closer inspection turn out to be absolutizations, or we come under pressure from others who treat what we may think are sincere Middle Way judgements as absolutizations. Judgements that start off as genuinely Middle Way ones then drift into absolutized belief, and in some of the more challenging cases, Middle Way practitioners are put under pressure from both sides, beleaguered and isolated. The wariness of agnosticism is needed in all these kinds of cases to avoid being deceived in our interpretations, even if the practice of all the other principles is also needed to help us do so appropriately.

Appropriation and lumping are perhaps the most common of these interpretative problems. In appropriation, a Middle Way approach is interpreted in terms of an absolutization fitting the ideology of the person appropriating it, so that the challenges of the Middle Way approach can be neutralized. For instance, I remember a conversation about the Middle Way with a Catholic monk in Ireland where he assured me that it was all in Thomas Aquinas. In lumping, a Middle Way approach is interpreted in terms of the rejected ideology of an opposing group, so that an easier rejecting or dismissing approach can substitute[1] for a more demanding Middle Way practice approach. For instance, Socialists who find mindfulness challenging as an aspect of Middle Way practice may insist on interpreting it as an ideological tool of capitalism to make workers merely adapt to exploitative work conditions (as opposed to changing them).

Appropriation and lumping seek out and exploit the ambiguity that will always be unavoidably present in Middle Way approaches, because of the avoidance of representationalism. That ambiguity is used to introduce absolutization in some form, without disrupting the appearance of a Middle Way approach. We may never recognize that that absolutization is present, unless we are wary as serpents, or we may recognize it only much later, when the effects of absolutized assumptions begin to reveal themselves, and it is then much more disruptive to reconfigure our approach.

The complexity of the Middle Way makes it constantly vulnerable to this kind of treatment, regardless of how consciously we try to follow it. In a few cases appropriation and lumping may indicate an active conspiracy to undermine the Middle Way, but in the vast majority of cases it is probably just a matter of entrenched cultural habits and of minds following an easier rather than a harder path. Those who appropriate or lump may or may not be able to learn a different interpretation if their approach is pointed out to them, but either way, blame is unlikely to be a helpful response to appropriation or lumping. Awareness of it, however, gives us many more options to respond to it: for instance, introducing crucial distinctions that help us to practically distinguish the Middle Way as we discuss the issues.

The processes of both appropriation and lumping are broadly similar, with one being positive and the other negative. Five variations can be identified in the way in which appropriation or lumping is done, listed below. I will focus on appropriation for the moment in discussing each of these, but they all apply equally to lumping.

1. **By definition**: a Middle Way approach is defined in absolutizing terms
2. **By application:** a Middle Way approach in theory is applied in an absolutizing way in practice

1   See I.5.d.

3. **By composition**: a Middle Way approach is seen as part of an absolutizing one
4. **By substitution**: an absolutizing approach takes the place of a Middle Way one
5. **By division**: an absolutizing approach is seen as part of a Middle Way one

1. **Appropriation by definition** operates at the abstract level to turn provisional generalizations into absolute beliefs, merely through translation into what at first might seem equivalent terms. For example, provisional statements about racial differences based on empirical evidence can imperceptibly slip into the absolutizations of race employed by racism, as soon as those statements lose the context that would help us to interpret them appropriately in changing conditions. Thus, for instance, Charles Murray's writings about IQ and race claim that it is merely an empirical fact that the average IQ of whites is higher than that of blacks, but that this should not prevent us treating people of any race as individuals.[2] The ease with which such claims can be decontextualized and used as tools of power is immediately apparent to his opponents, who are thus likely to interpret his arguments as disingenuous and motivated by racism.[3] There is nothing inevitable about such data being used absolutely and as a tool of power, but avoiding doing so requires continuous awareness of all the limitations of IQ tests as useful measures, the ways that they may be impacted by social conditions as well as genetics, and the ways that information about IQ tests can and should be separated from questions of social and political equality. Without awareness of such contextual information, generalizations about the IQ of races can be very easily appropriated for absolutizing purposes, with 'intelligence' shifting its implicit definition not just to cover the ability to succeed in IQ tests, but other features of individual understanding and capability that are then assumed to affect rights or other political priorities.

2. **Appropriation by application** takes an approach that is justifiably Middle Way in theory, but then, perhaps due to ambiguity in the description of its application, applies it absolutely in practice. For example, a Middle Way approach, as I argue in this book, can

2   Murray (2021).
3   E.g. Williams (2021).

be greatly supported by mindfulness. However, in order to practise mindfulness helpfully one also needs to interpret it as a Middle Way practice rather than a repressive practice. There still seem to be quite a large proportion of practitioners who interpret mindfulness as a method of 'controlling' one's mind in accordance with the ascetic religious tradition, or alternatively think of it as a 'treatment' for a specific medical condition, such as depression or chronic pain, that will subjugate that condition. This tendency may be exacerbated by definitions of mindfulness as a maintenance of concentration in the present moment,[4] rather than a *contextualization* of every aspect of our experience. Predictably enough, if we turn mindfulness into only a concentration practice rather than one of contextual awareness, it may create further psychological conflict. This unhelpful interpretation of mindfulness practice has at times created a backlash from those who see it as a dangerous or potentially harmful practice, justified by studies showing substantial proportions of negative effects from meditation.[5] Our theoretical understanding of the Middle Way needs to reach all the way down into our interpretation of its application, just as that theoretical understanding in turn needs to be shaped by an experience of equilibrium in practice.

3. **Appropriation by composition** takes a Middle Way approach to be a subset of an absolutizing one. This is obviously what occurs when the Middle Way is subsumed into metaphysics by tidying it into metaphysical categories – for example, if the Middle Way is treated as a type of naturalism. If propositions about 'natural' phenomena are assumed to be necessarily provisional, rather than judged on a case-by-case basis according to their provisionality, the idea of the Middle Way can then rapidly be subsumed into scientific method. Scientific method is assumed to tell us about 'natural' states of affairs, through an investigatory process relying in part on the social consensus amongst scientists rather than only on provisional modes of judgement. The Middle Way is then assumed to be subsidiary to a naturalistic scientific perspective, justified only as far as it participates in that perspective, rather than vice-versa, and the priority of provisional judgement itself as an aspect of the Middle Way is lost in wider assumptions.

4   Baer et al. (2019).
5   Otis (1984); Cebolla et al. (2017).

4. **Appropriation by substitution** puts absolutizations in the place of Middle Way concepts because they are easier to deal with. In *Absolutization* I discussed the substitution process in the development of absolutization, where less energy-demanding processes are substituted for higher energy-demanding ones.[6] Daniel Kahneman and his associates have shown the ways in which this explains the basic mechanism of bias.[7] It is hardly surprising, then, that this shortcut is extended into a *defence* of absolutized processes through their association with Middle Way concepts. Any bias can also be understood as a process of appropriation: for instance, the sunk cost fallacy. In the sunk cost fallacy, we can't let go of a failing project into which we have 'sunk' time, money or effort – whether this is a failing relationship at individual level, or a major engineering project taken on by a nation. When we do this, we substitute an easier continuing identification with the objects of our past effort for a harder recognition of a complex new situation. At the same time, this is an *appropriation* of the idea of the new situation by the continuing identification. It is our rationalization of the new situation in terms of the old identifications that marks that appropriation. For instance, I might say to myself 'There's still a chance that my original plans might work out, so it would be such a shame to give up now', despite a gathering weight of evidence against this. We appropriate by exploiting ambiguities in the situation to support our continuing absolutization, rather than weighing up the alternatives. In external debate, our opponents are likely to do exactly the same thing.

5. **Appropriation by division** takes an absolutizing approach to be a subset of a Middle Way approach, and thus diverts us into the absolutization under the illusion that it must be as provisional as its supposed parent category. For example, the traditional Buddhist understanding of the Middle Way as lying between 'eternalism' and 'nihilism' may be adopted on the understanding that it is a version, or an expression, of the Middle Way.[8] However, if one then got into polarized debates about whether Marxism was really nihilistic or not,[9] one would be starting to substitute this subset for the wider

---

6 I.5.d.
7 Kahneman (2011) part 1.
8 See Ellis (2019) 4.c & d.
9 See Ellis (2001) 3.i.

Middle Way. This is one prime reason why it is vital to understand the Middle Way as a principle of judgement rather than a navigation between specific metaphysical beliefs, as the claims we will then find ourselves making about those metaphysical beliefs, even though initially motivated by a desire to follow the Middle Way, are likely to end up dominating our attention and moulding the interpretation of our practice.

I will not go through the application of these same categories to *lumping* in the same detail, but here is an example applied to the first category. We can *lump by definition* when we define Middle Way positions as absolutized ones, and thus end up rejecting them when they could be helpful to us. I come across this frequently as a response from those who do not understand the Middle Way as a distinct option, but respond to particular features of it that they identify with one side or another of a metaphysical divide that they assume to be inevitable. For instance, an agnostic recognition of the concept of God as meaningful can lead to agnosticism being lumped with theism by definition, by atheists who assert that the concept of God must be meaningless and that the assumption of its meaningfulness is a theistic characteristic (using some absolute criterion of 'meaninglessness' rather than an experiential one). Alternatively, in political discussion, the Middle Way may be lumped in with pro-capitalist stances by definition if it fails to offer an anti-capitalist position, despite the ways in which absolutized capitalist assumptions may lie at the heart of the ways that capitalism can be damaging and problematic.

Lumping can occur by *application* if we assume that an application of the Middle Way is a practice typical of 'them' – 'the other side' – for instance that critical thinking is the preserve of irrelevant ivory-towered academics. It can occur by *composition* if we take the Middle Way to be a subset of what 'they' (the rejected group) believe – so it's 'really' a sort of idealism, or humanism, or some other rejected -ism. It can occur by *substitution* if we defend absolutization by taking the easier path of seeing the Middle Way in accustomed negative terms – for instance, as dismissible 'navel gazing' rather than as a complex practice. We can lump by *division* when we see a rejected category as a subset of the Middle Way: for instance, assuming that the Middle Way includes political moderation and that this is ineffective.

The five categories given here just provide some different possible ways into identifying both appropriation and lumping. It is not necessary to always classify examples of it exclusively in one of these sets of terms, especially when more than one may seem to be applicable. In practical terms, it is not necessarily important whether appropriation or lumping is compositional or divisional, for instance, as long as we can identify its activity.

The identification of appropriation and lumping as problematic defence mechanisms for absolutization also does not mean that all processes that might be identified as 'appropriation' or 'lumping' are necessarily unhelpful. The integration of belief (see 5.d below) is an aspect of Middle Way practice that involves seeking out the positive and helpful elements of beliefs that may be traditionally associated with absolutizations: thus, for instance, rather than rejecting the whole of Christianity, or any other religious tradition, as necessarily absolutizing because of its association with absolute creedal statements, we look more closely for aspects of Christian tradition that can be used provisionally and are compatible with the Middle Way. That process could be seen by Christian absolutists as 'appropriating' Christianity for what they see as a view alien to it. That such appropriation *for* the Middle Way is helpful rather than unhelpful can be seen only in the light of a wider understanding of the damaging effects of absolutization, and of the need to separate absolutization from other aspects of human experience wherever possible.

As an aspect of the practice of agnosticism, it is *awareness* of appropriation and lumping that serves us helpfully. One cannot prescribe how one should act in the light of this awareness – for example, how explicitly or strongly one should object to it when one encounters it. What is clearer is that if we remain unaware of appropriation and lumping, our intention to practice the Middle Way may very easily be hijacked by absolutizing tendencies, and we may gradually end up forgetting the whole idea of the Middle Way or its importance, under pressure from the absolutizing group. It is thus a crucial aspect of the wariness of serpents.

4.e. Awareness of Sceptical Slippage

> *Summary*
>
> Sceptical slippage is the tendency to interpret uncertainty or agnosticism as grounds for denial, when it actually offers no more grounds for denial than for positive assertion. This occurs because a more troublesome two-shift process is needed to reach an agnostic approach, because of the pressure of group biases, and because of the culturally transmitted ontological obsession. Sceptical slippage results in flips substituting for reforms, failed revolutions, and fissiparousness in reform movements.

'Sceptical slippage' is the term I have coined for a type of absolutizing appropriation – specifically the type that interprets agnostic positions as denials: for instance, agnosticism about God is interpreted as atheism, agnosticism about absolute sources of ethics is interpreted as relativism, and a failure to support a specific political ideology is interpreted as support for the opposite ideology. This kind of slippage is so common that the term 'scepticism' has for most people come to mean a negative position. As I argued in 1.b above, there is nothing negative about scepticism, as the mere questioning or doubting process applies just as much to negative claims as it does to positive ones. For some reason, however, human history reveals a common process of sceptical slippage. Some explanations can be advanced as to why this form of appropriation is particularly easy to slip into, and of course our awareness of this danger is required to avoid it.

Perhaps the most obvious explanation for sceptical slippage is that a two-shift process is needed to reach an agnostic position, whereas only a one-shift process is required to reach a denial position. Agnostic positions are thus more complex and take more time to reach, creating a correlation between reaching an agnostic position and potentially theorizable stages of psychological development (as discussed in 4.g below). The two-shift process is modelled by the Buddha in the story of his early life, with him first leaving the Palace ('going forth'), where he rejects the values conventionally dominant in that context; then secondly recognizing the limitations of his teachers and of ascetic practices in the Forest, to recognize the Middle Way.[1] Following a typical human pattern of development,

---

1 Discussed in detail in Ellis (2019) section 1.

he rejects the values in one context on discovering their limitations, takes refuge in an opposing context with an opposing ideology, and then in turn recognizes the limitations of that alternative.

In the two-shift process, the first shift is likely to be articulated solely in terms of a denial of the position rejected, particularly if an alternative group offers an opposing ideology that can be readily identified with. In the second, however, the denial position is questioned. This may result in a 'flip', in which the denial of the denial takes one back to the first position. However, if there is also sufficient remaining awareness of the reasons for rejecting the first position, the rejection of the second can alternatively provide an agnostic position in which the assumptions governing both extremes are questioned and rejected simultaneously. For anyone who has only gone through the first shift and not the second (or who has only 'flipped'), however, those who have completed the second will continue to be categorized along with those who have completed the first – for example, as radicals or rebels.

A further reason for sceptical slippage can be charted psychologically in outgroup effects. There are four established group biases, recognized by cognitive psychology, all of which tend to exaggerate our sense of the homogeneity of views both within and beyond our group. The ingroup-outgroup bias[2] leads us to judge the beliefs of those outside our group unfavourably – for instance, Christians rejecting Buddhist approaches as 'navel gazing'. Social proof[3] leads us to accept beliefs because they are shared by our group, and thus by implication reject alternatives because they are not shared by our group – so, for instance, teenagers will adopt peers' opinions on favoured types of music and disparage those of other groups. Groupthink[4] leads us to make judgements in a way that prioritizes the maintenance of harmony in a group over any other considerations, and thus also reject any considerations raised from beyond the group that do not fit the perceived priority of harmony in the group – so, for instance, the boards of doomed companies may pay no attention to warning signs about the conditions that will lead to their demise, even when they are obvious to others. False consensus[5] leads us to assume that our own group's views are the

2   Taylor & Doria (1981).
3   Asch (1956).
4   Janis (1982).
5   Ross, Greene, & House (1977).

norm, and thus that there is something intrinsically wrong with any other view – thus, in the US of the McCarthy inquisitions, any view that was not mainstream conservative or moderately liberal was deemed 'Communist', without any distinction being made between different types of socialism.

In all of these types of bias, the denial of our own group's view is likely to be given a single negative outgroup status, impeding us from recognizing any incrementality, or even sub-division, of disagreement within it. The 'no' of disagreement with the group is thus likely to be interpreted as a denial, not merely as a recognition of uncertainty. On the other side, the affirmation of our group's view is also likely to be homogenized, resulting in the appropriation of any ambiguous views to the group. When our own group takes a negative position in regard to the views of another group, then, that 'no', too, is likely to be interpreted as a denial, not as a recognition of uncertainty.

A further reason for sceptical slippage is our ontological obsession – that is, our concern with reaching descriptions of how things 'in fact' are, rather than maintaining provisional representations for practical purposes.[6] When we are dealing with propositions in terms of their 'truth', then Aristotle's law of the excluded middle applies: if a proposition is not 'true', then it is 'false'. Any degree of failure to match our assumed reality entails the falsehood of the proposition, no matter how small. This is all correct within the terms of its own, propositional, world – one in which we are for some reason entitled to completely ignore the implications of basic sceptical argument, and not worry whether or not any of our propositional sentences are actually capable of describing reality. If we bypass this, as most philosophers and many others have been trained to do, then we take an automatic absolutizing shortcut to debating the 'reality' of the situation. In the terms of that shortcut, all incremental beliefs about the mere probability of a state of affairs that we envisage are false beliefs, and sceptical slippage is baked into an entire world-view.

Sceptical slippage is thus created and maintained by a combination of our developmental limitations, the reinforcement of group identity, and philosophical culture, each reinforcing the other at every turn. If the philosophical culture is challenged, the group identification kicks in to defend it, aided by the need for the group

---

6   Also see Ellis (2019) 4.b.

to maintain the lowest common denominator – the one-shift that more of its members will be familiar with rather than the two-shift. Even if identification with the group that maintains sceptical slippage is successfully overcome, cultural assumptions of the ontological obsession may still remain unquestioned.

The consequence of sceptical slippage is the maintenance of a reinforcing feedback loop of absolutization in general, since if challenge always results in flips rather than the discovery of the Middle Way, we will merely oscillate from one extreme to the other rather than moving beyond the framing assumptions of the extremes. This oscillation can be seen at many points in human history, where ideological absolutes have been challenged, only to be replaced with their denials rather than with sustained or longer-term progress. Very often denial positions have been succeeded by a reversion to the original absolutization, once the limitations of the denial have become clearer. Our history is one of endlessly botched reforms.

There are many examples of such botched reforms, where a one-shift process has been assumed to be all that is required, and the framing shared by the pre- and post-reform beliefs has not been effectively questioned. Thus many conditions giving rise to the need for reform in the first place have not been addressed. Political revolutions such as the French and Russian Revolutions can, for instance, show this pattern: because they failed to address the psychological conditions that create unjust power structures, such structures re-asserted themselves after they had been formally abolished. Similarly in religious revolutions such as the Protestant Reformation: Martin Luther created a decisive shift towards individual judgement in the interpretation of the authoritative religious scriptures, but completely failed to question why those scriptures themselves should be accorded absolute authority. Those who wished to exert arbitrary power over others in the new Protestant order, then, only had to appeal to the Bible to do so, creating little advance on the authority of the Pope.

Such reactive movements can also create fissiparousness (a tendency to split into smaller fragments) as a further feature dependent on sceptical slippage. Once a justification for absolute claims is replaced with their denial, there is no longer any reason not to deny the denialist position as soon as any difficulties arise in it. Denying denialism on the original issue that was denied results in a flip back to the first absolute position, but questioning it on another absolute position can result, instead, in a third position: for example, Calvin and Zwingli agreed with Luther's rejection of papal authority, but split from him on church government, the nature of salvation, and other issues. Absolute denials can thus create fissiparous groups, all splitting with each other on more and more issues that are made the subject of absolute belief. As individuals, too, we may remain relatively consistent on one absolute belief, but flip between opposing positions on others, creating an internal fissiparousness.

Such fissiparousness may also result in relativism of values of a kind that is a further expression of absolutism. In a relativist (or subjectivist) view, absolute justifications continue to apply, but in a restricted zone, so that opposing absolutes can coexist acceptably. The fissiparous tendencies sparked by denialism may create so much conflict that a merely short-term pragmatic 'live and let live' solution to that conflict must be found, through the acceptance of multiple contradictory beliefs in the framework of an overarching relativist or utilitarian philosophy. However, relativism does not resolve the conflicts between the beliefs: rather it continues to accept their absolutization just as much as the earlier dogmatic traditions that may have been rejected. Such relativism may substitute a smorgasbord of options for a single dominant tradition, assuming the individual's freewill in choosing the absolute option they prefer, as is implicitly the case in some forms of multi-faith religious education (students are introduced to the absolute beliefs of Christianity, Islam, Judaism, Hinduism, etc., and it is said to be a personal choice which they accept).[7] However, there will be no justification in experience for choosing one of these absolutes over the other without it ceasing to be an absolute, since, as I argued in *Absolutization*, absolutization restricts options to the acceptance or rejection of itself.[8] We cannot match experienced options to experienced desires when both options and desires are denied, but only go through the motions of doing so. The supposed choice will be an arbitrary one between an array of empty labels, all of equal value.

The phenomena of sceptical slippage thus give rise to the need to explore its full implications in relation to a whole set of established philosophical and ideological positions built on denial. Broadly speaking, the trouble with not only relativism, but also materialism,

---

7   Ellis (1997).
8   I.1.d.

determinism, atheism, and nihilism is that they are most basically one-shift doctrines. Of course, there is a lot more complexity surrounding all such doctrines than this, because in many cases their proponents have tried to make them more adequate by appropriating some limited features of the Middle Way but identifying these with a one-shift position. I am not going to attempt to engage with all the complexity of argument around his topic here, but leave it for a later volume in this series (*The Practice of Agnosticism*[9]) that will deal in much more detail with these issues.

However, before we are swallowed up in the complexities of debate about the interpretation of existing ideological and philosophical traditions, the overall approach and purpose of the practice of agnosticism needs to be clear within the overall structure provided by the five principles. In this context, sceptical slippage needs to be recognized primarily as something we might do ourselves in the course of judgement. Simply encapsulated, we avoid sceptical slippage by recalling that *the failure to accept a claim does not necessarily imply its denial*. Everything else should be an application of this recognition as we apply it in our own experience.

4.f. Awareness of Unholy Alliances

> *Summary*
>
> Unholy alliances consist of normally opposed absolutizing opposites uniting in opposition to the Middle Way, so as to defend the wider framing for their opposition. This can happen at political or at individual levels. Normally opposed individuals or sub-personalities may unite to reject the Middle Way by caricaturing it as conventionally middle, as indecisive, or as representing a rejected outgroup (as the normally opposed are temporarily welcomed into the ingroup).

Although the traditional use of the term 'unholy alliance' merely implies an 'unnatural' or otherwise intrinsically wrong alliance, I propose to use the term in a more specific way. Unholy alliances, as I shall use the term, are alliances between supporters of theoretically opposing absolutizations, in joint opposition to any expression of the Middle Way. Such alliances generally reveal the superficiality and hypocrisy attending absolutized positions, when previous reviling of an opponent to which one was in polarized opposition suddenly gives way to tactical alliance. At this point it is revealed that the polarized opposition was not nearly as overwhelmingly important as it was purported to be, and that it is far less important, in the absolutist's order of priorities, than maintaining the absolutizing framework itself. At some level, when they form unholy alliances, absolutists recognize that the Middle Way is actually a far greater long-term threat to their position than the opposing absolutization.

Some of the earliest uses of the term 'unholy alliance' refer to alliances of Christian powers in Europe with the Ottoman Empire against other Christian powers: for instance, William Giles Dix employed the term in 1855 to protest against the British and French alliance with the Ottoman Empire against Russia during the Crimean War.[1] Here absolute Christian opposition to Islam turned out to be less important than the tactical desire to defeat a rival European power, even when that power supposedly shared the same Christian beliefs. In such cases there is no explicit challenge to the absolutizing framework itself, only hypocritical shifting between absolutized priorities. A political use of the term more closely matching the one I want to employ might be the Molotov-Ribbentrop Pact made

---

1   Dix (1855).

between Stalin's USSR and Hitler's Germany in 1939, whereby Poland was divided between the two powers. Here the historian Geoffrey Roberts has again used the term 'unholy alliance'.[2] Two totalitarian governments made a pact of self-interest, despite the supposedly extreme polarization of their ideological opposition to each other. In this case, too, the pact might be understood as joined against more integrative opposition to them both from democratic governments.[3]

That this pattern can also be reproduced at an individual level can be seen in the way we maintain the conditions for oscillation between absolutes whilst rejecting alternative frameworks. For instance, in a state of addiction to a vice, we can cling to the hope of total refuge from it offered by a fruitless moralizing solution, even after we have already experienced the reinforcing feedback loops of endlessly moving between addiction and renunciation and back to addiction. The insistence on an absolute solution that we are aware, at some level, does not work, is a more subtle way of maintaining the addiction whilst going through the motions of renouncing it. I once had a friend who used to give up smoking on a regular basis by throwing her cigarettes away and swearing that she would never touch another one – only to be back on them again the next morning. In such circumstances, our absolute desire and its fruitless absolute solution are in unholy alliance with each other against any kind of effective incremental solution to the problem.

Unholy alliances not only involve tacitly accepting an opposing absolute position that you are theoretically opposed to, but also developing a negative attitude to any manifestation of the Middle Way. If you're in alliance with your polarized opposite, this can no longer be done by lumping the Middle Way into the opposing camp, so instead it becomes necessary to develop an unattractive version of the 'middle'. This can easily be done by creating a straw man version of the Middle Way based on one of the many misunderstandings of it in circulation – as only conventionally moderate, as the result of weakness or indecisiveness, as inauthentic, or as beyond an acceptable ingroup. All of these negative caricatures of the Middle Way simultaneously help to establish a story about the basis of the unholy alliance as addressing universal conditions, as

2   Roberts (1989).
3   For ways that democracy is or can be integrative, see ii.6; IX.3; Ellis (2022) 6.g.

strong or realistic, as authentic, and as based in the ingroup. Let me take these straw man caricatures one by one.

To caricature the Middle Way as conventionally moderate is to interpret its 'middle', not as a navigation between absolutes, but as a moderate position between two extremes that are merely conventionally determined in a particular situation. For example, in one situation the opposing extremes might be people who want to eat big steaks and people who don't want to eat steaks at all, making the moderate position apparently people who only want to eat small steaks. This is an absurd 'moderate' position from a wider point of view, since eating small steaks still involves supporting what in most cases is the most unsustainable common source of food on the planet, using vast resources of land, energy, and water – namely grain-fed beef. In a steak-eating culture, eating small steaks is 'moderate', but the Middle Way avoiding absolutized defensive judgements will probably (again in most situations) involve eating no steaks at all, but rather something more appropriate. The assumption that the 'moderate' option must be correct is known as the fallacy of moderation, a fallacy that may be wrongly attributed to the Middle Way approach by both sides of an unholy alliance.

This form of straw man is related to a second one – that of associating the Middle Way with indecisiveness. Radical and urgent problems are likely to demand radical and urgent solutions, whether that involves leaping into a river to save a drowning child or taking radical measures to mitigate global warming. An unholy alliance may well appeal to a widespread recognition of that need, to then reject Middle Way approaches by associating them with practically inadequate, indecisive behaviour. Such indecisiveness is 'moderate' only in conventional terms and 'incremental' only in the sense of foot-dragging. When we look at the situation more carefully, we find that rapid and decisive judgement still needs to be *justified* by the best understanding of the situation available – an understanding that can probably only be reached by taking longer over it when the opportunity to do so presents itself (see 2.c above). To save a drowning child, we have to leap in immediately and risk the possibility of severe miscalculations (for example, perhaps the current is so strong that we will probably die too), but to have more confidence that we will not miscalculate in such situations, we need to think about them in general beforehand, and practise instantaneous responses that are as good as possible because of the slower training that we have undergone. An absolute basis for the decision is never better if it is still absolute in the wider analysis, once we have taken the wider context into account, and it is only our understanding of this wider context that justifies the decision. The Middle Way is thus only 'indecisive' in the sense of deferring judgement when it would be helpful to be so.

A third form of straw man used to attack the Middle Way from both sides simultaneously is the idea that it is inauthentic. A strong cultural association has developed between absolutization and 'reality', whether that reality is external or internal. Thus, to be absolute, it is often thought, is to be 'real' – not to qualify what one 'really thinks', but to state it straight down the line. The conflict between polarities is then thought of as honest and straightforward in a sense that the Middle Way is not. Of course, the only justification that can be given for such an assumption is circular: that is, that what we 'really think' or 'really feel' must justify what we judge, and our decisive judgements then tell us what we 'really think' or 'really feel'. What we shut off then is any other possible voices, of the kind that may make us aware that we were mistaken about what we thought we 'really felt'. There is no 'real' without begging the question,[4] just an assumption that our current view is the only one that counts. A deeper form of authenticity comes from the recognition of different voices that can emerge in our experience over time – from being prepared to face and accept our multiplicity. The Middle Way, when we try to find it, is thus not an avoidance of authenticity, but an attempt to find a deeper version of it.

A final target of the unholy alliance may be the outgroup. Two opposing absolutizations may be united in their appeal to the same wider ingroup, and in their rejection of the Middle Way as the position of a rejected outgroup. This may be typified by an unexpected acceptance of one person from what is normally the polar opposite camp, but who is accepted as an exceptional or honorary member of the ingroup. Their membership of the normally reviled opposing outgroup momentarily does not count, as long as they can be united against the Middle Way. For instance, a white racist may treat someone of another race whom he knows personally as an 'honorary white',[5] but simultaneously unite with them against a

---

4   See I.4.c.
5   Young (2009).

white liberal. Jung illustrates this conditional reconciliation in his *Red Book*, in the shape of an unexpected friendship between a hermit and a devil. The hermit decides that the devil is not so bad because he's 'a toned-down type of devil', whilst the devil accepts that the monk is 'hardly the fanatical type'.[6]

Awareness of unholy alliances as an aspect of the practice of agnosticism, then, involves the wariness of serpents in relation to all these ways of misrepresenting the Middle Way, as well as of the common features of positions that at first appear to be diametrically opposed. It is important not to apply that wariness with too much defensiveness of a kind that may end up by absolutizing the Middle Way, but nevertheless to persist in maintaining a clear alternative model, and to use every opportunity to offer it where its advantages might be understood. The practitioner caught in the middle between warring sides needs to maintain a studied neutrality between those two sides, at the same time as determined confidence in the possibility of a peace that adopts neither set of colours.

---

6   Jung (2009) Liber Secundus 33; Ellis (2020b) pp. 33–6.

4.g. Agnosticism and Psychological Development

> *Summary*
>
> Agnosticism requires a two-step process, and thus seems to require the capacities of the fifth stage of development in Robert Kegan's scheme. However, judgements do not always match capacities precisely, so this does not justify esotericism or an unqualified power hierarchy. Agnosticism also needs to be applied at the micro level (between opposing shortcuts when transitioning between levels of psychological development) as well as the macro level (between opposing metaphysical ideologies).

There is one final type of objection to agnosticism. That is that not everyone is ready to practise it. The capacity to consider the third option has to be developed, it seems, by working through the two absolutized polarities first. A two-step process of consideration requires the first step to be enabled before the second, and the incrementality of organic processes means that the second step, back towards the middle, cannot be immediately forced. To ask someone to practise agnosticism who has not yet developed the capacity to practise it is, it seems, to demand the impossible. In the terms of Robert Kegan, we would be 'in over our heads' when subjected to such a demand, like a teenager expected to take premature adult responsibilities.[1] If we are trying to follow the embodied Middle Way, we should avoid making any such merely abstract impossible demands, which in practice will only cause conflict and, worse still, create institutionalized failure by associating the demand of agnosticism with practical impossibility.

If some people are ready for agnosticism and others are not, this then also creates dilemmas of potential hierarchization and/or esotericism. Are we to say that only a certain elite capable of agnosticism should practise it? If so, what do they say to the others? How do we avoid the implication that such an elite should exert power over the rest, even if this is only the power conferred by privileged understanding? Not to try to share their understanding of agnosticism would also be another kind of use of power – the esotericism of withholding information from others.

---

1   Kegan (1994).

Agnosticism 163

To answer this objection, we need to put agnosticism in the context of human psychological development. To discuss it adequately, we then also need a scientifically based model of how that development works. Robert Kegan, drawing on the earlier work of Jean Piaget, seems to offer such a well-supported model, not only through the evidence that he cites, but also through the number of links that can be made between Kegan's approach and other approaches within psychology, such as those of the political value theory of Jonathan Haidt,[2] the cognitive bias theories of Daniel Kahneman,[3] and Jung's ideas about development in the second half of life.[4] I have already mentioned his work in connection with the continuity of training in 3.g, and a fuller account of it, and of its relationship to the Middle Way and to these various other approaches, will be given in the next volume of this series.[5] For the moment, in this chapter, I will focus only on the ways that Kegan can help us resolve these objections to agnosticism.

Kegan's model takes Piaget's understanding of the stages of child development and continues these stages into adult development, resulting in a total of five stages preceded by the zero 'incorporative' stage.[6] These are described by Kegan as follows:

1. Impulsive
2. Imperial
3. Interpersonal
4. Institutional
5. Interindividual

Each of these stages marks a balance in which human development plateaus, followed by disruption of that balance as we reach a *tipping point* (see 3.b) that forces us into a new set of cognitive and value priorities. Those priorities shift from desires and wishful thinking in stage 1, to a regularized model of the world in relation to individual desires in stage 2, to the prioritizing of social relationships in stage 3 (often reached in teen years), to an abstracted and consistent ideological model in stage 4, then finally to a recognition

---

2   Haidt (2012).
3   Kahneman (2011).
4   Jung (1960) §749 ff.
5   III.3.
6   Kegan (1982).

of the contingency of ideologies, and of pragmatic choice between them, in stage 5.

The early life of the Buddha readily symbolizes our progression from stage 3 (the Palace – a conventional and socially defined set of values), to stage 4 (the universal religious values of the Forest renunciants), to stage 5 (the discovery of the Middle Way). In terms of Kegan's stages, then, agnosticism is a position we reach when we have not only realized that our group does not have all the answers, but also that there is no ultimately 'true' set of value priorities to be discovered as the sole alternative to the relative values of groups. This simultaneously allows us to avoid the biases of that group, and to balance its dominant values with other potential values. We are more likely to become capable of such agnosticism in what Jung referred to as the 'Second Half of Life', when the absolutes that we adopted for effective adaptation to the world during earlier life begin to show their inadequacy.

So far, then, it may appear that agnosticism is at the top of a hierarchy above the two polarized absolutes that it avoids, and that the absolutization of beliefs before one reaches agnosticism is a necessary stage that one needs to go through before reaching it. However, this would be an over-simplification. Firstly, psychological stage theory applies to whole persons and attempts to describe the progression of their *capacities*. We do not always use the capacities we have developed, especially when we regress under stress, or in situations of strong social pressure. Secondly, we cannot rule out the possibility of us making judgements in advance of our stage – again probably with the assistance of a supportive social context. Agnosticism, as an aspect of the Middle Way, is a *judgement*, not a feature of character. We can talk in approximate terms of people in a particular stage making at least some of the kinds of judgements associated with that stage, but that primarily helps us to recognize the process we need to go through to be able to make agnostic judgements, not to justify inflexible uses of power according to a hierarchy with agnostics at the top.

That does not mean that agnostic judgements are not better judgements to employ when power has to be used – as it must in practice. The prime expectation that we should have of anyone in a position of power is that they should use it provisionally, and this also entails that they need to be able to question the absolutizations of the groups they encounter, thus also practising agnosticism.

However, the complexity of the relationship between character and judgement requires that we include checks and balances at every stage where power is used, from the democratic accountability of governments to the need for consultation and openness to criticism by spiritual leaders.[7]

If there is a hierarchy of states with agnosticism at the top, then, it is not a simple hierarchy, but one of interacting nested systems. As a feature of the judgement of individuals, it lies within the wider system of each individual's character, and this character in turn operates within a socio-political system that is influenced by judgement, but neither completely determined by it nor completely determining it. To direct that system responsively in changing conditions we need to set up adjustment systems – provisionality for judgement in the individual case and democracy at the socio-political level. We should separate out any associations we have between a hierarchy of psychological capacities and an imposed power hierarchy, because one does not imply the other – and would not be a consistent application of agnosticism.

Consistent with nested systems, though, the practice of agnosticism for the individual can be applied not only at the macro level, where we are exercising a capacity for agnosticism built up over a lifetime, but also at a micro level. Agnosticism is most needed at times of transition, where important judgements are made that influence our development from one stage to the next. Each stage has its own gravitational pull, as a result of our habitual prioritization of the values of that stage forming well-worn neural pathways. To be forced out of those pathways we need difficulty that incentivizes new approaches, but difficulty may also cause stress that leads us back to absolutized judgements. It is then easy to lunge in absolutized judgement either for the old status quo or for a new belief that is adopted prematurely. Someone rescued from alcoholism by a religious cult, for example, may easily either revert to alcoholism or embrace the absolute beliefs of the cult as an alternative.

To make our transition securely at each stage, we need to consciously avoid either of these extremes. Robert Kegan provides a detailed survey of the transitions between stages, identifying an interaction between each and a culture in which it becomes embedded. At each transition, the embedding culture needs to

---

7   IX.3.

simultaneously hold on, let go, and provide continuity.[8] It is easy to absolutize either the holding on or the letting go, but the transition depends on the framework that separates them being questioned even-handedly. Such questioning results in a new model being adopted that puts the assumptions of the old framework within the wider context of the new without simply rejecting the old – an integrative process of the kind I will explore in the next section of the book. For example, when a child moves from the imperial to the interpersonal stage during early adolescence, this is typically accompanied by a shift in priorities from the family as an embedding culture to a peer network, and thus the adoption of values that prioritize the approval of peers. Nevertheless, for an effective transition the adolescent should not wholly abandon the family context and its values, but maintain continuity between them of a kind that allows the family values to be situated within wider social values.[9]

A micro-agnosticism, even a micro Middle Way, is thus required at such points of transition. Kegan provides an engaging story of stage 1 to 2 transition that illustrates this. An eight-year-old boy decides to leave home and packs his bag. The parents avoid any reaction to this, and let him do so. He then sets off, but gets diverted into playing with friends whom he meets outside. As it gets dark, he dejectedly turns round and comes home, but his parents avoid humiliating him by making any mention of his failed plans to leave home.[10] The parents' restraint reflects the helpful cultivation of an open attitude in which the boy can appreciate both old values of family security and new values of greater self-sufficiency at the same time, without either being imposed against the other and creating a polarized reaction in the boy. Of course, in practice the parents needed to ensure the boy's safety, but they were wise enough to recognize that there was no immediate threat to this, and to prioritize the psychological value of allowing the boy to make his own developing adjustments. They did not need to insist on the value of staying at home, nor on the other hand bid the boy embrace a 'freedom' that he was far from ready for. Neither of these absolutized positions was likely to aid the boy's transition.

Micro-agnosticism can be cultivated in a particular situation, and supported by a culture, without every other aspect of that culture

8   Kegan (1982) pp. 121 ff.
9   Ibid. ch. 6.
10 Ibid. pp. 159–62.

being agnostic. For example, both the boy and his parents may have had absolute beliefs about other things – however, in practical terms the important point is that they did not apply those absolute beliefs to determining their response to the boy's behaviour. Macro-agnosticism, on the other hand, is consistent agnosticism between the ideological positions typical of stage 4 thinking in Kegan's account. Macro-agnosticism is the most helpful kind overall, because it supports the application of micro-agnosticism in all sorts of potential contexts. However, micro-agnosticism can also make a huge difference both to our judgement in general and to the way that judgement is allowed to develop. Whenever we apply the Middle Way by taking sufficient account both of conditions and goals in our judgement, we can help make that judgement more effective, whatever the context, even if we are a long way from the regularized agnosticism of stage 5.

5. Integration

5.a. Recognizing Conflict

> *Summary*
>
> Integration is a resolution of conflict, whether internal or external, that first requires a recognition of that conflict. Conflicts are created by systems having incompatible goals (or incompatible processes needed to maintain themselves). The same goals then recur regardless of changing conditions that block those goals, and in humans this takes the form of recurring feedback loops that conflict with more adaptive motives. The corpus callosum then allows us to repress, also producing other absolutizing phenomena. To integrate we then need to acknowledge differing desires over time and stop them hijacking our processes.

The final principle of the five is *integration*, which can be defined as the effective resolution of conflict to unify previously divided energies. For such a resolution to be *effective*, it cannot be imposed by one side over the other side, whether by insisting on one solution, by withholding information, or by denying the existence of the conflict. A process of integration needs to allow a unification of energies in pursuit of shared goals that were previously blocked by the conflict.

As we will see later in this section, integration can occur interdependently both within an individual (psychological integration) and between individuals or groups (socio-political integration). It can occur either as a long-term adaptation of character or as a temporary state (temporary integration). In its long-term form it can take complex incomplete forms (asymmetrical integration). It can also take different forms in relation to desire, meaning, and belief. However, before exploring this variety of integration phenomena, I want to focus first on the basic common process by which conflict is resolved, and the ways that the practice of the Middle Way enables it to be resolved.

To gradually build up a clear picture, I will begin in this chapter with the recognition of conflict. We cannot integrate conflicts unless we recognize them in the first place, and a failure to recognize them is a common reason for their integration being blocked. To recognize conflict, we need to have an understanding of what conflict looks like in various different forms at different levels. Once recognized, the basic process for integrating that conflict is *reframing* of the polarized absolutizations that are creating it, as I will explore in the next chapter. For effective reframing, we will find that all the other principles of the Middle Way that we have explored are crucial. This is where we need to thoroughly synthesize the more philosophical understanding involved in the other four principles of the Middle Way with the more psychological perspective required to understand integration.

Most basically, conflict depends on a system having goals, and on those goals being frustrated by blocking conditions. For a system to 'have goals' does not depend on some sort of teleological deduction about the goals it ought to have, but just an observation of the ways that reinforcing feedback loops maintain that system. Thus, an animal is a system that has to be maintained by eating and drinking, so we talk about eating and drinking as amongst its goals. Our goals may or may not be consciously represented, and may or may not be 'needed', but the continuing organization of the system to fulfil those goals, in our own case, is what we think of as desire.

If the fulfilment of that desire is blocked by any new condition, we are then *in conflict* with that condition. We remain in conflict as long as we are locked into the reinforcing feedback loop that leads us to seek the fulfilment of that goal. It's important to note, then, that at the most basic level conflict is not resolved by 'winning' in the sense of forcing our way past the blockage, if the conditions of conflict that produce it remain. It is resolved only by introducing new information so that the reinforcing feedback loop is transformed into a balancing feedback loop, with our habitual goal-seeking adjusted to slightly different goals.

Conflict can thus be modelled at a basic corporeal level. If, for instance, a planet is in orbit around a star, it could be said to be in a reinforcing feedback loop in which the goal of the planet system is to maintain it in orbit. If it then collides with a large asteroid, that orbital track can no longer be maintained, but is blocked by the new gravitational conditions. The planet can only continue in its orbit by adjusting to the impact that the asteroid has made on it. At an organic level, conflict could take the form of a cancer developing within the human body, mutating some of its cells so that they can no longer perform their previous functions to help fulfil the goals of the person. To continue in fulfilling their goals as far as possible, the person will need to accept and respond to the presence of the cancer, either getting successful treatment for it, or accepting eventual death.[1]

Conflict is thus rooted in systemic relationships in our bodies, and it is hardly surprising that psychological or intrapersonal conflict produces similar stress responses to those of any other threat. The regular elimination of a threat in conflict may sometimes be seen as part of a wider system that remains stable – for instance, we may swat a particular insect that threatens to suck our blood without eliminating that insect species from its role in the wider ecosystem. Swatting the insect, however, does not remove the systemic conflict, as long as other insects with the same goals are part of the same wider system.

In the context of the human experience, conflict is the result of the recurrence of the same goals in our mind-body system regardless of changing conditions. Those goals may keep recurring and being blocked because of reinforcing feedback loops in our basic mode of operation as living systems, and obviously there is nothing we can do about such conflicts. For example, if we are starving, but there is no food, we will keep seeking it and trying to remove all barriers to getting it. As living systems, we depend on wider systems, and features of those wider systems will at times block our goals, even to the extent of ending our experience as living organisms through death.

However, the capacity of our left pre-frontal cortex to develop representations of the world that are assumed to be absolutely true creates a continuation of reinforcing feedback loops of recurrent goals in accordance with those representations, regardless of changing conditions. This results in psychological conflict when our represented goals differ at different times, or in socio-political conflict when they are incompatible with the goals of other individuals. In *Absolutization*, I discussed the ways in which therapeutic psychology has modelled this conflict and recognized its importance: often as conflict between the conscious and unconscious mind.[2] However, it is not necessary to construct theories about the unconscious when

---

1 ii.1.c discusses corporeal conflict in more depth.
2 I.5.a.

we have contradictions that are conscious and evident over time – the only basis there has ever been for unconscious conflicts in any case.[3]

As I also argued in *Absolutization*, the method of psychological conflict is *repression*. In neuroscientific terms this probably reflects the operation of the corpus callosum in allowing the left hemisphere to inhibit the operation of the right.[4] As noted above in 2.e, there is also evidence for a neuroscientific distinction between repression and suppression, with suppression instead being dependent on judgements made in the right hemisphere. Since the left hemisphere specializes in the representation of goals, repressive inhibition allows continuing focus on the goal regardless of the new information coming in from the right hemisphere. Since the right hemisphere also mediates awareness over time, the effect of this may also be to inhibit the left hemisphere's awareness of its own goals and representations at other times. In repression, the role of the left pre-frontal cortex in representation is also looped with the motivational role of the limbic system, which contributes to absolutization by reinforcing rigid representations with craving or anxiety (feelings which are in turn reinforced by the rigid representations). Ikemoto and Panksepp suggest that motivational dopamine tends to be released by different parts of the brain for 'fixed instrumental approach responses', which make more use of the nigro-striatal dopamine system, as opposed to more flexible responses using the meso-accumbens dopamine system.[5] In the cases of both repression and suppression, the retrieval of more or less flexible representations in the pre-frontal cortex is a distinct but interlocking effect.

When one looped system at one time can repress another, it can continue trying to fulfil its goals regardless of the surrounding conditions, and even regardless of the contrary looped system occurring at another time with its representation of a completely contrary state of affairs. We thus get many of the other characteristics of absolutization that I also discussed in that volume – for instance, mental proliferation, fragility, projection, substitution of easier for harder processes, and confirmation bias.[6] We also get the phenomenon of 'flipping' discussed in 4.e: when a dominant left-hemisphere

3   Ellis (2022) 1.e.
4   Paradiso et al. (2020).
5   Ikemoto & Panksepp (1999).
6   I.1.a, I.2.c, I.5.b–d.

representation does finally give way to wider awareness, it is quickly succeeded by a contrary one reflecting the same structure but superficially opposed content. We thus get the oscillations of the smoker trying to give up, the political flips of someone caught between two party groups, or the phenomena of dramatic religious conversion.

From a practical point of view, the first step in addressing these conflicts is to recognize them. To recognize a conflict involves some, though not necessarily equal, recognition of the perspective of both sides of that conflict. Such recognition requires us to use a model that focuses on conflict as our immediate problem, rather than obscuring it in ways that pre-suppose the rightness of one side of a conflict and thus absolutize restricted values. This does not require us to accept values that we may find abhorrent, but to recognize that the justification of our rejection of wrong values is not the absolutization of particular values, but rather the integration of conflict.

That's why the use of the *integration model* is in my view central to understanding the Middle Way, and it follows through the psychological implications of the other four principles I have discussed. The integration model, in which we understand the development of good judgement as an effective response to conflict, avoids the recourse to metaphysical absolutizations that has been so widely employed in epistemology, ethics, and aesthetics – that is, in our understanding of the ways that our judgements can be incrementally justified. We do not have to appeal in a top-down fashion to 'truth', or 'reason', or God, or an enlightened perspective, or a revelation of nature, in order to understand justification. Instead, we just need to recognize conflicts and integrate them, so as to make our judgements gradually more effective and adequate to the conditions around us. Our embodied state means that we will never get any closer to 'truth' than our most integrated judgement about conditions – but a more integrated judgement is a clear advance on a conflicted, sub-optimized judgement.

To recognize conflict means to recognize our *experience* of conflict over time. That does not imply that we think of ourselves as eternally or essentially conflicted, only that we recognize the impact of conflict. Thinking of the mind as a city, for instance, populated by many different perspectives, may have a temporary value in helping us move away from a monolithic view of ourselves as essentially one (especially as our egos constantly insist on this assumption!).

However, we are no more essentially multiple than we are essentially single – our degree of singularity is instead a matter of ongoing development through integration. Less sophisticated presentations of the Buddhist doctrine of *anatta* ('no self') as a metaphysical 'truth' of multiplicity are just as misleading, and just as far from the Middle Way, as insistence on a single essential self.[7]

The context in which we are most likely to encounter and recognize conflict is the socio-political, so it may be a helpful practice to reflect systematically on the links between socio-political and psychological conflict. For instance, if I get into conflict with another individual because of disagreement about something, I am also in conflict with an element of my own experience that is in sympathy with that person, likely to emerge at another time. Instead of focusing the conflict only on the 'external' person, then, it is useful to reflect forward or backward in time to connect with similar feelings and values in our own experience as those offered by the other person. We can then understand the 'external' conflict not as a personal threat to ourselves as a whole, but as a conflict between two perspectives in our own experience.[8] Once again, that does not 'relativize' the conflict, because we do not then have to assume that the two perspectives are equally weighted in their justification, only to recognize that there *are* two perspectives that we could ourselves have.

To avoid interference in this recognition of conflict, we also need to recognize and avoid assumptions that are likely to pre-empt and interfere with it. These include the assumption that one of the desires in conflict is *intrinsically* good, rational, or 'higher order' in relation to another. Much of the accustomed vocabulary for conventional morality and analytic philosophy is thus unhelpful here.[9] If we are inclined to attribute absolute features to 'values' as opposed to desires, it may also be helpful to reflect that there is no absolute distinction between values and desires, only a probably greater complexity of rationalization. All our desires deserve recognition, followed by *incremental* judgement about the justification of the beliefs associated with them, rather than pre-emptive dismissal.

7   Ellis (2019) pp. 204–6.
8   ii.1.e.
9   ii.1.a goes into much more detail on these.

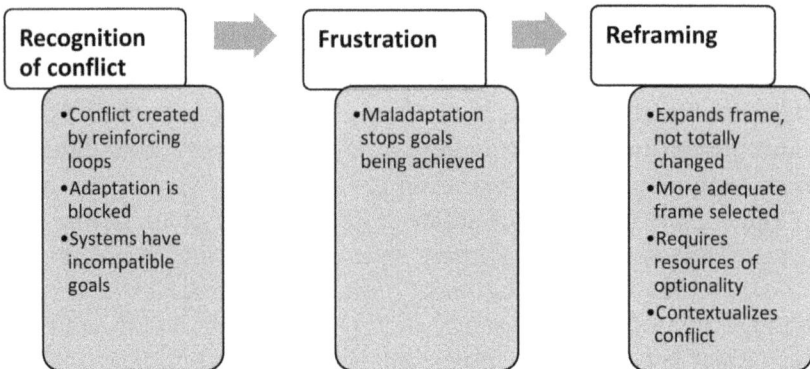

Figure 7. The process of integration: flow diagram.

The recognition of conflict is not an end in itself, but only the necessary preparation for integrating it, which is discussed further in the next chapter. The diagram here (**figure 7**) also brings together some of the key points about the process of integration from both these chapters. Given the ways that conflict is the psychological indication of absolutization, however, its recognition is essential for addressing all other dimensions of absolutization, including polarization, the exclusion of options, the fragility and disembodiment of belief, and the maintenance of the group binding that supports socio-political conflict. The recognition of conflict is also the vital first stage of any integrative practice such as meditation, the arts, or critical thinking. If you sit down to meditate, for instance, without acknowledging that part of you does not want to meditate, that part will hijack your practice rather than being welcomed into it.

5.b. Reframing

> *Summary*
>
> Framing consists of limiting assumptions that focus our attention on one thing rather than another. Even the most basic framing does not have to be seen metaphysically, as it can be questioned. Reframing is prompted by frustration created by conflict, making it possible (with optionality) to switch to a wider frame free of the conflicts of the previous one. We are always obliged to *expand* frames rather than being able to free ourselves totally of them – an error-led process of responding imperfectly to integrate conflict rather than a process of deduction from a frameless position.

Once we have identified conflict, the crucial act of judgement to integrate that conflict is that of *reframing*. Reframing is, of course, a metaphor, where the idea of a frame around a picture is paralleled to the assumptions we make when we make judgements. Just as we do not normally look at the frame, or think about it, when we view a picture, similarly, we remain unaware of framing assumptions unless we choose to focus on them. A frame may also limit our view of a picture, for instance cropping out certain areas, or creating a wider or more detailed view, but we normally focus only on what the picture is showing us rather than on these limitations, unless we make a special effort to include the framing in our consideration of the picture. In an interesting discussion of the idea of a frame, Gregory Bateson points out that both a concrete picture frame and the idea of logical framing in a mathematical set can be seen as externalizations of a more basic psychological framing, which helps us to focus our attention relevantly.[1]

In the discussions of philosophers, framing assumptions that we normally remain unaware of are often considered the preserve of metaphysics. This connection is most unfortunate, because it has led to the widespread assumption in philosophy that our framing assumptions are necessarily absolute, like the logical requirements of sets rather than the psychological role of frames. This is not necessarily the case, as we can extend our awareness to include framing assumptions, so as to either consciously accept them or question them. They can be treated provisionally just as any other belief can, even if we rarely want to question the most basic ones in practice,

1   Bateson (1972) p. 187.

and even if they are unquestioningly assumed by most people most of the time. For example, the 'truths' of mathematics, such as that 2+2=4, or our assumption of the consistency of time and space, are matters of such generally unquestioned framing. We do not normally need to question them, but there *are* possible perspectives from which we can do so. However apparently unquestionable the belief, it is still formatted through modelling, and dependent on schemas and metaphors to make that modelling meaningful to us. Other models are always possible, whether or not we can even imagine them at the moment. It is our openness to such alternative perspectives that can keep our view of them provisional, even if in practice we have no motive to abandon a given basic framing belief.[2]

The assumptions that Middle Way practice is specifically concerned to reframe are absolutizing assumptions – those that involve the belief that we have the whole story. Whilst such assumptions remain absolutizing, we are unable to consider alternatives. However, new experiences may make us frustrated with the old assumptions and thus motivate us to seek out new alternative framings. New alternative framings may then work better for us if they enable us to resolve conflict. The two mules pictures, originally from a pacifist poster (**figure 4**, discussed in 2.d), clearly illustrate this basic process: the mules become frustrated by their conflict and thus reach a point where they become able to consider new alternatives. In this case the absolute assumption is that they should each eat separate piles of hay at the same time, but the new framing is that they could instead eat each pile of hay together and in sequence.

What exactly is this frustration that sparks provisionality when we have become locked in absolutization? How does it then lead us to reframe? To understand this process more closely, it's important to let go of metaphysical assumptions of the kind that could short-circuit the organic experience of reframing in practice. Typically such assumptions are those of freewill or of determinism: either we assume that we only have to 'choose' the new alternatives in an otherwise neutral way (freewill), or alternatively that our framing is fated and unalterable, whether we are unalterably locked into the old framing or inevitably 'forced' into the new framing by 'external' events. There is no justification for either of these absolutized

---

2   See I.4.a for more detailed discussion.

Integration

assumptions as an interpretation of the process of reframing, which occurs in the complex system of the human mind/brain, where there will always be elements we don't fully understand. The process is ineluctably ambiguous, simply because of the limitations of our embodied standpoint. It is thus not a matter of 'rational choice', nor of divine intervention to set us on the right path, nor of 'natural' constriction to the wrong path.

The experience of frustration as a stimulus for reframing is well-established in the Buddhist account of *dukkha* – a term often misleadingly translated as 'suffering'. Experiences of suffering may indeed sometimes jolt us out of a rut of well-worn framing assumptions, but there is no guarantee that they will at all. Suffering may instead just make us more depressed or defensive of our old assumptions. However, there will need to be some experience of frustration or dissatisfaction with the previous assumptions to motivate us to engage with new possibilities. Together with this dissatisfaction, though, our motives for reframing may be largely positive, impelled by a new engagement with an alternative that has forced itself on our attention. For example, a student going to university for the first time will not necessarily need a strong dissatisfaction with the values of their previous home to be excited by new friendships and new ideas, offering whole new alternative perspectives to that previous home life. To actually start to switch to a new set of assumptions, though, there needs to be some degree of dissatisfaction with the old, even if it is only that the old is no longer working in a new environment.

This frustration is also not sufficient by itself, but needs to be combined with awareness of alternatives. Awareness of alternatives is not a matter of 'rationality', but of meaning or imagination, as already discussed in 2.a. Alternative neural links need to be present, and sufficiently accessible for us to fall back on them when our frustration pauses us in our normal progression down old tracks. The point of change can also be seen as the switch between a reinforcing feedback loop and a balancing feedback loop.[3] The reinforcing feedback loop continues in an old pattern of assumption (for instance, the two mules pulling against each other), until new information starts to modify the loop by adding in new elements. The new elements could consist in new metaphors, models, or concepts that we

3   I.2.a.

use to reframe our experience, from the mere possibility for the two mules that they could behave differently, to a more profound shift of guiding metaphor such as that undergone by someone who starts to see the maintenance of their health as an act of integrative maintenance rather than a battle.

Reframing as part of a process of integration is not just the adoption of any available new model, but the adoption of a model that releases us from absolutizing beliefs that previously created unnecessary conflict. Of course, there is then a question of how much, or for how long, the new model relieves us of conflict. As already discussed in 4.g, the new model does not in any sense have to be a final solution to the problem to offer a helpful reframing in the circumstances – rather it can be the reframing that the person concerned is capable of at that time. The releasing of one immediate conflict may then help to propel us into a new stage of psychological development of the kind discussed in 4.g: for instance, the recognition that we do not simply need to choose between the beliefs of two groups (in Kegan's stage 3) may propel us into a more consistent ideological stance instead (Kegan's stage 4). Such a move is integrative, because it is part of a *process* by which conflict is increasingly resolved. We do not need to be able to identify the end point of that process in order to engage in it.

If we can identify conflict and accept its presence to begin with, an error-led approach is then sufficient, without any need for deduction from a final point. An error, in the end, is a conflict between two perspectives – the one that produced the error and the one that is dissatisfied with it. We bridge that conflict, not just by using the error-aware perspective to enforce its 'correction' on the erroneous perspective, but rather by changing that aspect of the perspective of both sides that created the conflict – either by producing the error or by producing dissatisfaction with the error, or by a combination of the two. For instance, if someone is practising a particular skill, such as driving, and they make a grinding gear change, that is an error from the perspective of the person driving with their wish to drive well according to socially accepted standards. From the standpoint of a driving instructor cultivating patience with minor faults in his pupils (so as to focus more effectively on major ones), though, it is learning to ignore his dissatisfaction with that error that is most important. From an even wider standpoint, both the mechanical treatment of the vehicle and the psychology of effective teaching are important in that situation, and thus corrections in either or both have the potential to integrate conflict.

At a socio-political level, too, there may be resolutions of conflicts that are not yet sufficiently available to individuals. A larger question relevant to the example above is that of whether the two people concerned should be driving at all. The answer to such a question is complex, but merely raising it can be part of an integrative process. As long as a wider environmental perspective on the driving scenario remains off the agenda entirely, it is a potential source of conflicts: both the driver and the instructor may then find themselves confronted by protestors against inaction on climate change blocking the road. The moral resolution of the conflicts of priority there, again, is our ability to adopt a new model that is neither merely an absolutized understanding of the wrongness of driving from an environmental point of view, nor a mere rejection of the relevance of the wider environmental perspective from a narrower point of view. The environmentalist may be 'right' in the sense of having a bigger and more adequate picture, but nevertheless does not operate on the basis of understanding *all* conditions, so can still develop new and more adequate models (for instance, incorporating psychological awareness) for how to pursue environmentalist priorities.

Whatever our current frame, we are stuck with frames, and can only move to a more adequate frame that resolves immediate conflict. In the embodied condition, there is no such thing as a frameless position or a final frame. Nevertheless, the process of integration is of overwhelming moral and practical importance as the best response to each new situation, taking into account as many new perspectives as possible.

5.c. Responses to Intractability

> *Summary*
>
> Conflicts may be intractable because at least one side lacks motive or perhaps capacity to resolve them. At times practical situations require the use of power to impose our will, which can be justified by greater integration of judgement, but this should not be used as a shortcut. Intractable conflict can be addressed by using an array of different types of context, often in combination through practices that use them. These contexts may be locked together, but opening up one of them can breach the absolutizing of the conflict.

To some, talk of reframing as a way of resolving conflict may seem impossibly glib. Conflict is so deeply entrenched into our lives, that in some circumstances the idea of resolving it may seem an impossible fantasy. To some one living in the context of the Palestinian-Israeli conflict, for instance, the possibility of that conflict being ended by reframing may seem merely utopian. To reframe, those with both conflicting perspectives must have some motivation to move beyond the assumptions they are entrenched in. For an individual, there is always the possibility of new experience triggering frustration or an awareness of alternatives within the wider system that holds the conflict. However, in the context of socio-political conflict, where the conflicting assumptions are constantly reinforced by opposing groups, awareness of alternatives is constantly repressed.

There may also be cases in which others seem incapable of progress, and indeed, in some cases actually are. More complex modelling depends on the capacity for complexity in the individuals involved, and although it is very difficult to identify the limits of development (even, for instance, in those with specific learning difficulties), there may well be such limits. Whatever the underlying causes, we have all probably encountered situations of intractable conflict, in which others (as we may like to put it) 'won't listen to reason'. What this probably means is that they have no motive, or possibly no capacity, for reframing to a wider set of assumptions.

Intractable conflict may mean a war between two groups, such as Israelis and Palestinians, in which no available strategies to resolve disputes seem to work. It may mean a conflict between two individuals in which one has more power than the other (as with a boss and an employee), where the more powerful individual has no incentive to reframe and simply seeks to enforce their will within the frame that they have absolutely adopted. It may mean a psychological conflict within an individual in which the maladaptive effects of early trauma continually block all attempts at healing. A Palestinian who hates all Israelis, or a victim of childhood sexual abuse unable to develop a mature relationship, deserve our sympathy and help as far as we can offer it, but the intractability of both inner and outer conflicts is a matter of framing, not of simple absolutized evil in their respective abusers. Healing in such cases may require major social or political change, but such change, if it ever happens, may nevertheless not be sufficient.

How, then, should we respond to such intractability? Too often we do so with absolutized blame and an attempt to impose a solution through power. Such imposition in the face of conflict may be necessary in situations where there is strong evidence that the opponent does not have any capacity to reframe, and can be justified if the level of integration of our judgement clearly exceeds the other's. When a toddler attempts to run into the road, then, we do not 'reason' with them, we restrain them. The police do not attempt to reframe the perspective of criminals, they arrest them (although there is still the possibility of subsequent punishment of a type oriented towards rehabilitation – which often implies reframing). Gandhi's non-violent methods of political persuasion were calibrated to *persuade* the British administration in India, and succeeded precisely because there was a capacity for reframing in that administration – but such methods would hardly have worked in Nazi Germany, as Gandhi at one point admitted. Because there are some circumstances where power is necessary, however, and because it is also mentally easier than reframing, we get into the habit of using it in a range of situations where it is *not* the only effective option. We are more likely to overestimate intractability than to underestimate it, because there is so much complexity behind human behaviour and we do not give others the benefit of the doubt.

Intractability can be addressed in the long term, because it is not the result of any essential features on the part of anyone. Rather, it is the result of specific conditions that keep maintaining a reinforcing feedback loop in our judgements of others. Those specific conditions are those of absolutization, with its accompanying lack of contextual awareness of any kind. As a result, intractability *can* be addressed by introducing further context of any kind – bodily, social, spatial, temporal, experiential, aesthetic, moral, or intellectual. Such context provides an opportunity for reframing and thus integration, though of course there are no guarantees that it will succeed in breaking the reinforcing feedback loop of conflict. Eight such contexts are listed below, as well as illustrated on the diagram (**figure 8**).

- *Bodily* context is the kind developed in, for instance, yoga or meditation, where stress-related anxiety does not disappear, but rather is integrated into a wider context of bodily awareness that makes it less significant.
- *Social* context is a wider awareness of people's views beyond the group that has been a focus of absolutizing attention – for instance, travelling to unfamiliar countries allows one to reconsider one's attitude to the customs in one's own when they previously seemed unquestionable, as women from some parts of the Islamic world might find in relation to their personal freedom when moving to the West.
- *Spatial* context just involves looking in different directions or further away – as the mules started to do to realize that there were two piles of hay available to them.
- *Temporal* context makes one aware of how current conditions have been different in the past and may change in the future: for instance, we might look to the past to adopt some features of pre-industrial living because they are more sustainable.
- *Experiential* context is the awareness that we can have different kinds of experience from the kind we currently take to be normal: for example, religious experience may have a strong reframing effect on our attitude to 'ordinary' experience.
- *Aesthetic* context involves appreciation of sensory experience in a way that allows us to see conceptual beliefs as less solely dominant: for instance, immersing oneself in the beauty of a forest may help us to process otherwise obsessive grief.
- *Moral* context involves awareness of differing moral justifications apart from the one we may be inclined to absolutize – for instance, that abortion is not simply murder if one views it in the light of the effects of our actions, rather than only by applying an absolute principle about the value of human life.
- *Intellectual* context is an awareness of different possible theories or types of belief that one might hold when interpreting a particular situation: for instance, study might make us aware of both a scientific and a traditional religious view of a situation.

Integration 183

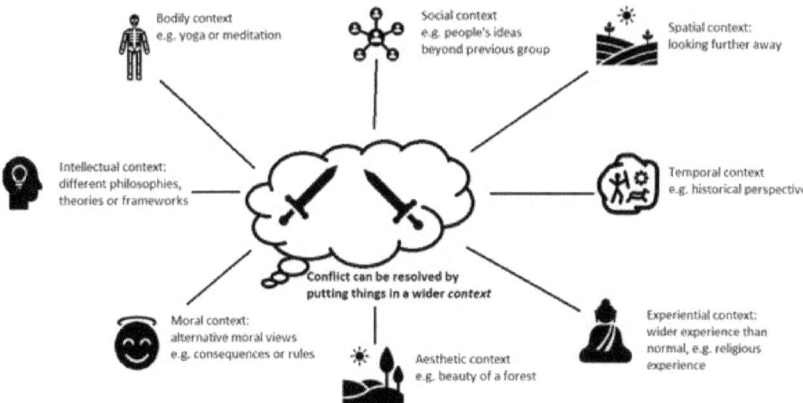

Figure 8. Eight types of context for the integration of conflict.

The type of context that we might try to use to stretch intractability depends very much on those that are available to us in that situation. However, if one type is difficult to access for any reason, there are nearly always others we can try. The two mules managed to integrate their conflict simply by looking around and becoming aware of the space around them – a simple approach that might work for anyone. However, in many other cases it is a more complex interpretation of the situation that needs to be contextualized. There, we might want to try intellectual or moral contextualization, but if that fails we could return to our body and its experience. We do not have to rely on one type of context alone, but can use one to help us access others: for instance, more bodily context may help us to develop a more open mental state in which we can start to grasp a wider intellectual context.

It is this variety of types of contextualization that makes different types of integrative practice so interdependent. Different types of practice specialize in opening out different kinds of context: for instance, meditation provides bodily and experiential context, the arts provide aesthetic context (and often many other kinds, such as moral context). Critical thinking and study in general may provide intellectual context. If we rely only on one of these types of practice without the others, the type of contextualization that might most effectively address the absolutizations we are stuck in at the moment may not be available to us. A greater repertoire of types of contexts gives us more opportunities to contextualize.

These varied interdependent practices will also need to be undertaken as an aspect of Middle Way practice, if they are not to facilitate further absolutization that will undermine the integration process. For example, it may well be claimed that belief in God gives an important context to many people that allows them to overcome conflicts. However, without rigorously applying scepticism and provisionality to such beliefs, one may fail to differentiate belief in God from an appreciation of the meaning of God. It is God as meaning that provides experiential context, perhaps linked by association to many other types of context – aesthetic context in the ambience of a church or mosque, temporal context when contemplating God's eternity, or the social context of a religious community. There are many established ways of providing context that are unnecessarily attached to beliefs that undermine that contextualization in the longer term, so that, for instance, we find a temporary respite from our addictions in the social context of a religious community, but then start to defend the boundaries of that community by ignoring the wider contexts beyond it.

Intractability, in the end, may consist in the locking together of a variety of dimensions of experience to prevent wider contexts being glimpsed. For example, a person may refuse to compromise because of the principles of her group (for instance, she may be devoted to the kosher rules of orthodox Judaism). She can't see a wider social context due to the exclusivity of the orthodox Jewish group, which is in turn locked together with a limiting of intellectual context (she never learns about alternative views), supported by constricting social interpretations of anything that might provide experiential, bodily, or aesthetic context (for instance, religious experience is seen as threatening unless it is approved by religious authorities, and art is discouraged or even prohibited). However, when locked in in this way, any one of these types of context may still provide a window beyond all of them. Intractability is not for ever, and it is not locked. You may not be aware of when and where it will be released, but there are too many different windows in human experience for the blinds to be closed on all of them for ever.

5.d. Integration of Desire, Meaning, and Belief

> *Summary*
>
> A division into the three levels of desire, meaning, and belief offers a helpful practical analysis of integration, though these levels are highly interdependent. Integration of desire occurs when the energies previously directed towards incompatible goals are united. The bodily context of mindfulness enables this temporarily. Integration of meaning is the unification of a previously fragmented associative response to symbols, developing understanding in both of the interdependent 'cognitive' and 'emotive' senses. This enables the integration of belief, in which previously opposed beliefs become mutually acceptable, and thus the absolutization that divided them is overcome in the long term.

To further understand integration in its relationship to practice, we can analyse it into three elements: desire, meaning, and belief. A process of integration at any one point includes all three of these elements, but its practical cultivation is more likely to focus on one or two of them at a time. Integration in general is also integration of desire, in the sense that it unites flows of energy that were previously divided. This flow can be engaged with directly through practices that work with embodied energy. Integration is also integration of meaning, in the sense that it unites our associative responses to stimuli into more complex patterns that enable new possibilities to be considered. This uniting of associative responses depends on the unification of embodied energy, but can also be worked with directly through any practice that connects new symbols to experience. Thirdly, all integration is also integration of belief, in the sense that beliefs that were previously opposed to each other become compatible. This compatibility (which does not require any kind of formal identity of beliefs) depends in turn on new potential beliefs being meaningful to us.

I will now discuss each of these elements of integration in more detail, but it needs to be noted that the purpose of doing so is practical. We can see from this kind of analysis why, for instance, mindfulness practice can have an integrative effect, and how this operates indirectly to help reconcile opposed beliefs. Similarly, it can show how the arts are helpful both to general embodied well-being and to the resolution of conflict, and how critical thinking that resolves absolutization of belief can also help to support more embodied types of awareness. These types of practice, usually considered in isolation from each other, need to be viewed as interdependent parts of a wider human system.

Integration of desire

Desire (to begin with the first element) is energy experienced in our bodies that connects goals with the motive required to pursue those goals. The striatum is the part of the brain that seems to be most closely associated with our base motives. These are then mediated through the representations of our pre-frontal cortex, and drive our nervous system to activity whenever our representations of the conditions around us support a belief that we can contribute to the fulfilment of a goal through activity. Desire is a normal and unavoidable aspect of organic life, and it is entirely fruitless to try to fight desire in the fashion of the ascetic.[1] However, desires can be integrated or unintegrated.

Unintegrated desires are ones that dominate our awareness, in line with our represented beliefs at one time, but that then conflict with desires at another time. Desires conflict because they are each associated with incompatible represented beliefs: for example, I might desire to eat cake at one moment, and then feel guilty about it (developing a contrary desire) the next. If the energy of the desire to eat cake and not to eat cake can be united in terms of compatible beliefs with a wider context, this conflict is integrated.

We can sometimes integrate our desires (and thus our beliefs) by working directly with the desires themselves to put them in a wider context. If we can do this, the flow of energy associated with a particular conceptualized goal does not disappear and does not need to be blocked: but instead it is no longer isolated. The desire for cake, for instance, is experienced *in the context of* an awareness that at other times we might feel guilty about eating cake. That awareness does not remove the goal, nor predetermine the action we will take (we may still decide either to eat cake or not to eat cake), but just makes the judgement we will arrive at a more broadly-based one. Because the flow of desires is a larger one (a majestic broad river rather than a rushing torrent in a narrow ditch) the beliefs on which it is based will also be more adequate ones. To make the flow of desires larger, we will usually work in some way or another with

---

1   See Ellis (2019) 1.e on the Buddha's asceticism.

our embodied awareness, to give a bigger context to our direct aesthetic consciousness of what it feels like to have that desire.

To integrate our desires directly, then, what we need is *mindfulness*, which can broadly be defined as a direct contextual awareness of any given thought, feeling, or action. When I get up or sit down, I am aware of the movements of my body in doing so. When I breathe, I am aware of my breath. When I engage in a train of thinking, I am aware that I am thinking. When I experience a burst of sadness, I am aware of that emotional state. This awareness is not just a narrowly focused, alienated commentary on myself, but an awareness of a wider *aesthetic* context in which the object of awareness is contained. It is not a conceptual commentary by which I just turn getting up and sitting down into an intellectualization of getting up and sitting down. Rather it is the wider experience of getting up and sitting down *in a body* in which muscles expand and contract, skin is in contact with surfaces, and my sensual impressions constantly change as I move. Such awareness is not an end in itself (though we should find it enjoyable), but it is a context in which all our conceptualized ends can be placed. When those ends conflict, each one is then no longer solely dominant, but placed in a space where we have more chance of examining the assumptions of each.

The integration of belief may be enabled by the integration of desire, but it is not always so. The unification of flows of energy in wider aesthetic awareness is a temporary state that can be developed particularly through meditation, but may also be supported by embodied practices such as yoga or tai chi – or even by recreational activities such as walking or painting. Whilst engaging in such practices, and for a limited time afterwards (probably no more than a few hours), our sense of conflict or frustration may be alleviated, and we may feel more open, energetic, and positive. However, such states are more an opportunity to integrate our beliefs than they are a long-term integration (I will discuss them further in 5.f below). After a short while, more deeply entrenched patterns of conflict and reinforcing feedback are likely to return. However, whilst our desires remain temporarily integrated, we have the advantage of a wider aesthetic context to our beliefs that may easily enable a wider context of belief. For a while, our absolute assumptions are not the whole story, but we have not yet developed an alternative, more complex story to put in their place.

Integration of meaning

The second element of integration, integration of meaning, forms an intermediate layer between desire and belief – one that is often ignored because it is reduced to one or the other, but also one that it is equally important to recognize and address. The main reason for meaning being ignored is our strong intellectual tradition of falsely separating cognitive from emotive meaning, so that the emotive aspect of meaning becomes merged with desire as 'feelings', whilst the 'cognitive' aspect of meaning (a misnomer in itself) becomes merged with 'sense-making' (a term that blurs meaning with belief) or even 'knowledge'. However, the cognitive and emotive aspects of meaning are totally interdependent, neither ever appearing in experience without the other.

Meaning can be fragmented when different resources of cognitive-with-emotive meaning are out of contact or connection with each other: this is what we experience as 'not understanding' something or someone. To integrate meaning is to bridge a gulf of understanding in one or another respect. This is a process that on the one hand is distinct from merely having a wider aesthetic awareness of what we previously did not understand, and on the other is distinct from forming beliefs about it. However, we cannot integrate meaning without first having an aesthetic awareness of what we find meaningful, and we cannot integrate belief without first integrating the meaning of the beliefs we are integrating.

To understand the integration of meaning requires an embodied meaning framework of reference: it will make no sense in a representationalist framework. Embodied meaning has already been introduced in 1.d above.[2] If we understand meaning as embodied, we understand meaning as the associative response we have to new experiences – ones that are neurally linked to symbols of one kind or another. For instance, when I look out of my window and see a tree, that tree has a meaning for me because it is associatively linked, not only with my previous memories of looking at the same tree, and my experiences of other trees and associated contexts, but also with symbols that are associated with what I am seeing, such as the word 'tree' (or more specifically, 'oak', or less specifically, 'plant'). Words are not the only symbols, though: I may associate the tree with visual images of trees, or with sounds, including music. Our

---

2   Also see I.3; iii.1; IV.

understanding of more complex ideas and verbal propositions is built up from these basic associative elements through a process of schematization (association of sets of symbols in various embodied situations), metaphorical extension, and cognitive modelling, so that the meaning of a sentence like 'My family tree includes some Scottish connections' then includes the symbol 'tree' in interdependence with several other such associations in long-established complex further associations, brought together in grammatical relationships. This basis of meaning and its implications will be discussed in much more detail in volume IV of this series.

Unlike the (fragmenting) conflicts of desire or belief, the fragmentation of meaning is not strictly a conflict. Different meanings are not seeking to eliminate each other, but are merely disconnected. One reason that we fail to *understand* (in both a 'cognitive' and an 'emotional' sense) can be simply that we have not previously made any associations between a symbol and any meaning – as is the case, for example, on encountering foreign languages that one has never learnt to any extent. However, a further common reason for failing to understand is a lack of connection: whether we see that in the 'cognitive' terms of having forgotten the meaning of a word (or of a set of verbalized ideas), or in the 'emotional' terms of failing to sympathize with another's perspective sufficiently to engage with it. When we are dealing with someone else's beliefs, this sympathetic engagement is a stage prior to agreement with those beliefs, and often involves the recognition of the person as being sufficiently like us to have beliefs that are worth considering. As we overcome absolutized dismissal of another, we begin to treat them 'as a person' and also with provisionality: as we do so, then, we have begun to integrate their meaning and the meaning of what they say.

As we make those neural connections, recognizing a symbol, or set of symbols, as meaningful in their embodied context, we integrate meaning. This requires some prior integration of desire, because my attention needs to be directed towards the newly meaningful symbol, and I need to stop ignoring it by repressing my attention towards it because of conflict. If the integration of meaning arises from an integration of desire in relation to a person, we may call it compassion – my view of the person changes, not because I necessarily agree with them, but because my energies are united in relation to them. My view of myself as a person with goals correlates with my view of them as a person who also has their own goals: a process that neurally can be explained by the operation of mirror neurons.[3]

If the integration of meaning is solely about a symbol whose meaning we start to access, we experience a falling of barriers in response to our new motivation to understand it. We may then make a link with a schematic or metaphorical meaning that we did not make before. For instance, a student struggling to understand a new concept may experience an 'aha' moment when a teacher explains a difficult concept using a new metaphor: but this will only work if the student first identifies sufficiently with the process of learning as integrated with her other desires. Such moments may also require a personal connection of some kind, as the student recognizes that the teacher as a person shares some of her goals and is trying to be helpful.

The integration of meaning is thus strongly associated with education in the widest sense of the word. Indeed, education could be defined as the development of new meaning, whether with the assistance of others or without them. Unfortunately, however, education is still far too often seen as a cultivation of 'knowledge' instead – an assumption that institutionalizes absolutization and interferes with the learning process (see 6.f below).

The imagination is also central to the integration of meaning, as we only come to understand new symbols by engaging with them provisionally – either as isolated symbols, or in a fluid and hypothetical form of representation. The imagination is basically synthetic – it always connects previous ideas in one way or another, whether in the form of a composite idea (such as a fantastic beast), an elaborated hypothetical scenario, or a set of interacting images or sounds drawn from different areas of past experience. The stimulation of the imagination through the arts (either in creation or appreciation) is thus an ideal way both to connect new symbols with meaning and to integrate ones we may already have encountered (these two kinds of process cannot usually be clearly distinguished in practice).

Integration of belief

The integration of belief consists in the reconciliation of conflicting beliefs. The conflict is psychological, and consists in representations

---

3   Woodruff (2018).

that are assumed to be irreconcilable, whether or not they are strictly irreconcilable in logical terms when stated as propositions. Beliefs also do not have to be explicit (indeed rarely are), but are rather the assumptions that form judgement either for action or for further belief. All that is necessary to reconcile psychologically opposing beliefs is provisionality, not propositional agreement. Provisionality implies that both of the beliefs to be reconciled incorporate enough complexity to be associated with an awareness of their own uncertainty, and thus that there is at least some probability, however minuscule, that other beliefs are correct. Where two opposing beliefs are associated with such an awareness, a basis is created for further investigation to produce a practically acceptable mutual belief.

Mutual acceptability does not necessarily mean compromise. In some cases, an acknowledgement by one side that a belief is not total can lead to a new examination of the weight of evidence, followed by a recognition that this overwhelmingly favours the other side. In a complex issue like climate change, for instance, a climate change denier needs to recognize that although they may be able to find evidence that apparently supports their position, this is not the whole story, and the *weight* of evidence overwhelmingly favours the acknowledgement of anthropogenic climate change. The acknowledgement of not having the whole story is the crucial point at which the denier may well move, not to a compromise position (except, perhaps, to temporarily save face), but to a position that largely favours the beliefs she has previously rejected. In an internal conflict of beliefs, too, we may shift quickly towards recognizing a belief we have repressed (such as acknowledging that one has become overweight) largely by simply recognizing that our previous beliefs (together with any partial evidence we may have used to rationalize them) were not the whole story.

It is at this point that beliefs become integrated (as well as provisional, incremental, and agnostic). As this is a psychological phenomenon, it is not a fixed state, although it is a discontinuous one, because it consists of the overcoming of absolutization. We could still conceivably revert to unintegrated beliefs, although the new links we have made reduce the chances of this, and give us the capacity to create and build on further provisionality. The changes that have taken place, then, are longer-term than those that we could ascribe to integration of desire alone. Our energies can be united as a result of our beliefs being reconciled, but those energies could be temporarily withdrawn and the new neural tracks will remain, even if they then become gradually disused. We will feel much more fully able to act on new integrated beliefs if our desires are also integrated, but we have also set up a longer-term infrastructure that will help those desires to flow down more helpful channels.

This integration of belief can only occur if an integration of meaning through the imagination has already occurred. To be able to adopt new beliefs that acknowledge alternatives, we first have to be able to represent the alternatives in some form. Without that prior exercise of the imagination on the half-developed frontiers of our beliefs, the new beliefs cannot develop. Before we can build a road into the wilderness, we first have to beat a path and survey the terrain.

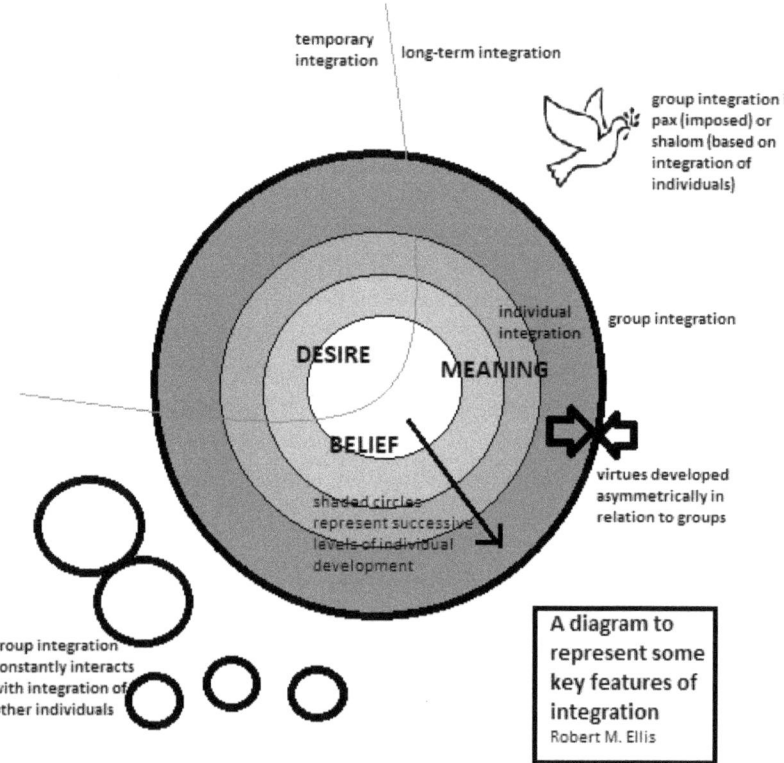

Figure 9. Some key features of integration.

These three levels of integration offer the basis of my account of practices in section 6, where their full practical value as organizing principles may become clearer. Although no aspect of integration can be completely isolated from the rest, manageable ways to develop it do usually require us to focus on one of these levels at a time, and I will be working through a number of specific practices in section 6 to show how they can all contribute in different ways to integration (and thus the Middle Way) as a whole. Like other analyses of complex phenomena, however, they offer only one of many possible ways of cutting the cake, which could in future be superseded by a more useful analysis.

Before we directly discuss practices, though, these three levels of integration will need to be related to some other features of integration which are discussed in the next three chapters. These are also schematically represented in the diagram here (**figure 9**).

5.e. Individual and Group Integration

> *Summary*
>
> The integration of individuals nests within that of groups, interdependent but differing in complexity. Both are subject to conflict and integration, with the representations causing conflict in groups being an aggregation of those of individuals. Formal or informal agreements create group beliefs that can be imposed or integrated, creating two kinds of peace: pax and shalom. Pax is superficial and temporary, but idealized shalom can also be disruptive, so both kinds of integration need to interact.

Integration is a systemic, nested phenomenon in which the integration of larger systems involving desire, meaning, and belief is interdependent with the integration of smaller ones. The integration of an individual is a smaller system associated with one body and one shifting focus of action, but that smaller system in turn nests within a whole complex set of wider systems involving other individuals. The challenge for these systems can be called 'group integration', where a group is considered to be any set of associating people, from a pair to the world population. One could also call this 'socio-political integration'.

To begin with, it is a challenge for us to keep both the individual and socio-political levels of discourse in focus at the same time, and there is a long history of reductions, unhelpful dismissals, and unjustified supervenience claims along the boundary between the socio-political and the psychological. However, there should be no dogmatic priority between these two levels of integration: each requires the other. Individual integration can be very quickly undermined by socio-political conditions, whether this is conflict in a personal relationship, or a violent political conflict creating massive disruptive stresses in our psyches. Socio-political integration, too, is constantly sabotaged by the conflicts within individuals, resulting for instance in exploitative personal relationships, bullying, criminality, corruption, and vulnerability to group brainwashing. Reductive sociology (often including Marxist theory, and some social psychology) fails to address the ways that socio-political conflict demands psychological solutions, whilst psychological approaches that ignore or dismiss the social and political sphere are highly vulnerable to unforeseen disruptions from without.

Integration

At the same time as keeping the two types of integration in relation to each other, it's also important not to always assume that they are the same, or that they will follow exactly the same patterns of development. There is a long-established philosophical tradition (particularly associated with Plato) of paralleling the harmony of the individual with the harmony of the body politic (that is, the state), or even of the whole universe. That parallel can be useful as long as it remains a provisional one, open to adjustment in the light of evidence of the differences between psychological and social systems as well as the similarities, rather than assuming that the two systems must be the same in every respect *a priori*. The key difference is obviously that socio-political systems have an additional step up in complexity, being made up of many individual systems that are in interaction with each other. The relative predictability of social, economic, and political systems depends on the averaging out of individual responses, all of which tend to respond to human needs; so whilst individual systems can vary greatly according to their genes, environment, and patterns of judgement, socio-political systems vary only to the extent that these individual differences are consistently shared amongst a wider group.

However, there is one key similarity between individual and socio-political systems that I want to focus on here: namely, that both are subject to processes of conflict and integration. Just as individual conflict consists of incompatible represented goals, so does conflict between individuals and between groups. Just as for individuals, these represented goals consist in beliefs that may or may not be held absolutely. For an individual, a single focus of attention means that conflicting views have to succeed each other over time rather than being the subjects of awareness at exactly the same time, and the same can be the case for a group: however, the fact that the group can have many simultaneous focuses of attention also means that conflict can become more obvious, with incompatible beliefs being expressed or acted upon at exactly the same time. This is what makes group conflict generally more obvious to us than conflict within individuals. The representations that create both kinds of conflict, however, are the same, and are held by individuals: for example, if two rival gangs, the Jets and the Sharks, hate each other, this hatred is an emotional state held by each member of each gang, and in each of these cases associated with representations of the members of the rival gang as hateful.

Group conflict can be made much more intractable, however, by the group binding uses of absolutization. There, as I explored in *Absolutization*, groups use absolutization as a shortcut to bind themselves together for the achievement of common goals.[1] Absolutized beliefs may be associated with authoritarian leadership that exploits an uncritical following, or it may consist of absolutized beliefs that have been adopted individually by all members of the group. The power of 'religions of the book' like fundamentalist forms of Christianity and Islam lies particularly in this capacity to motivate each individual to an absolute end that can be to some extent independent of leadership. Group binding can maintain strong continuing conflict in an individual even in the absence of the immediate influence of the group that created it, as we may see for instance in the continuing guilt of those brought up in an authoritarian religious group, but who then renounce it.[2]

Just as conflict can take both individual and group forms, then, so can integration. The process of integration, as in the individual case, depends on the reframing of the assumptions that make represented goals incompatible. However, the assumptions that we count as those of a given individual in a social context are those that have been communicated because they are dominant at the time when a judgement about a socially prioritized belief has been made. In a larger group, a further similar process has to be undergone to create a socially accepted group judgement – whether this is the formal agreement made in a meeting or the initiative of one individual in an informal group of friends that others then accede to. Integration at a group level is often thought of in terms of the mere compatibility of these dominant beliefs on both sides of the conflict, but this is only the starting point. For its longer-term sustainability, it also depends both on the integration of the groups on each side that judge the dominant beliefs, and the integration of each individual in those groups.

An analysis of two types of peace – pax and shalom – is quite useful here.[3] Pax is peace that is socio-politically imposed, and thus consists of no more than a possibly temporary agreement between the dominant beliefs on each side. Shalom is a deeper and more sustainable peace in which the integration of individuals is also taken

1   I.5.e.
2   Matthews & Salazar (2013).
3   Harries (1990); ii.1.g.

into account. However, too much emphasis on the integration of individuals (especially if this is accompanied by deluded absolute beliefs about how this can be done) at the expense of immediate social order can also produce more conflict, as we find in the intractable conflicts that can arise between well-intentioned religious or political ideologies. Christianity, for instance, is in theory a religion of peace, but in practice has sponsored countless wars because of a naïve insistence on the salvific value of its own particular symbols of integration as ends in themselves, regardless of the actual sociopolitical effects of Christian activity. Pax, on the other hand, is a very limited and temporary truce subject to changes in conditions both in societies and in individual psychologies. The *Pax Romana* and the *Pax Britannica* were both peaces imposed on subject populations which then fell apart when the conditions changed – however, they were more successful for a period of centuries than most attempts at establishing *shalom* have ever been, because at least they established some of the starting conditions for further integration.

We should thus not underestimate the intermediate value of the skills of diplomacy that may establish an immediate agreement between the dominant beliefs in a given context. However, it's also important not to assume that such an agreement will then last for very long, given the ways in which human desires and beliefs constantly change under the influence of new conditions, both external and internal. Making immediate peace is only the starting point for both socio-political and psychological forms of integration, both of which can make an important contribution to the continuance of that peace. The further continuance of peace is also a required condition of addressing almost any other large-scale conditions, for instance responding to global environmental challenges.

At the socio-political level, integrative practices involve some means of creating a bigger context to the judgements made either by individuals in relation to others, or by groups collectively. Such a bigger context is created by some kind of formal process that helps to maintain that bigger context even when we would otherwise be in danger of falling into absolutization. Thus, for instance, a friendship creates a bigger context over time for the interaction between two people, so that both parties are less likely to develop absolutized beliefs about the other. A formal process of conflict resolution, such as mediation, puts a particular conflict in a wider context, both through the overall framing and the process of mediation, which may involve requiring both partners to listen to and acknowledge each other's position, feelings, and needs. Democracy, operating at the level of large group decision-making, requires those decisions to be put in the context of wider consent from the whole community.

Of course, this larger context will not enable us to integrate conflict unless it is used to reframe the conflicting beliefs that each side has about the other. For instance, you could bring two conflicting parties together for mediation, but the mediation could fail, because one or both sides refuse to re-examine crucial assumptions. It is very easy to hijack a formalized process to present the appearance of an effort to make peace, whilst actually remaining attached to fixed beliefs that will only accept submission from the other side. This may take the form of 'refusal to compromise', but underlying this is the persistence of entrenched absolutization. As already suggested in 5.c, we may be able to make progress here by using different types of contextualization. Negotiations between organizations or governments may fail at a formal level because both parties feel obliged to stick to certain entrenched positions that have been reinforced, but personal discussion between two leaders may be able to break through this. When socio-political integration fails, too, we can always go back to individual and psychological integration – perhaps an aesthetic experience, an intellectual breakthrough, or a bodily experience can break through the rigidity of an individual, which then makes socio-political progress possible.

In 6.c–h below, I will discuss each of the complex relationships between socio-political and individual practices at each of the three levels of integration. The key general point, however, is to constantly understand each in the context of the other. We do not only change the world by changing ourselves, nor do we only change ourselves by changing the world: the two levels are interdependent.

5.f. Temporary Integration

> *Summary*
>
> Temporary integration is a bodily state that abates absolutization and conflict only for as long as it lasts. This is not just a state of suppressive concentration, but rather one in which conflicts are contextualized due to relaxation, as in the Buddhist *jhanas*. However, temporary integration does not change the long-term neural tracks of belief, which will require a critical thinking and judgement process. States of temporary integration need to be invested effectively to support long-term integration, but instead they can be easily reified and absolutized.

Temporary integration is a state in which our habitual conflicts temporarily cease, because of specific conditions operating for the moment in our bodies. However, when our bodies return to a more habitual default mode, this temporary integration will cease. This can be contrasted with long-term integration, which changes the habitual default mode in which we operate.

In Buddhist tradition, temporary integration is specifically discussed in terms of *jhana* (or *dhyana*) as a hierarchy of identifiable absorbed states that can be created by meditation.[1] What marks these clearly is dwindling signs of conflict and its effects on the whole body system, whose energies then become unified. The first level of *jhana* is described in terms of subtle pleasurable sensations in the body, accompanied by directive and evaluative thought. At the second level this thought is said to fade away, although this may just mean that it becomes more subtle. At the third level this develops still further into equanimity, an obvious sign of the cessation of the effects of immediate emotional conflict. At the fourth level the meditator is beyond distinctions of pleasure or pain, which we can interpret as being no longer attached to obsessive states seeking pleasure or avoiding pain. There are also descriptions in Buddhist tradition of preparatory states prior to the first *jhana* and 'higher *jhanas*' beyond them (though these become increasingly abstract). Whatever one might think about the details of this Buddhist analysis, it offers a pioneering account of temporary integration as a human phenomenon, and shows its incrementality.

---

1   *Majjhima Nikaya* 111: Ñanamoli & Bodhi (1995) pp. 899 ff. Also ibid. 39.15 ff.: pp. 367 ff.

The Buddhist description gives us a general idea of how temporary integration can work for us: it provides a surge of energy in a context of relaxation, it is usually dependent on short-term integrative practice, it can be developed in increasingly subtle forms, and it combines 'cognitive' and 'emotive' aspects, with an increasing emphasis on the latter as it becomes more refined. We can also include in temporary integration states the 'flow' states described by Czikszentmihalyi,[2] the creative and inspired states of artists, poets, and composers, and the elevation we might feel after a particularly inspiring talk or conversation.

The distinction between 'temporary' and 'long-term' integration is not very precise, as it is impossible to specify a particular length of time after which integration ceases to be temporary. However, in practical experience, the distinction is usually fairly clear. Temporary integration involves a mental state that is temporarily more energized because the conditions creating conflict have been relaxed: for example, due to a meditation session (or just a few deep breaths, or a walk) stilling a loop of proliferating anxiety. This is not merely a stimulated or a concentrated state: such states may actually exacerbate conflict by feeding the dominant sub-system in our mental state to the exclusion of others. Getting stimulated on coffee, for instance, does not necessarily create temporary integration. Temporary integration does not merely result from more energy being put into a habitual task with fixed goals, but more likely from the suspension of habitual goals to allow longer-term ones to take over, as occurs in what we are likely to call a 'practice'. A temporary integration state may only fade gradually, but it does not involve a change of our normal beliefs, because the causes of conflict, and the psychological disposition to it, are still present.

The distinction between integration of desire on the one hand and integration of meaning and belief on the other does not map precisely onto that between temporary and long-term integration. One could sometimes, for instance, have rather short-term experiences of integrated belief before regression to our more habitually unintegrated beliefs. Nevertheless, we can often identify the difference between temporary and long-term integration according to whether our experience of it primarily takes the form of a burst of newly unified energy, or a change in the beliefs that habitually modify our

---

[2] Csikszentmihályi (1990).

judgements. The glow that can arise from a session of a practice that integrates desires, such as yoga, is primarily one of immediate embodied feeling. If we then go on to some other, narrower, task (say, filing of papers), we do so with a broader awareness than we would have had previously, so that, for instance, we may notice some new sensual feature on the surface of the filing cabinet, or be able to tolerate an interruption from someone else that would otherwise have been irritating, by giving it a bigger emotional context. We are able to do this because the energies that were previously locked in repressing alternative feelings are now available to us, so a wider range of neural connections are fired up and sensitized in greater connection with each other.

In contrast, a longer-term process of integration will not necessarily feel like this at all. It may be a process of integration of meaning, in which case our experience will be one of increased understanding; or one of integration of belief, in which case there will be a change in the assumptions of our thinking. There are some contingently supportive relationships between these different elements of integration, though, which also reflect contingent support between temporary and long-term forms of integration. When our energies become more unified, it becomes easier to direct our attention in a way that makes new understanding possible, but we can still have the experience of comprehending what someone is saying and engaging with it strongly, but without any particular experience of unified energy (integration of meaning in some cases largely independent of integration of desire). Similarly, when we have an experience of new understanding, we have new resources with which to re-examine our interpretation of experience (integration of meaning contingently aids integration of belief). Similarly, too, when our energies become more unified, it becomes easier to re-examine our assumptions (integration of desire contingently aids integration of belief).

Thus the long-term integration process may occur in a 'dry' way that we experience primarily as a process of thinking rather than feeling (even though the two cannot be entirely separated). It may also happen slowly and largely unconsciously, rather than as a conscious breakthrough where we may wake up one morning and realize that our approach to life has changed. Nevertheless, temporary integrations can be extremely helpful in enabling this long-term process, by giving us perhaps a succession of moments in which we are more open to new possibilities, so that we then gradually build up momentum towards a longer-term and more sustainable shift. When a bigger shift occurs, we may no longer recall most of the moments of greater openness that enabled it, but even so, practice will have enabled that longer-term shift by supporting those moments of greater openness over a period of time. This is why meditation and other allied practices can actually make a huge difference to our beliefs and approaches to life, even though particular kinds of shift are not guaranteed.

This contribution of experiences of temporary integration to a longer-term process can be facilitated by a conscious practice of *investment*. 'Investment' is a term now primarily used in relation to money, but we also talk about 'investing' time or effort into a project that yields particular goals. Rarely, however, do we talk about 'investing' mental states, which is probably the most important type of investment. To invest a state of temporary integration is to use it in a way that consciously facilitates longer-term integration, particularly by using the access of energy we may experience from temporary integration in ways that are more immediately directed towards the integration of meaning and/or belief. To take a simple example, if we finish a session of meditation feeling a 'glow' of renewed energy, it is then good to apply that energy to a creative project or to challenging study.

Just as it might also not be wise to invest financially when one lacks the resources to do so, a converse principle of investment prudence also applies to suggest that we should not try to develop long-term integration without some temporary integration to power us. For instance, if we are trying to think and design creatively, we should beware of doing this at times when our more general embodied awareness is relatively closed – perhaps because we are tired or overstretched or dulled by some mechanistic activity. It may be better to actively prepare ourselves for an embodied state of greater openness to match an activity that demands it. Thus a helpful order of morning activities might well be meditation followed by study, rather than study followed by meditation.

It's thus also important to recall the ways in which temporary integration can facilitate the practice of the other four of the five principles. To practise scepticism and provisionality by recognizing uncertainty, we will need enough confidence to consider alternatives rather than absolutizing at each point of judgement. To practise incrementality, we need to be able to apply the energy needed to consider incremental alternatives to habitual absolute ways of thinking. To practise agnosticism, we again need the confidence to consider alternatives to absolute dualities that are constantly reinforced by groups. Whilst temporary integration does not guarantee that we will find alternative possibilities sufficiently meaningful, or that we will have a critical perspective on our current beliefs, it does provide us with the immediate awareness and energy we need to apply those facilities when we have them.

However, temporary integration states can also be easily absolutized instead of being used in this helpful way. We normally do this by reifying them into proofs for absolute beliefs. There is a long history of the religious interpretation of temporary integration states as revelations that then justify truth-claiming propositions. Mystical and religious experiences are experiences of temporary integration – not *just* experiences of temporary integration, for understanding them in that way does not reduce their meaning and its importance by one iota, but nevertheless experiences in which vast new potentiality may open up for us because of the integration of desires and beliefs that were previously in conflict. In *Archetypes in Religion and Beyond* I discuss such experiences, and their relationship to the God archetype as a source of inspiration, much more fully.[3] There I also discuss the culturally entrenched *projection* of that archetype: that is, the tendency to constantly assume that a highly meaningful integrative experience somehow justifies absolute beliefs – whether these are about God and his will, or about enlightenment and a 'final penetration' to 'reality', or whether they are about 'Nature'. There is no necessary link whatsoever between such meaningful experiences and such absolute interpretations of them, apart from the mere cultural habit that makes the link almost unquestionable and apparently obvious to many people.

We can also inflate and reify temporary integration experiences in more personal ways just as personal experiences. Even if we don't think that it tells us about God's will, we can find temporary integration pleasurable, and thus adopt the belief that getting more of it will give us more pleasure. So we pursue it as a goal that then undermines the conditions needed for its achievement because of the absolute focus it creates. It has become part of the informed

3 Ellis (2022) 4.f.

tradition of Buddhist meditation practice to recognize that getting obsessed with *jhana* actually makes *jhana* less likely – more broadly, the purpose of meditation is not to have good meditations. This is a version of the hedonic treadmill or hedonic paradox recognized in psychology, whereby the narrow and continual pursuit of pleasure often undermines its achievement.[4] When we identify any kind of pleasure state just as an object to be gained, we tend to forget that it is a mental state dependent on a complex system. In 5.a above, I have already discussed the relationship between systemic conflict and reinforcing feedback loops, and here we just need to recognize that even the temporary integration of a system can set off reinforcing feedback loops in reaction, as the old arrangement of the system tries to reassert itself. In psychic systems, those reinforcing feedback loops take the form of absolutized interpretations of the integration state that in fact incorporate the startling new experience into an existing conceptual order and neutralize its effects. The system of social power linked to individual repression that is found in absolutization is extraordinarily successful in preventing us from changing by hijacking our conceptual belief systems.

Overall, then, it is important to appreciate the positive importance of temporary integration when invested in support of long-term integration. However, it must neither be confused with long-term integration, nor idealized and projected so that it gets processed back into a set of absolute conceptual beliefs that at best neutralize its benefit. Temporary integration is an *experience* – one that can have great meaning and value for us, but only an experience.

---

4   Fujita & Diener (2005).

5.g. Asymmetrical Integration

> *Summary*
>
> The process of integration is evidently not simply a single-track escalator from messy conflict to a completely unified character, but is subject to contextually-dependent asymmetries. Our virtues mark a positive degree of integration linked to a context, but are only incrementally unified through a process of working on our weaknesses. A concept of asymmetry is important when discussing integration, to avoid projecting someone's integration into a basis of unconditional authority (falling into a 'guru trap'), and to prompt us to focus more on specific judgement rather than character as a more reliable locus of integration.

The final major issue in understanding and interpreting the idea of integration is that of the relationship between a habitual integration in an individual's judgements, and that individual's character as a whole. Individual humans are, to put it mildly, inconsistent. Often they are described as 'irrational', but the problem here is not usually to do with whether or not we can correctly derive one proposition from another following logical rules: it is simply that our basic assumptions (conscious or unconscious) vary in different contexts. Nor is this usually just an easily identifiable moral problem of somehow abstractly 'deciding' to act wrongly, as people tend to think when they accuse others of 'lying' in response to inconsistency in claims and actions. We can easily fail to follow through on a promise we made or a principle we adopted, and in one situation we can be quite blind to the relationship between our thoughts and feelings there compared to those in another situation. Thus, even when we feel we have achieved some integration, we can be dismayed at the sudden recognition of how far we still have to go. An otherwise harmonious relationship can still descend into fractious backbiting under sufficient stress. An otherwise highly aware spiritual leader may still be unable to resist the sexual temptations that are offered by his social standing. The reformed alcoholic of twenty years, who has built a whole new life without alcohol, can still slide back under the influence of a meeting with her old drinking friends.

It would be easy to conclude from these inconsistencies that we are not really as integrated as we thought, but instead we should take them as indications that integration is not a single phenomenon in relation to character. The reason for this is that our previous judgements about integration that we or others have achieved are still justified, and following the Middle Way, we should not simply assume that our weight of experiences of integration is null and void – rather we should fit both kinds of observations into a larger picture. Our failures of integration are not just a failure to proceed smoothly along a single track that culminates in the perfect unity of our whole character, but rather an indication of the entire complexity of integration phenomena. We can be genuinely integrated in relation to our habitual response to a particular range of experiences, yet still be inconsistent in relation to others where less common stimuli are encountered.

This is perhaps particularly evident where there are relatively strong boundaries between different environments, such as a work environment and a home environment. For instance, some psychologists are highly integrated in their professional lives, but still show surprising signs of inconsistency (perhaps being hijacked by emotions of pride or irritation) in their personal relationships. The cognitive bias of *deformation professionelle* (the tendency to get stuck in modes given to us by our jobs)[1] reflects this boundary and its effects: we can be genuinely highly adapted, and highly complex in our functioning, in one particular range of environments, yet struggle to adapt beyond that range.

The term I have adopted for this kind of inconsistency in the development of integration is *asymmetry*. An asymmetry is simply a leaning in one direction or another in the way that we grow (think of a tree growing in relation to a prevailing wind), not a failure to grow at all. The idea of asymmetry might well help us to understand the integration of character in a way that is positive, despite its complexity, since asymmetrical integration is still achieved long-term integration, even if it is patchy and imperfect. It can also be a prompt to return to the more basic context of integration, which only occurs at a specific point of judgement. To talk of the integration of character at all is only a crude and approximate way of talking about the integration of judgements, aggregated into habitual patterns.

Judgements of character as a whole are very much the preserve of the virtue ethics tradition in philosophy, which goes back to Aristotle, and has more recently been developed by such figures

1   Taylor (1975).

as Alasdair MacIntyre in his landmark creative book *After Virtue*.[2] Virtue ethics identifies 'virtue' (that is, good habits) as the good characteristic in individual character by which ethical issues should be judged. However, this tradition of thought has struggled, not only with the obvious question of what justifies 'virtue' universally rather than only in the social conventions of a particular group, but also with how that overall 'virtue' in a particular character relates to specific 'virtues' within it. To be courageous, for instance, may seem 'virtuous', but then so may be being patient. If we are not to distinguish courage only as a virtue for warriors but not for nurses, and patience as a virtue for nurses but not warriors, we need some way of integrating the apparent contradiction between these virtues (the problem of 'the unity of the virtues').[3]

The concept of asymmetrical integration can help with this by reconciling virtues with virtue in general. Virtues are not just group-prescribed qualities, but instances of integration in relation to a particular field of habitual stimuli: so, for instance, we may learn to be courageous in situations where wider awareness tells us that our fears are unjustified by the weight of evidence, like overcoming a fear of flying. In a different situation, however, we may encounter the limitations of the integration that our courage represents: for instance, we may still be frozen by social anxiety at a party. Our virtue or integration is asymmetrical, even though it is well developed. To progress further with the virtue of courage, we may need to integrate it with other virtues, such as patience, which we may need to apply to our own progress as well as to our children. Courage and patience in isolation from each other are not 'unreal', or merely relative, virtues, but they represent integration that lacks symmetrical development.

It is important that we have and use a concept of asymmetry in relation to integration to guard against idealizing and projecting it. As with any phenomenon in a complex system, integration is difficult to judge, and subject to a lot of uncertainty, whether we are trying to assess our own or others' integration. Insufficiently cautious judgements about our own integration, based on our mental states and responses in a limiting sphere of conditions, may create an absolutized view of ourselves as integrated that we are then

2   MacIntyre (1981).
3   i.7.d; VIII.5.

unable to adjust when our integration unexpectedly fails us – this could be described as the 'guru trap'. Insufficiently cautious judgements about others' integration, again based on a limited sphere of conditions, may also lead to an absolutizing of authority. If we assume that someone who is more integrated is generally wiser than us (that is, makes more adequate judgements in the face of varying conditions), but we fail to consider any alternatives to this view when there are grounds to doubt it, we are starting to absolutize their authority.

This raises the whole question of the nature of absolutized authority as an expression of power, and the ways this can be distinguished from incremental credibility: a topic I will expand on in the fifth volume of this series.[4] The key point here is that integration *is* a genuine basis for authority as an embodied relationship of justified trust. However, such authority depends on the embodied states of both people in the relationship concerned, not just on an abstracted and absolutized idea of a leader's level of integration supporting his or her social status. Recalling the likely asymmetricality of integration can help us to avoid idealizing authority in this way. Incremental authority is probably better called *credibility*, a term that seems to put a bit more emphasis on our fallible responsibility for judging the likelihood that we or others are right, based on a weight of experience. The assessment of credibility is a skill of critical thinking, which I will discuss further in 6.g below. In many cases, gurus and other leaders deserve a fair degree of *credibility*, probably based on their reputation, experience, and expertise. However, the likely asymmetry of their integration should always give us grounds for caution, so as to avoid not only throwing ourselves unconditionally at the guru's feet, but also the reaction of deciding later that he has feet of clay and heaping disproportionate opprobrium on him.

Asymmetry of integration may not be very effectively addressed just by continuing with the same range of practices that helped us to achieve the integration we have so far. Rather, when we recognize asymmetry, it may well be a signal to vary our practices, because different aspects of integrative practice address different types of conditions and different areas of experience. Indeed, asymmetry may well be a result of relying too much on one type of practice rather

4 V.2.

than another. So, for example, a strong meditation practice may equip us effectively for integrated judgement within a particular type of quiet, orderly, and civilized environment (such as a retreat centre). However, if we don't sufficiently question the assumptions that shape that environment, it won't help us cope with judgement in a more chaotic and stressful environment, such as that created by war or environmental breakdown, or even work as a school teacher, social worker, or aid worker. To avoid falling back on very defensive stances in that kind of environment, we might need to engage with new symbolic resources for those kinds of experiences to make them meaningful (for instance, through the arts and imagination) and develop skills of critical thinking and critical feeling that help us question inappropriate assumptions that we have imported from a more sheltered environment.

Robert Kegan's theory of psychological stages also helps us to understand integrational asymmetry. In 4.g above, I discussed how each stage of development is a plateau, an arrangement of the human psychic system that creates temporary stability in a particular set of conditions. Those conditions clearly include not only 'external' conditions that we are adapting to, but also the conditions of organic development imposed by our bodies, which make it difficult to reach a given stage before a roughly appropriate age. Each psychological stage can also be seen as a stage of integration, in which the conflicts of the previous stage have been resolved – for example, the 'institutional' or ideological stage 4 resolves the conflicts between groups that we began to experience in the 'interpersonal' stage 3, by trying to develop universal models. However, the integration achieved in each stage is also asymmetrical, because it does not address every remaining conflict in our experience. Even when we have moved on from a merely group-based stage 3 way of thinking to an aspiration for universality, we will still find further conflicts between our supposedly universal models and those adopted by others (as illustrated, say, by political conflicts between universal models like those of liberalism, socialism, and conservatism).

Practice of a kind that overcomes integrational asymmetry has to work on our weak areas. These can be identified by feedback from others, as well as by reflection on the conflicts we encounter and by more formal means such as character typing. Psychological typing systems such as the Myers-Briggs Type Indicator, or the Big Five Personality Traits,[5] can help give us an indication of our asymmetries: whether, for instance, we are more integrated alone or in interaction with others (introversion vs extroversion), in more cognitively-driven 'thinking' as opposed to 'feeling', or in observation as opposed to theoretical modelling.

Focusing on our weaker areas is hard, as our strengths have developed precisely because we have constantly reinforced particular neural pathways at the expense of others. It is quite easy to start thinking of a demand to work on our weaker areas in absolutizing terms as an imposition from without, and thus create a new conflict. The Middle Way always needs to be applied by resisting an over-emphasis on an idealization of the more whole person we might wish to become, as well as complacency about the person we are (which can also merge in the delusion that we are the idealization). Instead, working on our weaker areas needs to be a positive extension of our strengths. For instance, introversion offers typical strengths of independent thinking and greater sensitivity, but a limitation of connection and communicativeness: but no introvert is entirely uncommunicative, and confidence in communication just requires practice in communicating. When judging how to relate to others in groups, the introvert can gradually integrate the conflicts represented by diffidence by building on the strength of independence and extending communication skills on his or her own terms. Nobody should require an introvert to magically become extrovert or vice-versa, but asymmetries in the ways we have grown up can be compensated.

Nobody's integration is likely to be completely symmetrical: we will all grow more or less crooked, because we start off facing in a particular direction and impacted by the conditions of our background. However, it is possible to adjust our development in response to a recognition of that limitation, by focusing our growth in some ways more than others. The result will not be a perfect fulfilment of human potential, which is why I think it is important not to deduce our pattern of growth backwards from an idealized perfect example. 'Enlightenment' as a model of complete integration can work for us as an inspiring concept or symbol, as long as we

---

5   Combined in an online personality test at https://www.16personalities.com/ (accessed 2021).

don't form beliefs about our own growth on the basis of deduction from our idea of an enlightened being. The Middle Way can only operate by starting from where we are, both as individuals and as social groups, and guiding our judgements from that point.

6. Practice

6.a. The Middle Way as a Framework of Practices

> *Summary*
>
> The practices discussed in this section of the book all contribute to an effective long-term response to absolutization. All need to be shaped by the five principles. The Middle Way as a whole provides an account of why these practices are beneficial and how they interrelate. It can also become a ready basis for archetypal symbolism to inspire our practice. The Threefold Practice is a taxonomy for Middle Way practices based on the levels of integration (desire, meaning, and belief) in connection with whether they operate at individual or socio-political level.

This final section of the book aims to bring together an account of what it means to practise the Middle Way in application of the five principles. Although I have mentioned specific practices that contribute to the general practice of each principle as I have gone through this book, for a fuller understanding of the issues we also need to consider how each practice contributes to a Middle Way framework. This involves approaching things more from the standpoint of the practices themselves.

The Middle Way framework as a whole consists of a set of explanations for why certain practices, especially in combination and in relation to each other, are helpful to overcoming absolutization and thus addressing conditions. In *Absolutization* I have already discussed the concept of practicality as a criterion for any effective response to absolutization.[1] The aim of any Middle Way *practice*, as I described it there, is to both address absolutization directly and undermine the conditions that give rise to it. However, to ensure that a particular type of established practice, such as mindfulness or study, does this, we also need to specify *how* that practice can do so, and what limiting factors might make it less effective.

Of course, there are moments when we need to stop pontificating and just get on with a practice: to deal with that hindrance to

1   I.7.

meditation, plant that tree, or re-engage with that difficult person. However, these efforts may be readily undermined by absolutization if we do not also pay regular attention to the context and framing of that practice. The context and framing are what determine that we do a practice *as* a Middle Way practice, in relation to other supportive practices, and justified by beliefs that remain compatible with the provisional interpretation of experience.

The five principles can be used as a kind of checklist for any practice we may undertake. Does it take uncertainty into account? Are the beliefs it relies on provisional? Are its judgements of qualities and attributes incremental? Have we avoided getting sucked into dualistic framing that may be promoted by competing groups? Does the practice have integrative psychological effects, overcoming conflict whether inner or outer? Thus, for instance, we need to undertake meditation on the basis of provisional beliefs about what it will achieve for us, rather than absolute beliefs coming from the instructions of a guru accepted only on authority. We need to understand that meditation as having an incremental effect on our mental states, rather than fixating on a discontinuous goal that it will achieve for us (such as *jhana*, or even 'enlightenment'). Even if the community of meditators sets up dualistic beliefs that distinguish them from other groups (such as the belief that non-meditators must be unhappy), we need to avoid either accepting or absolutely rejecting such claims. Our experience of meditation also needs to be directly engaged in overcoming conflict as we encounter it, rather than reinforcing beliefs that actually create conflict.

Most importantly, the Middle Way can provide coherence for a range of practices that are already widely undertaken, and that we may recognize in one way or another to be beneficial, but where a larger account is needed of *how* and *why* they are beneficial. For instance, people may recognize the benefits of meditation for relaxation, concentration, or even relief of pain and anxiety, but not recognize its wider role in integrating and justifying our judgements. The arts are often justified in terms of enjoyment and creativity, but their role in integrating *meaning*, and the value this has for all our judgements, is rarely mentioned. The value of critical thinking is also too often circumscribed within a framework of academic success measured by formal academic assessments, which may lead us to underestimate its continuing role in all our day-to-day judgements. In all such cases, the Middle Way provides a fuller and longer-term justification for such practices that makes them part of our development over a whole lifetime, not just the recourse of a particular limited need or socially-defined situation.

Such a larger framework also offers a longer-term reminder, incentive, and inspiration for undertaking the practices. If we consider the motivations we have for undertaking and then continuing with a practice in the press of day-to-day concerns, what we need most is a synthesized view of them which we can then evoke quickly and powerfully by means of symbols. In *Archetypes in Religion and Beyond* I offered a more detailed account of how such symbols operate.[2] Typically in a practitioner both in religion and beyond, it is prompted by the symbols of their tradition – for instance, a Buddha, a Christ figure, an identification with nature, or a commitment to scientific ideals. For this to help us maintain a set of interrelated practices, we need to have a set of associations with that symbol that radiate from it to a variety of concerns that are quickly evoked by it. For Buddhists, for instance, recollection of the Buddha can quickly evoke the Eightfold Path, which then gives a list of interdependent types of practice that fulfil a commitment to the ideals represented by the Buddha figure. Even if your ideals are only expressed in more abstract, conceptual ways, they will still be symbolized by particular people, places, objects, and writings that will continually reinforce those ideals for you. This is archetypal symbolism in action.

The Middle Way itself offers an archetypal symbol of a specific kind – that is, one that combines our recognition of unfulfilled open potential with a practically realistic engagement with current conditions both within and beyond us.[3] Whilst the God archetype alone is in constant danger of merely being projected as an ideal (which is why it is so often turned into a supernatural figure), and practical realism alone is in constant danger of losing any inspiring vision, the Middle Way combines practical idealism with practical realism, holding them both in constant tension, and making that tension itself into a symbol. Our immediate and embodied relationship to that symbol can arise through its schematic relationship to the experiences of following a path and of balance – basic experiences we have from infancy that can then be built metaphorically

---

2   Ellis (2022) 1.a *et seq.*
3   Ibid. 4.g.

into symbols such as those of the Middle Way. Accessible symbols of the Middle Way may thus include navigating a narrow strait, crossing a narrow bridge, the Buddha's acceptance of food (which brought realism into his idealized quest), or the ambiguous humanity and divinity of Christ. In some cases, though, subtle practitioners of a particular tradition may already associate all the symbols of that tradition with the Middle Way – for instance, for a scientist, the whole laboratory, institution, and set of colleagues with which they work may represent and reinforce the provisionality of the scientific method at its best.

With the Middle Way as an inspiring symbol for a set of practices, then, we also need a process of analysis or classification to be able to unpack the range of what that inspiring symbol may remind us to do from day to day. That means that we need something of a taxonomy or classification of Middle Way practices, which is what I aim to provide in the rest of this section. That taxonomy will try to remind us of the range of practices we *might* engage in, from which we can then select the most appropriate practices for our circumstances.

This taxonomy will be based on two criteria. The most important of these is the integration levels – that is, the ways in which forms of practice can focus more on desire, meaning, and belief. As I have already discussed in 5.f, this also tends to correspond very roughly with whether the integration that can be achieved by the practice is temporary or long-term. The categorization of practices using this criterion also interacts with one of individual and socio-political practice. This is concerned with how far a practice is focused on individual development, as opposed to the wider development of a group or its traditions. Socio-political development can also be seen as a form of investment from an individual point of view, just as individual development can also be seen as a form of investment from a socio-political point of view, as the conditions of society constantly interact with our personal habits to influence judgement.

The chart provided here (**figure 10**) brings together these two axes in relation to each other, attempting to show how a broad range of practices can contribute to wider Middle Way practice as a whole. This chart will form a basis of reference for the more detailed discussions in the remaining chapters of this section of the book. Of course, the list of practices in it does not cover every possibility, but it should be wide enough to illustrate the range of how the Middle Way can be applied in practice.

The Threefold Practice in Middle Way Philosophy

	Individual practices	Socio-political practices
Integration of Desire Temporarily unifying energies to boost attention and creativity, and avoid conflict	• Mindfulness-based meditation • Bodywork: e.g. yoga, tai chi, martial arts, pilates, dance • Sport and exercise • Immersion in green environments • Recreation to vary activities • Many forms of psychotherapy • Ethical avoidance of intoxicants	• Mediation and conflict resolution • Use of provisionality in discussion • Political campaigning • Friendship • Care • Social activities that support human solidarity • Voluntary work • Active listening (e.g. Samaritans) • Ethical practice avoiding violence and aggression
Integration of Meaning Broadening the symbols we understand and relate to, in ourselves and others	• The arts: visual, musical, literary, performing (appreciating and creating) • Reading and listening • Focusing • Active imagination and visualization • Loving-kindness meditation • Exploratory discussion on the edge of our echo-chambers • Learning foreign languages • Education and study • Humour • Travel	• Most forms of communication • Ritual: religious, civic, or social • Teaching and promoting the arts • Meaningful education (cognitive and emotional) • Political support for arts and meaningful education
Integration of Belief Resolving conflicting assumptions to address conditions better	• Critical thinking and bias awareness • Philosophy • Scientific practice and research • Most forms of education and study • Autobiography • Reflective meditation practices that promote awareness of assumptions • Cognitive behavioural therapy	• Critical dialogue • Philosophical teaching and communication • Political dialogue and negotiation • Responsible journalism

Figure 10. The Threefold Practice in Middle Way Philosophy.

6.b. The Threefold Practice

> *Summary*
>
> The Threefold Practice structure models the interaction of practices in a similar fashion to the Buddhist Threefold and Eightfold Paths, except that it takes more account of meaning, and is based on an incremental integration model, rather than a discontinuous enlightenment model. This makes it more compatible with support from scientific and systemic sources. The ways that all the practices address conflict should become clearer if we think of them in relation to all the five principles.

The Threefold Practice can be seen as an adaptation of already established Buddhist models for interdependent practice, such as the Eightfold Path and the Threefold Path. Traditionally the Eightfold Path combines 'Right' or 'Perfect' (*samyak*) Vision, Aspiration, Effort, Concentration, Mindfulness, Action, Speech, and Livelihood, whilst the simpler model of the Threefold Path condenses these into Wisdom, Meditation, and Morality. What is particularly valuable about these models is that they establish the idea of interdependent sets of practices operating in combination to aid human development (notwithstanding the bizarre fact that some Buddhists have interpreted them sequentially).

They particularly establish an interdependent relationship between meditation practice (in a broad sense) and ethical practice, and between both of these and judgement (i.e. wisdom). Ethical practice is often seen in the Buddhist model as setting up the basic conditions for working with mental states by eliminating disruptions to the refinement of mental states. Working with our mental states (i.e. meditation) is also not an end in itself, but a way of cultivating the character traits that enable better judgement, in addition to feeding back by facilitating ethical practice. It is easy to see, for instance, how defects in ethical practice can disrupt the integration of mental states: think of drinking several glasses of wine every night, or quarrelling routinely with your partner. It is also easy to see how disruption of mental states can in turn make us less ethical, as for instance we become impatient, irritable, and unaware of our prejudices.

However, there are several limitations to this traditional Buddhist model that I seek to address in the model I'm suggesting of the Threefold Practice. One is that Buddhist discourse does not explicitly tackle meaning at all – not surprisingly given that an explicit understanding of embodied meaning has only started to be developed since the 1980s, and the dominant representationalist assumptions about meaning have affected Buddhist tradition as well as Western thought. Of course, the arts do feature prominently in some schools of Buddhism, and the way has been paved for a change in this approach by some Western Buddhist thinkers who have an intense relationship with the arts as an aspect of their practice, such as Sangharakshita and Stephen Batchelor.[1] However, none of this recognition of the importance of the arts has resulted in any effective adaptation of models like the Eightfold Path to give an explicit role to the arts or similar practices in cultivating meaning.

Another thing I am aiming to do in the Threefold Path model is to base a practice model squarely on the incremental integration model, rather than on a model of 'enlightenment' or of a breakthrough to 'reality' as the starting point for thinking about spiritual development. The obvious weakness with the traditional Buddhist justification for practice models in terms of progress towards enlightenment is that it entrenches a large discontinuity in our thinking, that can then readily become the starting point for the deduction of absolutizations. The effects of this can readily be seen in the discontinuous authority given to those who are believed to be 'enlightened' (or to have reached 'stream entry' or 'satori' or any other discontinuous goal), which can then be readily abused. In contrast, the integration model is continuous and incremental, and does not need to be dependent on any kind of belief in total integration. We can become more integrated, even in temporary and asymmetrical ways, and we can understand this in terms of genuine development along a universal but provisional path.

The integration model has the advantage of being much more compatible with psychological, neuroscientific, and systemic models, being based on a resolution of conflicts within the psyche (or mind-brain-body), seen within the system created by our neural network. To provide empirical justification to a practice model of this kind, then, we just have to show how practices reduce conflict – whether this conflict appears primarily as motivational variation over time, as fragmentation of meaning, or as incompatibility of belief. The three levels of integration *primarily* address each of these

---

1   E.g. Sangharakshita (1988); Batchelor (2020).

levels of conflict, but never exclusively. In any practice, there will always be limitations on how far we can use it to achieve a particular degree of integration without the others.

The reduction of conflict (or of the fragmentation that provides a key condition for it) is the common theme that runs through all the practices listed in the chart at the end of the previous chapter. In some cases, such as bias awareness, the arts, or ritual, this may not be immediately apparent, because these are not our accustomed ways of talking about these practices. We may tend to talk about bias as a maladaptation or as a source of falsehood, but in a world where all sources are uncertain to some extent, it is the way that bias prevents us from reaching sustainable resolutions to conflict that is more practically important (see 6.g). Those conflicts may be the internal ones of failing to consider a repressed alternative view, but also overlap constantly with conflict at the socio-political level between individuals or groups. Groups conflict because the group's way of judging does not allow for the consideration of the alternative possibilities believed in by other groups: for when those alternative possibilities are accepted, the accompanying desires can be made compatible. The arts help with conflict at an earlier stage of this process – that is, the stage at which we simply need to be able to imagine what a repressed perspective is, and what other conditions, symbols, and ideas it might be built on (see 6.e). The resolution of conflict, I argue, should be the common currency of our understanding of helpful practice.

Although of the five principles, integration here takes centre stage, all the other four remain constantly in the background. We cannot resolve conflict if we are certain that we have the right answers, so scepticism is required. We then need to be able to try out new motives, meanings, and beliefs that would integrate conflicting assumptions, requiring provisionality. Entrenched conflict can usually be traced back to absolutizing assumptions in the way we are thinking about a person or an object or their qualities, of a kind that incrementality is required to resolve. If we cannot adopt a resolutely agnostic position, we may also not be able to overcome entrenched conflict because of the assumptions insisted on by groups that dominate the discussion. All of these principles thus come into play in all the practices listed in the Threefold Practice chart, enabling us to differentiate helpful use of these practices from other use of them. For instance, sport and exercise can be used in highly integrative ways, overcoming the conflicts engraved into our bodies by the enforced narrow application of our bodies in certain limited ways and inactivity in other ways. Think of the effects on our bodies if we spend all day sitting at a computer screen, and the degree of release offered by exercise at the end of such a day. However, sport can also be readily used for absolutizing ends as it is hijacked by tribalism, obsession with particular achievements, or alienation from one's body – application of the five principles is constantly needed to check whether we are using the practice of sport in a sustainably helpful way.

In the remainder of this book, then, I will survey the practices on the Threefold Practice chart in a way that shows how these approaches can be applied in each case. By the end of the following six chapters, it should be amply demonstrated how all the practices work together, how they can all be understood as resolving conflict, and how that resolution of conflict also interacts with all five principles of the Middle Way.

6.c. Individual Integration of Desire Practices

> *Summary*
>
> Individual integration of desire practices work on reducing the immediate press of conflict in our experience. This can be initially through ethical observance focused on dealing with major conditions that produce conflict, such as addiction. Some everyday practices, such as ordinary recreation, help to prepare the ground by reducing the stress of inner conflict to some degree. Bodywork, mindfulness, and psychotherapy, however, provide much more direct and focused methods for reducing conflicts of desire in immediate individual experience.

The integration model can be most immediately identified and used in integration of desire practices. Some of these are concerned with avoiding the kinds of conditions that produce immediate conflict in ourselves. Others are concerned with actively building our awareness of other parts of ourselves. Still others directly address socio-political conflict, or seek to address the conditions that create it over a longer period, and this last category will be considered in the next chapter.

The types of practice that try to avoid the conditions for conflict in ourselves can be broadly identified with self-care and ethics with regard to oneself. Addiction is an obvious example of conflict within oneself over time, so the general avoidance of intoxicants is an example of a basic moral practice that seeks to avoid creating such conflict. Here it's worth noting that, as in any precept of abstention that one might adopt, the motive needs to be integration rather than rule-following or conformity. Puritanical teetotalism can create more conflict, despite its recognition of the damaging effects of alcohol, by absolutizing the opposition to it and repressing the desire for alcohol. Abstaining from alcohol or other recreational drugs is not a good in itself – but their effects on our bodies can be damaging both in very big and in small ways. To pursue an abstention practice integratively, we need to do it for the sake of the part of us that wants the intoxicant as well as the part of us that wants to abstain. The indulgent part of us needs not to be denied but to be satisfied – in some deeper way. A principle of abstention should work primarily as a reminder of that deeper satisfaction, to recruit all our energies towards a more sustainable goal.

The same principle can be applied to less serious types of addiction, which can still result in conflict. We can get into reinforcing feedback loops with any kind of activity that produces pleasure (or the relief of pain or relief from a sense of conflict) in the immediate experience, but which then conflicts with our awareness of longer-term needs: this can come from a time-eating computer game, a person we are over-dependent on, the anaesthetic of mindless television, or aimless phone-checking and internet browsing. There are a variety of specific techniques one could employ in response to such addictions, but they all involve facilitating awareness of the context which can then assist us in changing the conditions. If the context includes awareness and recognition of both sides of our conflict, we stand a chance of success as long as we maintain that awareness. As soon as we slip into thinking of the addiction merely as a problem to be solved separate from us, though, we start to lose the energies that are tied up in the other side of the conflict, and thus slip back into it.

The variation of our activities (what we tend to call 'recreation') is also a basic practice that avoids the increasing repression that is created when we keep ourselves under the motivation of one over-dominant belief for too long. Many people have some sort of recreation, whether this is playing golf, going for a walk, constructing a model railway, or knitting, and these balancing activities can help with keeping conflict at bay to some extent, even if they do not very directly address it. The alienation of the factory worker, as noted by Karl Marx, is a classic case of the repression that results from the continued enforced focus on one limited type of activity. This leads to social as well as psychological conflict, and the replication of such alienation as a routine part of many school systems ought to be a matter of great concern to us.

The value of green environments for psychological health and development has also been shown by recent research.[1] This again can be attributed to avoidance of the conflicts created by highly artificial environments, which constantly force our awareness and motivations in some directions and not others: one cannot play in a busy street, dig in concrete, or listen to birdsong in an underground car park. The value of exercise, too, lies not only in maintaining general health, but in limiting the conflict created by inactivity, in

---

1   Berto (2014).

which our body is effectively caged by the obsessive dominance of one part of us.

Looking after more of ourselves thus becomes the most basic element of integration of desire practice, before we get on to practices that positively build our awareness of different parts of ourselves when this has been neglected (as it nearly always is, to some extent). Bodywork practices such as yoga or tai chi do this primarily through awareness of the body, either in its tensions or its movements. Given the ways that conflicts become associated with tensions in different parts of the body, bodywork practices can help to release these, creating a glow of unaccustomed well-being, in contrast to a previous state strained by our being forced into certain postures associated with absolute beliefs. As already mentioned in 1.b, Damasio's somatic marker hypothesis[2] helps to show how absolute beliefs, associated with repressive experiences, can become associated closely with specific bodily states: a point that is already obvious to those who do bodywork practices.

Mindfulness, as a general cultivation of awareness, is an awareness of the body as well as associated thoughts, emotions, and beliefs. As a practice, this has already been discussed at a number of points in this book (1.d, 2.b & c, 3.f, 4.d, 5.d). To extend our awareness beyond an obsessive starting point, some kind of contextuality is required, and the body provides the most immediate of such contexts (though not the only possible one). Our bodily tensions are associated with specific obsessions, so it is by relaxing the body that we are likely to gain bodily contextuality. Emotions, moods, and preferences are also readily recognizable through their associated bodily states, and the practice of interoception (internal sense awareness of bodily states) helps us to focus on these so that we join conscious wider awareness with the identification of that feeling state.

In meditation practice, mindfulness is cultivated directly through systematic relaxation, body awareness, and reflection on emotions, in relation to an object of attention. Where the object of attention is non-conceptual (for instance, the breath, or a candle flame), it helps us to contextualize obsessive feedback loops of rumination that are accompanied by an immediate absolutizing tendency (when we ruminate, we assume that the object of rumination is

---

2   Damasio (1996).

the only important thing to focus on). Rumination is a sign of conflict. Stilling those loops of rumination helps us to develop increasingly integrated awareness over time, allowing concentration on an object without repression of other thoughts. The contextuality may be offered primarily by the body and general interoception, as in mindfulness practices, or alternatively by a new imagined context, as in visualization practices.

Meditation practices are also often associated with forms of archetypal inspiration (for instance, a recollection of God, or of the Buddha) that also assist in creating a wider contextuality. Prayer may also have meditative effects if it is primarily a contextualization using God as an inspiring symbol (as it seems to be, for instance, in the Christian mystical tradition), rather than just a repetition of conceptual beliefs. The practice of prayer in general has been positively correlated to measures of well-being.[3]

Many forms of psychotherapy also work directly to give a wider context to conflicting desires as they appear in our experience. For instance, internal family systems therapy can help those with a past trauma to recognize and engage with the conflicts it has created through encounters with sub-personalities. These may take a variety of symbolic (probably archetypal) forms.[4] The boundary between integration of desire and of meaning in such therapies is, of course, a fuzzy one: one could describe what is happening as encountering neglected meaning linked to symbols in one's own experience, or one could describe it as encountering and reconciling energies that take a symbolic form. However, the value of integration of meaning does not depend on such a process of reconciliation, only on encountering new meaning, whereas these therapies primarily get their value from integrating desires (and thus resolving psychological conflicts).

These approaches to the integration of desire vary considerably in their degree of directness, and need to be applied appropriately to the situation of the individual. Mindfulness meditation has been foregrounded frequently in this book, helping to shape the whole approach in it, because it is probably the most direct and most universally applicable form of integration of desire practice. However, it is also a challenging practice, and we may well need less direct

---

3 Poloma & Pendleton (1991).
4 Schwartz & Sweezy (2020).

practices to prepare for it, such as effective personal ethics, recreation, or bodywork. For those in especially disintegrated states of the kind usually associated with mental illness, psychotherapeutic or even psychiatric attention may also provide a necessary preparation for even being able to engage with mindfulness.

6.d. Socio-political Integration of Desire Practices

> *Summary*
>
> Socio-political integration of desire practices are closely interdependent with integration of meaning and belief too, but primarily focused on reconciling interests. Mediation techniques resolve conflict directly, whilst provisional discussion extends the conditions for mediation more broadly and can even be applied in political campaigning. An ethical avoidance of violence removes an immediate disinhibition and entrenchment of conflict, while the positive practices of care and friendship develop relationships that can provide the conditions for integrating conflicts, both internal and external. Active listening and volunteering also provide some specific practices that can support these conditions.

At the socio-political level, integration of desire practices become even more interdependent with the integration of meaning and of belief. Reconciling our desires with those of others requires us to also adjust our beliefs about them, and often also to extend meaning so that we understand and engage with the symbols used by others. Nevertheless we could primarily call them integration of desire practices where their main focus or purpose is the reconciliation of differing desires between different individuals or groups. As we integrate desires in our relationship with others we not only create greater harmony between individuals or groups, but also integrate the conflicting desires in ourselves that are represented by others. Thus, for instance, if I quarrel with a friend, but then make the effort to engage with her view and recognize the extent to which the friend was trying to engage with conditions when I disagreed with her, I am also simultaneously engaging provisionally with that friend's meaning and beliefs as they are represented in my own mind. In practice, then socio-political integration of all types is inseparable from individual or psychological integration – a point that is often ignored by discussions that limit themselves to one or the other.

Integration of desire practices at the socio-political level begin most obviously with any type of mediation or conflict resolution. This type of practice is geared towards reconciling incompatible desires because these cause conflict, not only beliefs (where we could disagree abstractly without actually conflicting) or meaning (where we could share all our symbols and engage fully, but still disagree). It does not require opponents to reach agreement about everything, but works at the flashpoint of conflict, whether at the level of a row between neighbours or at that of a war. One highly effective form of mediation which is readily compatible with many other integration of desire practices is non-violent communication (NVC).[1] This often begins with inducing opponents to recognize each others' positions and the needs behind them. The justification of what is a 'need' is an obvious difficulty with NVC, but in practice the process of discussing each others' needs obliges us to recognize others' desires, whilst also accepting a justification of those desires in a form that aspires to universality. The beliefs that create the conflict are thus reframed through contextualization, as the desires of the other are put into a wider context that includes our own desires, even if they are very different from ours.

Provisionality in discussion is another kind of practice where the focus shifts from the assertion of beliefs that can only take one particular type of propositional expression, to the possibility of reconciling opposing beliefs in a pragmatic framework. In section 2 above, I have already discussed many of the forms such a practice can take, especially including probabilizing and weighing up. The challenge of provisionality in discussion, however, lies not just in thinking provisionally, but in communicating provisionality so that others can recognize it and avoid responding absolutely. One can attempt to send out signals of provisionality through the language one uses, such as hedging ('as far as I'm aware…', 'on the evidence so far…', and so on) or individualizing ('in my opinion…', 'I think…', rather than just stating something to be the case). There is no guarantee at all that provisionality markers in one's communication will be picked up and responded to, as they depend on the other person's own capacity for provisionality, but using them may increase the chances of provisional discussion occurring.[2]

A provisional discussion, when it occurs, can readily reconcile conflict because it is focused on the practical situation rather than an abstracted difference of view. When the people in discussion are focused on reaching a practical solution, as they often are in an everyday problem where the goals are widely agreed (for instance, how best to get an injured person to hospital), they are likely to discuss

1 Rosenberg (2002).
2 For further discussion of provisionality markers, see https://www.middlewaysociety.org/provisionality-markers-keeping-the-lines-of-discussion-open/

practicable options and then resolve any disagreement quickly on practical criteria. However, when our goals are more remote, and our views about how to reach them dependent on conflicting representations of the situation, absolutization can prevent any practical framing from emerging. What is required to shift this is for both sides in the discussion to consider a wider variety of options, and to recognize critically that none of these options is obviously 'true', even though some of them may fit the evidence better and thus be more practicable (see 2.a above). Once the obsession with truth and falsehood is relaxed in this wider context, both sides are better able to use a practical basis of judgement, and thus reach agreement.

Political campaigning, when used as a practice in harmony with the Middle Way, is an extension of the practice of provisional discussion into a wider arena where we also seek to address the wider conditions that support provisional discussion. Political campaigning can obviously take a wide variety of forms, including for instance debating in public forums or on social media, making videos, advertising in other ways, and canvassing from door to door. It may be in direct support of a candidate seeking elected office, or more indirectly promoting a view on an issue of political importance on behalf of a pressure group. Such campaigning often degenerates quickly into polarized conflict between political opponents, but to help create the conditions for the integration of desire in wider society in the longer term, it is unavoidable.

Because of the complexity both of political issues and of our own starting points, it is quite possible to sincerely seek to apply the Middle Way to political beliefs, but end up with completely different views about policy, and completely different ideological stances and party or pressure group affiliations from someone else doing the same. The relevant question when we seek to apply the Middle Way to these matters is not whether we all agree to start with, but how we address the conflict. Since political campaigning is often framed in terms of conflict, it is vital to reframe it instead as provisional discussion for shared practical ends. Our views about policy and our group affiliations can never be final ends in themselves in a provisional political discourse. Rather they are means to bring about a shared resolution of practical issues in society.

The practice of agnosticism then becomes vital. When political debate turns rapidly into *ad hominem* attacks, diversions, and overgeneralization appealing to narrowly interpreted 'evidence', it is the pressure of two polarized groups in conflict with each other that can rapidly drag us into similar responses. However, it is quite possible to adopt a determined and consistent opposition to the damaging and corrupting policies of an opponent, whilst staying focused on this long-term practical goal. Courage is required above all, along with commitment to a long-term vision that resists the assumption that the only way to avoid catastrophic governance by an opponent lies in conflictual attitudes. It does not, if only because those conflictual attitudes lie not just in the socio-political realm but also in yourself. Every piece of political name-calling etches the acceptability of such practices deeper into the neural networks both of yourself and others, and thus entrenches conflict more deeply. It is only by neglecting long-term psychological conditions that practical political strategy narrows into conflictual attitudes.

Political campaigning is actually a crucial practice for the future of the world, but it's even more crucial to do it with provisionality and agnosticism. That means focusing primarily on practical policy, focusing criticism on damaging policy or conduct rather than on opponents as individuals or as groups. Some of the practices of critical thinking which I will discuss below in 6.g will also be vital when making judgements about the beliefs to adopt and about how to argue for them. When integrating desires within an individual, a wider context is provided by the individual psyche (or mind-brain) as a whole, and when trying to do so at a political level, that same context is provided by constitutional arrangements that allow elections and decision-making in a democracy. The importance of those constitutional arrangements should never be underestimated, because they are crucial tools for integration.[3]

Political conflicts, like personal ones, are only solved by reframing beliefs into provisional forms in the long term. Perhaps, for instance, a party with a more provisional outlook wins power and improves the constitutional arrangements for future decision-making, or develops the education system to support integrative practice. Along the way, though, there may be temporary integrations in relation to each other, shared by the individuals who are participating in political discussions. In a tense negotiation between two leaders, a personal rapport develops and enables them to reach a better agreement, or a worse-placed candidate stands down to avoid

3   IX.1.

draining votes from a more provisionally-motivated candidate who might otherwise lose to an absolutizing one. These temporary integrations need to be invested for longer-term progress, just as *jhana* experiences need to be.

There is obviously a great deal more to discuss here to offer an adequate approach to the complexity of political constitutions, ideology, and activity. I am aiming here only to offer an indication of the ways that political campaigning can be an integrative practice despite any impressions to the contrary. Further detailed discussion of politics will follow in volume IX of this series.

In addition to these three relatively direct practices for integration of desire at socio-political level, there are a number of more indirect ones. These are not so much focused on reconciling conflict immediately as on creating better long-term conditions for such conflict to be resolved. These long-term conditions are obviously found in human relationships, and all such indirect practices are focused on building (or at least not disrupting) human solidarity within our relationships.

The least direct of these practices is the avoidance of violence and aggression as an ethical practice – a practice obviously reinforced both by many religious injunctions and by criminal law. Although there are some over-extended uses of the term 'violence', I take it to mean physical actions that directly harm by killing, injuring, or otherwise violating bodily integrity. Actions that are psychologically damaging, let alone mere criticism, are not 'violence' in this sense, whether or not they are morally justified.

Physical violence is obviously a result of conflict, but specifically conflict that is disinhibited.[4] Conflict is then no longer played out in representations of hypothetical realities, but in the direct imposition of one person's will on another. Not only violence itself, but aggression accompanied by a credible threat of violence, can do this. If all conflict is due to absolutization, violence shows us the most intense negative effects of absolutization, because violence or the threat of violence creates a strong absolutized response in its victims. It may not be entirely impossible to suffer violence without emotions of hatred that absolutize the opponent by reinforcing cycles of unquestionable beliefs about them, but it is extremely difficult.

4   ii.1 g.

The need to avoid violence, in response to a *prima facie* principle of conduct, is thus obvious. We do not have to justify the avoidance of violence with metaphysical beliefs about the unalterable sacredness of the person, or of divine commands against violence: it is enough to recognize that violence ramps up and entrenches conflict. To create anything like helpful conditions for the resolution of conflict, then, we must make a serious moral effort to eschew violence when we are tempted to use it or to threaten to use it.

That does not imply any need to treat violence as absolutely wrong or to embrace pacifism, but rather offers us a prompt to always put violence in a reflective context, with a strong tendency towards its avoidance. The occasions when violence may be justified require a much more detailed discussion, of the kind I will offer in volume VIII of this series on ethical issues.[5] In brief, however, the relationship between violence and conflict gives us a general principle: if violence is judged to have a long-term overall integrative effect given already highly conflicted conditions (as, for instance, in cases of self-defence), it may be justified. However, the judgement about this also needs to be at least as integrated as the contrary judgement.

The avoidance of violence is thus a practice rather than just a rule. As a practice it is interdependent with the general development of our judgement so as to be able to effectively judge those occasions when violence may be justified, as opposed to the overwhelming majority of cases when it is not. As a practice, it avoids the introduction of what are normally highly disruptive conditions into human solidarity. The same may be said of other common basic moral principles, such as abstaining from theft, damage to property, or sexual transgression, which are not themselves necessarily violent but which are likely to have similar disruptive effects on relationships, aggravating both external and internal conflict.

However, there are a range of far more positive practices that help to build up human solidarity in general, enabling communication and creating better conditions for the positive development of integration as well as the negative avoidance of conflict. This can potentially include almost any human social activity – for instance, initiating a conversation, making a phone call, organizing a group event, or just participating in these things with a positive sense of

5   VIII.8. Also see Ellis (2011b) section 10.

their potential integrative effect. Beyond this, we can talk of the more specific practices of *care* and *friendship*. These involve a more deliberate cultivation of human solidarity over time.

In any human social activity, the positive value of that social activity as a potential integrative practice needs to be set against the danger of it merely reinforcing group biases. On the one hand, human relationships can be used in a way that both supports the basic conditions of integration and stimulates us towards questioning our assumptions and adapting to new conditions. On the other hand, the absolutizing function of groups can readily take over in any such situation, so that the dominant desires of some repress those of others and create a similar internal repression amongst all members of the group. Central to the practice of working with any social activity and making it integrative is awareness of that danger, and using provisionality, incrementality, and agnosticism to avoid it. However, there is nothing inevitable about group biases. Human beings meeting together do not have to repress one another. They can always meet creatively and develop solidarity as a more integrative state of relating, rather than yielding to the temptation of absolutized group authority.

By *care*, I specifically mean the practice of practically and psychologically supporting anyone who is vulnerable, for instance due to infancy, old age, sickness, or disability. Of course, our motives in offering care may not be that we are explicitly thinking of it as an integrative practice. We may just think of it as a social duty, but to also think of it as an integrative practice adds a further exploratory and developmental aspect to it that may itself help to alleviate psychological conflicts created by the possible repression of a socially imposed duty of care. As a positive integrative practice, care can help to overcome the conflicts created by any individual's basic needs not being met, which is likely to trigger desperation or even trauma in the affected person and disapproval from others. The carer, too, has to constantly re-examine their assumptions about the person they are caring for to care for them effectively, being open to even quite subtle signs of their changing needs. We may all begin with different levels of instinctual disposition towards care, but these feelings can always be developed in response to new experience, overcoming any tendency towards absolutized views of a person. Merely having spontaneous feelings of pity or kindness is not itself integrative practice, but developing and applying them to reduce the conditions for long-term conflict is.

Similar points can be made about *friendship* as a practice – one that has been discussed positively through the ages since Aristotle and Al-Ghazali.[6] Friendship differs from care in creating a much more equal relationship of association, not only focused on relieving need or suffering but also potentially on shared enjoyment. Friendship can be developed with anyone capable of engaging in mutually responsive communication, from a stranger to a close relative, but is obviously more effective as a practice when it is incrementally deeper and more sustained. A friendship becomes deeper the more friends communicate about desires and beliefs that are important to them, or share experiences that express or inform those desires and beliefs. It becomes more sustained as they do this over time. Both depth and time help to make the friendship an integrative practice, because more development in both these ways helps the friends to stimulate each other into greater optionality. We have probably all experienced how conversations with a friend can influence us to develop new interests, and with those interests come new goals, new meanings, and new potential beliefs with which to engage with the world around us. Friends help us adapt to the conditions of the world.

In addition, of course, friends can care for each other and support each other, having all the positive effects of care discussed above as friends seek to support each others' needs. On the other hand, friends can also challenge each others' beliefs in a way that avoids absolutized responses, because the challenges can be offered within the wider context of a relationship of mutual support. The Middle Way needs to be found in any friendship between support and challenge: if there is no support, any challenge may destroy the friendship, but if there is no challenge, the friendship will not be integrative, and indeed may turn into a neurotic relationship of a kind that merely maintains shared absolute beliefs.

The relationship between friends can also be discussed in archetypal terms, since friends may well have archetypal functions for each other. This can be helpful as long as the archetypal functions are clearly distinguished from the individual, and used as sources

---

6   Both recommended as prompts to reflection on friendship: Aristotle (1953) VIII & IX; Al-Ghazali (1980).

of inspiration rather than prompts for projection. The archetypal functions that may be served within a friendship could be those of the hero (inspiring effort towards a goal), the anima/animus (inspiring engagement in relationship with otherness), or the God archetype (inspiring engagement with a much wider, unknown potential). Any of these, however, can readily turn into projection as soon as we stop being aware of them as sources of inspiration for *us*, and instead start to confuse the symbolic function with the person themselves.[7] The inspiring exemplar of achievement then becomes the person who saves us, before whom we are passive. The fascinating other (often, but not always, of the opposite sex) then becomes the answer to all our longings, the perfectly beautiful or good person who compensates for our specialized limitations rather than helping us to address them. The exemplar of the kind of person we might grow into then becomes the guru who can tell us all the answers, and to whom we yield power over our own judgement. Projection means that these are no longer integrative friendships, but instead absolutizing conduits of subordination to the power of the group mind.

These differing dangers are obviously concentrated in particular types of formalized social relationships. Heroic projection is likely to occur in everyday parenting, teaching, or training where one person is much more capable than another in a particular respect. Anima/animus projection is very likely to occur in the context of sexual or 'romantic' relationships. Projection of the God archetype is likely to occur in the context of a relationship between spiritual teacher and disciple.[8] However, friendship can also be practised in the context of any of these relationships, as it can also in purely 'utilitarian' relationships like that between shopkeeper and customer. All we have to do to practice friendship in these relationships is firstly to maintain basic care and support so that the basic conditions for human development are present, and secondly to both offer and accept new stimulus that helps us to treat our desires and beliefs provisionally. Over time we also need to be sufficiently wary of the possibility of absolutizing that relationship, so that we can maintain that practical helpfulness.

---

7   See Ellis (2022) 2.a.
8   Ibid. 4.c, d, & f.

Finally, a couple of more specific practices can be mentioned within the broader contexts of friendship, care, and social interaction. These are actively listening and volunteering. Perhaps these are most often expressions of care, but they can also both be expressions of friendship. Active listening involves a set of receptive skills, whereby one prompts and encourages another person, but focuses the conversation on them. It is especially suited to those in need of care and support, and is thus obviously familiar to professional listeners such as psychotherapists and teachers. The Samaritans organization in the UK provides a telephone service for anyone in need of a listening ear. This practice obviously works systematically to address the basic needs of a speaker and help them get a wider perspective on their conflicts. It may also offer new optionality to the listener.

Volunteering as a practice is a way of removing a particular type of common repression in human relationships – that of the economic *quid pro quo* in which labour is exchanged for money. When that relationship of employment or contracting is a more or less equal one, there is no reason why it should not be accompanied by friendship. However, inequalities in the relative economic positions of the provider of labour and the employer of labour often create conflicts and absolutizations, including alienation on the part of the worker and complacent absolutization of economic beliefs on the part of the employer. To volunteer, when the economic conditions permit one to do so, is to substitute a human relationship of friendship for any of these economic constraints. Of course, one's motive in volunteering may also be one of care. Similar arguments could be made about any form of generosity or use of an unconstrained donation economy: not that this frees us from all economic conditions (volunteering may often be seen as a middle-class privilege), but that it frees us from certain common conflicts that are often created by those conditions.

It may seem that we have travelled a long way here in exploring integration of desire practices, from meditation as an individual activity to social arrangements such as those of volunteering. However, what all these activities have in common is the ways in which they can effectively address conflicts in desire. Unlike the practices of integration of meaning and belief that we will examine next, they are not primarily focused on changing meaning or belief, even though they remain interdependent with our meanings and beliefs. Thus, for instance, care, friendship, or volunteering can still be helpful practices for those who are caught up in an overwhelmingly dogmatic community (such as many religious groups), even if the degree of integration they can provide is constrained by their failure to address issues of meaning and belief.

6.e. Individual Integration of Meaning Practices

> *Summary*
>
> Integration of meaning practices help us both extend our 'cognitive' range of symbols and our 'emotive' engagement with those symbols, to overcome fragmentation – gaps of understanding. The beauty of meaning and archetypal beauty found in the arts can help to do this, as well as developing integration of desire through aesthetic beauty and integration of belief through concepts. Focusing practice, loving-kindness meditation, and exploratory discussion can all also help to integrate meaning. Travel can be integrative as long as it actually extends experience, whilst learning foreign languages (and learning in general) help to integrate meaning more at the 'cognitive' end of the spectrum. Humour helps to integrate meaning through ambiguity, as long as we 'get the joke'.

Integration of meaning practices operate by extending both our understanding of, and our engagement with, symbols. Since 'cognitive' and 'emotive' types of meaning are in practice entirely inseparable, we can safely assume that the horrendously over-used distinction between them is always only a matter of degree.

Sometimes the integration of meaning is primarily a matter of understanding new symbols, in the sense of having further associations with them that enable us to find them meaningful: for instance, learning a new word in Welsh. My emotional engagement is required for this, but it is primarily a matter of learning to understand a new symbol. At other times, though, it is primarily a matter of 'understanding' in the sense of *engagement* with symbols that we already have some associations with, but where those associations have not been sufficient to helpfully engage our attention where it is needed. An example at this end of the spectrum would be finding new interest in a familiar set of words used by our partner: perhaps she keeps telling you about her back pains, and you have been understanding her abstractly and sympathizing vaguely, but then one day your own back pains suddenly help you empathize with her much more than previously. You then 'know exactly what she is talking about' (in the acquaintance sense of 'know'). Your bodily states and emotions are then contributing much more to your understanding of the meaning of her words.

Integration of meaning practices need to work with the whole of this range of meaning. At the 'cognitive' end of the spectrum would be aspects of study and education that help us to understand new words, phrases, and propositions in context, for instance learning foreign languages or unfamiliar disciplines with specialized vocabulary. At the 'emotive' end would be practices like the Buddhist loving-kindness meditation (also known as *metta-bhavana*) which systematically work at extending our emotive engagement with others and what they represent to us. More towards the middle of this spectrum would be the arts, which often both extend our range of symbols and help us to imaginatively engage with them in new contexts. All these practices are integrative, because they help to overcome the fragmentation of meaning.

The fragmentation (lack of integration) of meaning is not conflict,[1] but nevertheless the integration of meaning provides a key condition for the integration of desire and belief. This asymmetry between the different levels of integration is perhaps one reason why people do not often associate integration of meaning practices with the resolution of conflict. However, despite the enormous complexity of the systems we are dealing with, it is not difficult to trace some correlations between the development of integration of meaning and the reduction of conflict. One such correlation is between the development of education (the main business of which is understanding, not 'knowledge') and the reduction of conflict – particularly the most extreme forms of violent conflict at a socio-political level. One of the greatest achievements of Western democracies during the twentieth century has been the wider education of a larger proportion of citizens, and this development has been accompanied by a decline in violence and overt conflict in society, as Steven Pinker has demonstrated.[2] The arts have formed a relatively small part of that spread of education, but not an insignificant one. The arts are only the most open-minded tip of the educational iceberg of people understanding each other better – which they can also do through natural and social science and humanities, all of which constantly introduce new concepts, theories, and perspectives. Pinker particularly suggests the development of the novel as a making a major

---

1   iii.2; IV.3.
2   Pinker (2011), esp. pp. 832–6.

contribution to the decline of violence in society, by extending imaginative sympathy with others.[3]

It is clearly not the case that people who speak each others' language don't conflict, nor that people who mutually empathize can't misunderstand each other. However, if we stop falsely dividing the cognitive from the emotive and consistently view these developments of meaning *together*, it becomes easier to see how developments in both kinds of meaning together can be decisive in opening new optionality. It is only when new symbols are meaningful that we can imagine with them. It is only when we imagine that we can consider new options, and it is only by considering new options that we can overcome the binary lock of absolutization with its constant restriction of those options. This dependency operates whether we are thinking of meaning in terms of non-linguistic symbols, discrete words or phrases, or propositions, because all of these depend on meaning as association built up into increasingly complex structures.

The way that the arts contribute to integration of meaning is potentially a large subject worthy of much fuller discussion than I can give it here. Volume VII of this series will provide much more of the basis for this by offering a theory of beauty and of the differing ways that the arts contribute to beauty. In brief, the key point will be that there is not only one kind of beauty, and thus also not only one kind of way in which the practice of the arts can create beauty and contribute to integrate through that creation. It is seeing both beauty and the purpose of the arts only in one set of terms that has led to the increasingly common denial of any universality in the human experience of beauty, and thus also of the idea that the arts can have a helpful purpose of cultivating beauty (whether or not that helpful purpose is always fulfilled to any extent). In volume VII I will argue that there are actually four different types of beauty: beauty of impact, beauty of meaning, archetypal beauty, and cognitive elegance.[4] All these types of beauty can inspire us, but they do so in differing ways. It is thus also important not to reduce the arts to the cultivation of only one of these ways, as the arts can be sensual, symbolic, archetypal, or conceptual, or various combinations of these.[5] Sensual art has an immediate aesthetic impact but little

3   Ibid. pp. 210–13.
4   VII.1.
5   VII.3.

further association: think of a Zen garden, or Mark Rothko painting. Symbolic art is beautiful because its associations: for instance, an Odilon Redon painting or Schubert's *Winterreise*. Archetypal art is beautiful because of the specifically archetypal function of its symbols for us: think of a Renaissance painting of the Annunciation. Conceptual art is only beautiful in terms of the elegance with which ideas are combined or revealed: think of Marcel Duchamp's *Fountain* (a urinal) or a detective novel.

The integrative function of the arts, then, depends for its operation on the kind or kinds of beauty that it cultivates.[6] Sensual art can integrate through mindfulness, directing our attention directly towards colours, forms, notes, melodies, or the sounds of words, for instance. This sensual experience provides a wider context for our awareness in much the same way that the breath in mindfulness meditation provides such a context, potentially having at least a temporary integrative effect. Symbolic art integrates through play, enabling us to encounter and try out new links between symbols and meanings, whether we are appreciating new meaning in someone else's work or creating our own. Symbolic art thus extends optionality. Archetypal art integrates by providing inspiration in our active engagement with new potential or long-term intentions, prompting us to contextualize our limited thoughts and feelings in a larger vision. Conceptual art can integrate by challenging our beliefs directly and prompting us to think critically.

The sensual aspect of the arts thus works at the level of integration of desire, and the conceptual aspect at the level of integration of belief. However, in between these, the symbolic and archetypal aspects of art can integrate meaning by imaginatively extending both our understanding and our engagement with meaningful symbols. All of these symbols increase our optionality, but the archetypal ones also provide inspiration over time. This would be the case across the types of arts: visual, literary, musical, and performing, which differ only in the types of symbols they employ and in how they are created and presented. The linguistic symbols used in writing may have a more complex relationship with our immediate bodily experience than the symbols used in the visual arts, or the sounds, harmonies, and melodies used in music, but they still basically get their meaning from this relationship. This would also be

6 VII.4.

the case regardless of whether we are creating or appreciating art. The appreciation of the arts requires us to make the symbols used by others meaningful in our own experience, whilst their creation requires us to select or even create symbols for ourselves which are made more deeply meaningful in the process.

For example, let's take the fairly common scenario of a woman painting a mountain landscape 'from life' – that is, she is sitting in an Alpine meadow with an easel and a palette painting what she sees before her. As any artist will be aware, this is not a process of mechanical copying, since at every stage the artist needs to interpret what she is seeing and express it symbolically using the medium she is using. In this case, the medium is paint: features like the glint of snow reflected from sunlight on a mountain peak, or the complex dark green of a forest seen from a distance, need to be symbolized in that medium. When she, or later viewers of the painting, see the way she has applied the paint, they associate it with similar experiences of seeing mountain views: it *means* a mountain view to us, even though the colours and forms do not (indeed cannot) precisely 'represent' what the woman has seen. It may also mean other things – for instance, a warm memory of a mountain holiday in childhood, or a vast symbolic painting (like some of those by John Martin) in which hosts of angels with their archetypal meaning emerge from mountain tops. The integrative effect of creating and viewing the painting is not limited to the symbolic and archetypal levels, as we may also be moved by the forms and contrasts in it at a sensual level, and we might also analyse it conceptually. However, the symbolic meaning of the painting in relation to our experience is important to it, even though it does not set out to be a 'symbolic' painting. It is an integrative experience because it creates and evokes new meaning, adding further complexity to our interpretation of future experience.

Another kind of example might be that of reading a novel. Here any sentence or even any word may potentially integrate meaning, as we may learn new words or deepen our appreciation of the meaning of ones we are already acquainted with by seeing them in new contexts. However, the overall impression that the novel makes on us is more likely to be at the level of its content: character, plot, background, or metaphor. Of these, it is probably character that has the most profound effect, especially in literary novels where characters may better reflect the complexity of the people we experience in life. The words devoted to a particular character, often in interaction with other characters or with varied situations, provide another level of symbolism at which we understand and engage with a further level of meaning in relation to persons. Whether we have met Adam Bede, Mr Micawber, or Gandalf the wizard in the context of a novel, the complex way these characters are evoked through words creates new potentialities in us for identifying, describing, and imagining new dimensions of character in our experience. The more complex the relationships between different aspects of character, the more we are ourselves set up to appreciate such complex relationships.

Beyond the areas that we are likely to explicitly identify as 'art', other practices can also contribute to this process of integrating meaning. We are, of course, not necessarily dependent on the arts to develop increasingly complex capacities to symbolize the world and people around us, because we can also do this directly by associating new language, visual representations, or sounds with what we observe. Reading non-fiction that we may not regard as 'art' (although it has its artistic dimension – as for instance does this book) may do this. Watching, listening, and reflecting on what we observe can also do it, and these are of course part of the skill-set of the effective novelist. Making notes, sketching, or keeping a diary also helps to keep us linking those observations to new potential symbolizations of them.

The process can also be aided by directing attention closely onto the bodily, emotional, and imaginative sources of meaning to more fully allow new meaning to emerge into our experience. This is the practice of *focusing* as developed by Eugene Gendlin[7] and now widely taught. Focusing can be done alone like meditation, or with a mentor more like therapy. When done with someone else it involves exploratory dialogue to encourage close attention to sensations and feelings, so as to gradually open them up to description. The process of experiencing meaning and relating it to symbols is central to it, so it is an exercise in the integration of meaning, extending our engagement with symbols by working from the experience end of the association.

As already mentioned, loving-kindness meditation (*metta bhavana*) from the Buddhist tradition is a further example of integration

---

7   Gendlin (2003).

of meaning practice, this time focusing on widening the meaning of a person for us so as to cultivate positive emotion. This practice works by sitting in meditation and recalling (in turn) oneself, a good friend, a neutral person, and an enemy. In each case one systematically works to expand one's habitual view of that person through imagination, associating symbols of that person (their name, image, etc.) with a wider range of experiences that will give a bigger context to our awareness of them. The practice begins with easier cases (oneself and a good friend) and then moves on to more difficult ones where our views may be narrowed and reactive (an enemy). Traditionally, there are four variants of this practice in Buddhist tradition (known as the *brahma viharas*), which focus respectively on *metta* (loving-kindness), compassion in response to suffering, sympathetic joy in response to good fortune, and equanimity in response to changes in fortune. This range of practices obviously further extends the range of meaning that we associate with a person to allow a wider awareness of them to inform our associations. With a wider view, we are then likely to spontaneously feel more positive emotions of an expansive kind.

The way in which we engage in discussion with others can also offer a practice for the integration of meaning. Exploratory discussion that is on the edge of our habitual interests or emotional range is much more likely to break new ground for us, helping us to engage with symbols that we may only have vaguely heard before, and that are of much deeper interest to others. Exploratory discussion could be about the views of someone who thinks very differently from us, but quite likely it will also have a more personal angle, that helps us to give a wider context to those views through awareness of people's life experiences and feelings. Such discussion is on the edge of the 'echo chambers' that have often been remarked in online discussion, but that also operate offline – that is, our tendency only to communicate about familiar subjects with people who already agree with us.

The value of travel as a practice follows from this, as it puts us into contact with unfamiliar people and unfamiliar situations. As the traditional truism has it, 'travel broadens the mind'. We are likely to encounter many new symbols, as well as expanding the range of experiences to which we apply familiar symbols. The unfamiliarity of the situation is likely to add intensity to our experience and make it more memorable. Of course, the mere act of travelling to another place does not by itself make travel an integration of meaning practice: we need to *use* our experience of being in a strange place in an exploratory way, rather than confining ourselves to familiar types of company in familiar types of environment that are merely transplanted elsewhere. That may mean going to see new places and things, or communicating with new people, or both. It is also likely to be of greater value if we stay in one place long enough to explore and appreciate it, and if we deepen our explorations at least in one particular way (for instance, looking closely at the art, or talking in detail with one local person).

Ethical judgements about travel have been called into question in recent years, particularly with regard to the high CO_2 emissions of air travel. In discussions about travel, however, its value as a practice for the integration of meaning is rarely considered. This is not to conclude that air travel is always justified, but that the value of travel used effectively for the integration of meaning needs to be weighed against other ethical objections to it. Much air travel is not used effectively for integration of meaning, if it is used for short international meetings that could be conducted by video conference, or for holidays of a kind that involve little contact with unfamiliar people or cultures. Where it is used effectively for this purpose, however, we need to weigh up the issues rather than absolutizing our objection to all travel.

The learning of foreign languages, whether or not this is accompanied by travel, is perhaps the most relatively 'cognitive' integration of meaning practice. Learning, recalling, practising, and applying unfamiliar vocabulary and grammar is a highly demanding academic practice, but of enormous value for the integration of meaning. Moreover, the more different the new language is from your native language, the more this is the case. Different languages use habitually different cognitive models, dependent on differing schemas that develop in different environments, and differing paths of etymological development which reflect different metaphors.[8] These differing cognitive models create separate neural tracks that enable us to think quite differently when using another language, and thus add substantially to our symbolic resources and the optionality of our judgements. Studies of bilingualism have confirmed this point by showing the advantages that bilingual people have in learning,

---

8   Lakoff & Johnson (1980).

particularly in being able to resolve conflicting cues more easily.[9] Although they may be slower in retrieving vocabulary, this slowness can in many ways be seen as an advantage, a prompt to provisionality as a range of different possible meanings are considered.

To a lesser extent, however, any study or learning can to some extent produce the same effect. Whenever we learn about a new topic, we learn new symbols and either create or deepen meaning. The more different this is to the disciplines we may already be familiar with, the more new understanding we will develop. However, the extent to which education is a practice of integration of meaning does depend on the application of scepticism. If we believe that what we are learning in education is 'knowledge', then the meanings of the terms we use have to be rigidified to match the 'reality' we think they truly refer to, constantly undermining our capacity to use terms differently and thus to think differently. A model of education as developing understanding rather than 'knowledge' is thus vital to its use for integration.

The culture of over-specialization in modern academia (already discussed in 2.d) is another factor that tends to constantly limit the value of learning as an integrative process. Whilst some degree of specialization offers practical advantages (shown by the ways they have enabled social and economic development), especially in skilled professions such as medicine, engineering, etc., this is constantly at the expense of individual development and creativity of thought. The practice of integration of meaning for anyone in a highly specialized academic or professional role, then, will often consist in not being confined by that specialization, and regularly engaging with other areas of experience.

Finally, we should also mention the value of *humour* as an integration of meaning practice. Most humour involves ambiguity of some kind, that unsettles our fixed meanings,[10] but within a manageable and controlled context in which we do not feel threatened (that is, as long as we continue to interpret humour as such, 'getting the joke'). Puns unsettle the meaning of words, slapstick the meaning of actions, satire the meaning of authorities and institutions. The skill of comedy, then, involves constantly relaxing the boundaries of meaning for one's audience whilst maintaining a

---

9   Bialystok (2009).
10 Bekinschtein et al. (2011).

wider boundary of safety and reassurance. This can have a continuing integrative effect, as long as we do not get stuck in humour as an end in itself and fail to consider meaning and belief seriously as well. In 2.e above, I have already discussed how humour can be part of a skilful suppression or 'mature defence' and help to create provisionality. However, we also need to beware of the ways that humour can also be used to gradually make absolutizations acceptable, as occurs in the apparently 'jokey' introduction of attacks on individuals or groups that are then reinforced as prejudice within a particular group.

6.f. Socio-political Integration of Meaning Practices

> *Summary*
>
> Meaning is integrated at the shared socio-political level through communication in which all participants share sufficient of the meaning of symbols being employed. Ethical failings in communication, like lying, disrupt that shared meaning. Ritual also depends for its communal integrative effects on shared meaning, which needs to be ensured by ritual leaders rather than relying on representationalist assumptions. Longer-term integration of meaning practice is supported by education in the arts, and by meaningful education in general taking embodiment into account. The further conditions for these require political support, and politics itself also requires meaning integration.

Whilst individual integration of meaning practices are valuable because they develop the links between symbols and meanings in our neural systems, socio-political integration of meaning adds a further level of complexity, that is additionally developing the links of shared meaning between individuals. The distinction is clearly an incremental one, since all the practices I have discussed at individual level also have a socio-political dimension. Obviously, for instance, in the arts, activities like reading a novel, acting in a play, or painting are all communicative. Their significance is not merely a matter of developing the links in our own mind-brains, but also of enabling a similar development in the mind-brains of others. When others' meaning develops in similar ways, communication can be said to have occurred. That communication has an importance of its own at a social level, which indeed is so obvious to us that we often tend to neglect and ignore the individual level and judge development only in its more obvious externalized forms.

It is worth saying a little bit more here about the distinction between meaning and communication, because of the common tendency to try to reduce meaning to communication, or deny that meaning can occur without communication (in philosophical terms, this is the Wittgensteinian turn[1]). However, meaning is an experience and is not only linguistic. In infancy we begin with undifferentiated meaning that gradually becomes more

---

1   IV.2. Wittgenstein's perspective is particularly given in Wittgenstein (1967). For a fuller discussion of it see Ellis (2001) 4.e.

differentiated.[2] The stimulus of language and communication from others is crucial to us being able to differentiate meaning and link it to linguistic symbols, but to attribute meaning itself to that stimulus is to mistake the order of dependency in our development. We can learn to use language *because* we find things meaningful, not the other way round. Communication then depends on all individual parties to that communication finding its symbols meaningful, and clearly, having different bodies, they will not find it all meaningful in exactly the same way. We do not always understand others sufficiently when they try to communicate, and they do not always understand us sufficiently, but the criteria of sufficiency are practical. Applying the principle of incrementality to communication, it is safe to assume that some degree of misunderstanding always accompanies some degree of understanding.

Socio-political integration of meaning, then, consists in understanding that accompanies the misunderstanding. For example, if I talk to you about Wales to try to communicate my experience of its hills and valleys, woods and rivers, but your experience of it is mainly of the industrial or post-industrial south of the country, the word means slightly different things to each of us. However, as I communicate more of my experience, our respective understandings of the meaning of Wales, which did start off with some overlap, move even closer together. Our communication is creating integration of meaning, both within each of us and between us.

How far communication in general is an integration of meaning practice, though, obviously depends on the degree to which that communication supports mutual understanding. If my main aim in communicating is to assert power or status, for instance, I may do my best to avoid sharing any meaning with you. Instead, I will assume a representationalist meaning to what I am saying, and that it is solely your responsibility to understand, not mine to aid understanding. I may then use ingroup language or jargon that excludes you from understanding, in order to assert that power. The opposite tendency is to assume a powerless perspective, from which it is only my responsibility to understand, and your utterances have all the truth or power, or both. I then adapt myself to your language and make all the effort to interpret it. To find the Middle Way here, I need to bear in mind that communication requires understanding

2   Johnson (2007) chs. 1–4.

on both sides, so that I both maintain the integrity of what I want to say, and make reasonable efforts to make it comprehensible to you.

On the one hand, then, there is a positive practice of communication so as to enable integration of meaning, but there are also particular bad habits of communication to negatively avoid because they interfere with integration of meaning. These have been well identified in the Buddha's discourses, where he finds four kinds of speech practice to avoid: false speech, harsh speech, malicious speech, and gossip.[3] All of these can be applied to any medium of communication, not just speech. All of these, on closer examination, can be found to affect the integration of meaning in communication, so we do not need to depend on the Buddha's or anyone else's authority to have a reason to practise in this way. False speech disrupts trust between people over time, when propositional claims are found to be inconsistent, and thus interferes with integration of belief. Harsh speech adds an aggressive, power-based element to communication that interferes with integration as its aim and may cause reactions. Malicious speech attempts to reduce a person to an absolutization to be eliminated or subordinated, rather than helping others to understand their complexity. Gossip here means sharing unnecessary negative claims about someone else in their absence, and thus creating an unbalanced group assumption against them that they are unable to correct.

'Truth' in communication needs to be understood as truthfulness rather than as a representation of an ultimate reality we do not have access to. If we are truthful, we are inspired by an archetype of truth to continue to revise our representations of the world so that they fit our own and others' experience as closely as possible.[4] Provisionality is thus crucial to truthfulness, and claims to have propositional 'truth' in practice tend to undermine truthfulness because they create rigid vested interests. Consistency in such communication is important to its truthfulness, showing an aspiration towards universal adequacy in our beliefs, and one of the applications of provisionality is to correct inconsistencies when we recognize them. The Buddha's wise advice to Prince Abhaya was not to communicate 'truth' without benefit to the hearer[5] – a piece of practical advice that again suggests the pragmatic framing needed

3   *Majjima Nikaya* 117:7: Ñanamoli & Bodhi (1995) p. 936.
4   Ellis (2022) 6.c.
5   *Majjhima Nikaya* 58:8: Ñanamoli & Bodhi (1995) p. 500.

for 'truth' in communication. Speaking 'your truth' because you believe it strongly is not good enough: it is necessary to consider the likely impact of what you are saying, particularly whether it will reduce or exacerbate conflict.

However, the issue of harsh speech is treated slightly differently in the Buddha's advice to Prince Abhaya. Harshness is very obviously a matter of interpretation, and communication that is not pleasing to its recipient may at times be necessary. The Buddha thus states that he will judge the time when such speech is necessary, provided it is truthful and beneficial.[6] This is obviously a crucial point when any kind of criticism is communicated. Criticism will not succeed in changing anyone's belief or practice if it is interpreted as absolute and thus provokes an equally absolute reaction. Thus when offering criticism, one needs to judge whether there is a reasonable chance of it being interpreted in a wider context that will make it beneficial. Provisionality is thus crucial to critical communication of this kind.

Apart from communication in general, socio-political integration of meaning can also be created by shared ritual. 'Ritual' here can mean religious ritual, such as a church service or a rite of passage, but could also be a political or civic ritual – think of the opening of the UK parliament. Groups of any kind, particularly more formalized ones such as workplaces or societies, also have rituals – for instance, welcome and goodbye ceremonies, or celebrations of success. Families also use ritual – for instance birthday parties. Any social activity is also likely to have ritual elements – for instance, the courses of a meal and the etiquette involved in eating it politely.

For shared ritual to integrate meaning, its meaning must be sufficiently shared by all participants in the ritual. If this criterion is met, then rituals can inspire everyone present with an archetypal prompt of shared values and goals, or at least have a general bonding effect. However, the major reason why rituals are often ineffective or a source of conflict is representational assumptions surrounding them. If the leaders or sponsors of the ritual assume that its meaning is entirely determined by the tradition from which the form of the ritual derives, then they run a big risk that at least some of the participants will be alienated from it. The reason such alienation is likely simply follows from embodied meaning – each individual makes meaning in their bodies, it is not created by groups except

6   Ibid.

incrementally through communication. People may either not understand the intended significance of the ritual, or, even if they do, still experience ritual as an imposition of power by the group that determines its form and message.[7]

My own experience of sitting bored and alienated in church services from an early age offers one common example of this. That my experience is far from unique is suggested by continual declines in churchgoing. The alienation of non-voters from the ritual and shared ideals of democracy offers another: for example, even the record high turnout of 67% in the US presidential election of 2020 left another 33% of voters disengaged.[8] The increasing number of families created by couples who choose not to marry also suggests that the marriage ritual may have little meaning for an increasing number of people, especially given that legal and financial advantages for marriage continue.[9] Broadly, in Western democracies the value of ritual is widely perceived as being in decline, even though the human need for socially shared meaning is as great as it has ever been. Instead, the stakes have risen: we now expect ritual to be meaningful, and vote with our feet rather than tolerating alienating ritual.

The practice of effectively shared ritual means that leaders and organizers of ritual need to think far more provisionally about the form it takes with regard to each group of participants. Minor modifications to a format that is rigidly prescribed by tradition (such as modern hymns or slightly different liturgies) are not sufficient for this purpose. Instead, each new ritual needs to be considered anew and negotiated. That does not mean that the ritual will not draw on tradition, which is after all a major factor in the meaning of the ritual for the participants, but it does mean that the prescriptions of tradition should never trump a new assessment of the meaning of the ritual for participants. This is, of course, unlikely if the ritual is strongly associated with absolute beliefs and is taken to reflect those absolute beliefs, so the renewal of ritual can hardly be separated from the need for agnosticism about metaphysical claims.

---

7   See Ellis (2022) 3.e for further discussion.
8   https://www.census.gov/library/stories/2021/04/record-high-turnout-in-2020-general-election.html (accessed February 2022).
9   https://www.theguardian.com/uk-news/2019/aug/07/cohabiting-couples-fastest-growing-family-type-ons (accessed January 2022).

The socio-political integration of meaning also encompasses creating the conditions for individual integration of meaning in other respects, whether through the arts, education, or political activity. Teaching the arts, supporting and developing meaningful education, and giving political support to the arts and to meaningful education could all be seen as particularly contributing in this way.

Teaching of the arts is obviously central in enabling practice of the arts, particularly where that practice either depends on a degree of technical skill (as in learning a musical instrument) or where guidance can help people to appreciate aesthetic or symbolic distinctions they might otherwise miss. Teaching is more obviously crucial for producing art than for appreciating it, but nevertheless it can help provide a whole new context of awareness when, say, reading a poem with an understanding of poetic techniques, or listening to a piece of music with an understanding of its structure. Such understanding can become an end in itself displacing the art (creating a closed literary critical culture, for instance), but can also be effectively integrated with an appreciation of the art as a meaningful experience. Such teaching combines the integration of meaning that can occur through communication (extending our depth and breadth of meaningful symbols) with that which can occur through the arts (creativity in synthesizing new symbols).

By 'meaningful education', I mean education that develops greater understanding and thus integrates meaning. Unfortunately there is also such a thing as meaningless education, consisting of rote learning of 'facts', or even excessive bureaucratization of supposedly autonomous learning. Meaningless education can still help to develop meaning, but largely by accident as a side-effect: so, for example, a particularly curious student set to rote learn all the classifications of zoological taxonomy would probably still manage to relate these to her experience of animals and thus extend her understanding of symbols meaningfully. However, an alienated student might learn the classifications in the abstract only for a test and then promptly forget them. Ellen Langer's research has shown the ways in which mindful learning is far more effective than mindless learning.[10] As she defines mindful learning, it is learning that makes novel distinctions: but this is another way of talking about the linking of new symbols to experience. Good modern educational

---

10 Langer (1997).

practice does, of course, generally appreciate the ways in which student attention needs to be engaged, but this recognition is still continually undermined both by testing regimes that encourage mindless learning and by an entrenched cultural assumption that education is about imparting 'knowledge'. Even if it were somehow the case (in defiance of the unanswerable arguments of scepticism discussed in 1.a) that we 'knew' anything, we would still have to go through the processes of first finding it meaningful and then believing it before we could do so, and education still too often skips these preliminary stages in its haste to create 'knowledge'.

Meaningful education, then, consistently treats students as embodied persons who need to make neural connections of meaning as a basic condition for examining any subject, rather than only occasionally recalling this point and trying to squeeze it into a framework that is still absolutized in various respects. At the most basic level, that means learning by activity and/or through immediate sensual experience, so as to engage the whole human system in the meaning that needs to be associated with new symbols. However, it is also possible to make active learning into a reactive dogma that alienates through unnecessary and imposed recursion to the basic sources of meaning. Sometimes too many videos and group exercises can also be a waste of time. Progression to more complex levels of understanding gradually improves our capacity for increasingly receptive learning, so the Middle Way needs to be applied at higher levels to constantly adjust the balance, not to go through unnecessary reversion to the basic embodied conditions of learning on the one hand, but also not to jump too far ahead into abstraction on the other. The means of assessment also need to be consistent with the means of learning, rather than forcing the learning into a more abstract frame to help students pass the test.

Such principles can apply whether we are merely learning on our own, whether we are studying with the guidance of a teacher on a course, whether we are teaching, or whether we are contributing to political debate about the purpose and organization of education. The five principles of the Middle Way apply directly at all these levels: we need scepticism to challenge the knowledge model, provisionality in fitting the education to the student's dynamic level of integrative development, incrementality in seeing all learning as a matter of degree, agnosticism in resisting opposing group dogmas in education, and integration in recognizing the progressive interaction between cognitive and emotive elements improving our capacity to learn.

At the political level, we can help to support sufficient prioritization both of the arts and of meaningful education.[11] These both contribute long-term to the conditions for integration, and thus to the overcoming of conflict and the addressing of wider conditions (including social, economic, and environmental conditions) in society. However, it is easy to forget the long-term value of such relatively subtle practices in the face of immediate economic and political pressures. We constantly need to remind ourselves, for instance, that helpful environmental or social reforms are unlikely to succeed without the wider support of the majority of the population, yet the population will not give this support if they do not have the capacity to understand these wider conditions, and they will not understand them without a wider capacity to imagine a range of possibilities. Politics fails in the long term without democracy, and democracy fails without meaningful education.

Finally, it is also crucial for politics itself to be meaningful.[12] Political life is full of ritualized and institutionalized elements, from handshakes and speeches to the organization of who will speak in legislatures. As these ritual elements have often developed organically as part of a complex social fabric (mixed with occasional moments of design, such as the creation of the US constitution), it is very easy to forget their importance as part of a wider system for the resolution of social conflict.

We thus not only need to preserve, and where necessary thoughtfully reform, political institutions and their rituals, but also to constantly interpret and explain them so that others will understand them. For instance, one of the major difficulties with the EU for British voters, as revealed by the Brexit vote in 2016, was the lack of meaningfulness of EU institutions for British people. This is in turn due to a lack of interpretation and familiarization of these institutions and their purpose, not only in the UK education system, but also in most of its media. Without that meaningfulness, it makes little difference to keep telling people why they should believe in the value of the EU. Abstract belief is useless without meaning to support it.

---

11   iii.8.c & d.
12   iii.8.b; IX.5.

6.g. Individual Integration of Belief Practices

> *Summary*
>
> Integration of belief is the process of making conflicting beliefs compatible by reframing. The process of reframing thought and feeling can be described as critical thinking, of which only one element is reasoning, but which also requires justification from experience, recognizing context, avoiding biases and fallacies, interpretation, and credibility assessment – all of which are processes of contextualization rather than reasoning. Critical thinking skills can be practised in the context of any academic discipline, as long as the discipline does not constrain the assumptions that can be questioned (which in practice it often does). Cognitive behavioural therapy, reflection practice, and autobiography also provide further kinds of contexts where critical thinking skills can be used but should not be constrained.

The integration of belief is the level of integration that matters most in the long-term, because it changes how we act and the future conditions we create. However, it is also entirely dependent on the integration of desire and of meaning: we will not be able to adjust our beliefs without a more integrated motive that leads us to do so, nor if we lack understanding of symbols in which to represent a new alternative belief.

Belief does not only consist in explicitly held claims, but also implicitly assumed ones that may be expressed in our other claims or in our actions.[1] We may live as though a particular claim is correct or incorrect, either absolutely or provisionally, but when two claims are incompatible, conflict emerges and can be resolved through integration of belief practice. Integration of belief practice allows us to adjust conflicting beliefs so that they are *compatible* (not representationally identical) through a process of reframing. By becoming aware of prior assumptions that justified our incompatible beliefs, and treating those prior assumptions provisionally, we can adjust either or both of the conflicting beliefs in line with a wider understanding of the conditions that gave rise to them. Note that this may result in an outcome that looks much closer to one of the opposed prior beliefs than the other, if it turns out that one belief addresses the long-term conditions better than the other: for instance, an addict can only resolve their conflicts by sustainably

1   iv.1.b.

giving up the addiction, not by just reducing the amount taken as a compromise between taking the addictive substance and not taking it. Integration of belief should not be confused with compromise.

In practice, this reframing requires a sufficiently intellectual awareness to clearly consider both sets of beliefs and compare them with a wider context, even though this is not a solely intellectual process and not only a matter of 'reasoning'. Given that reasoning only tells us about the formal relationships between propositions, and nothing about the embodied and emotional context in which those propositions are interpreted, it can play a part by increasing our awareness of the relationships between possible beliefs, but is very far from being the key process in the integration of belief. Nevertheless, it is also difficult to integrate beliefs without intellectual clarity about their scope and mutual implications. That is why integration of belief practices are generally ones that have been associated with academic practice and thus with 'reasoning'. It is very important, though, not to assume that because of this association, academic study as usually pursued is either necessary or sufficient for integration of belief. The difficulties are similar to those of claiming that because Buddhism often offers a path of integrative development, and has made a huge contribution to our understanding of that path, therefore Buddhism *is* the path. It is not. Similarly, academia has made a huge contribution to our understanding of the integration of belief, but that does not mean that it *is* integration of belief. Awareness of this point should both offer a prompt for humility in those of us who have invested heavily in academic study, and a source of confidence for those who have become alienated from it.

Individual integration of belief practice largely consists in what we can call 'critical thinking'. 'Critical thinking' is a concept that has emerged in recent decades in the context of academic teaching and practice, and is pursued to some extent as a separate discipline – one that focuses on skills rather than any specific content. However, argument rages as to whether critical thinking is best approached as a distinct discipline, or as part of 'content' disciplines. The answer to this is obvious for anyone who has learned widely transferable skills like foreign languages, mathematical calculation, or even the use of tools. Critical thinking is just another such skill, and, provided it is understood provisionally, it can be taught and learnt using example content that is then transferable to other content. The idea that a skill can be restricted to particular content is a strangely constricted form of absolutization: it is no more the case that critical thinking skills learnt in history cannot be applied to physics, for instance, than that having learnt to use a saw on pine wood you could not use it on oak. The teaching and learning of critical thinking skills is clearly invaluable both within the academic system and beyond it, precisely because of that flexibility.

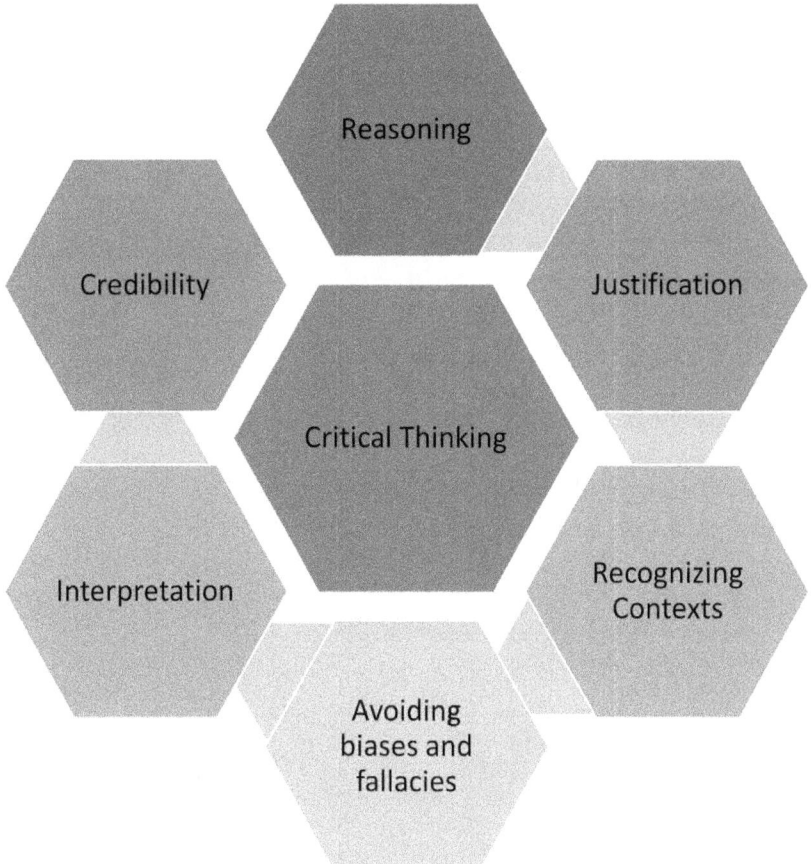

Figure 11. Critical thinking.

However, to fully understand both that flexibility and the relationship of critical thinking to integrative practice, it is necessary to decouple it from its appropriation by the ideas of 'reasoning' and 'rationality'. Where experts have attempted to reach consensus on what the skills of critical thinking are, they have usually given heavy emphasis to reasoning in various guises such as 'inferring', 'analyzing', and 'evaluating'.[2] However, my own account of the skills of critical thinking, developed from experience of teaching the subject in colleges as well as reflection on its relationship to Middle Way practice, suggests that reasoning is only one of six interdependent skills that form it: reasoning, justification, recognizing contexts, avoiding biases and fallacies, interpretation, and the assessment of credibility (**figure 11**). All of these skills apart from reasoning are in some way or other concerned with contextualization, seeing a given possible belief not as the only alternative but in relation to other possibilities.

Reasoning consists in creating connections of implication between different propositions, whereby if one is taken to be true, another is also taken to be true. This involves recognizing categorial and propositional identities in a representation, not the wider implicit relationships that may be thought of as an aspect of 'reason' by some, and that can be neurally distinguished as involving more right-hemisphere processing.[3] This wider 'reason' is included in the other five areas of critical thinking skill listed below here. Given that the meaning of all propositions depends on the embodied state of the individual rather than only on the words in the proposition, all such connection depends on communicative assumptions about shared meaning. Nevertheless, it can be helpful to trace these logical relationships to aid awareness of the assumptions that are being made when we try to justify a proposition. The study of patterns of reasoning can also help us to grasp to what extent the assumptions made in an argument support (or fail to support) a conclusion. For instance, the assumptions may justify the conclusion jointly, so that both have to be acceptable to support the conclusion but one by itself does not. Take this little argument:

> *Martha has taken her umbrella, so she must have gone out thinking it was likely to be wet.*

What is missing from this piece of reasoning is another assumption, namely that people only take their umbrella if they think it is likely to be wet. This assumption might turn out to be wrong: for instance, Martha might want to use her rolled-up umbrella to

2 Facione (1990).
3 McGilchrist (2021) p. 176.

brandish at aggressive dogs, or open it in hot weather to use as a parasol. Indeed, she might have an entirely different understanding to mine of the meaning and purpose of an umbrella, and may not even understand that it can be used to keep rain off. Although this may seem unlikely in a context where we share a lot of cognitive models and cultural norms with another person, there are some circumstances where we might need to consider such possibilities in relation to the other information available to us. The process of considering what other claims must be assumed true to support the conclusion here can thus be useful in helping us identify assumptions we have missed, and this can be pursued into much more complex logical deductions than this one. However, without imagination *in addition*, I would not have been able to consider the possibility that Martha might want to use her umbrella for other purposes. Reasoning can be useful, but is of no use whatsoever in isolation. The imaginative process is synthetic, and this needs to accompany the analytic process of reasoning.

Justification is a skill that is often confused with reasoning, but can be used entirely independent of it. It consists of the skill of being able to match beliefs with appropriate experience that increases or decreases our confidence in the acceptability of those beliefs. The idea that our experiences are necessarily put into propositions that then justify other more general propositions has given rise to the idea of 'inductive reasoning', but induction is a completely different process from (deductive) reasoning, so calling it 'reasoning' only appears to serve the rationalistic purpose of appropriating all justification to deductive reasoning through association, and thus making us assume a false certainty. Induction is simply an association between experiences and assumed beliefs that is constantly made by many animals as well as humans: for instance, if a cat associates the sound of a tin-opener with being fed, it will believe that the tin-opener is a sign that it will be fed, and behave accordingly. We do not have to reduce the cat's response to a determined stimulus-response mechanism in the manner of Skinner or Pavlov, nor do we on the other hand have to attribute 'rationality' to the cat: instead, avoiding the false dichotomy of freewill and determinism, we can admit that we do not know to what precise extent the cat is aware of or might change its beliefs, but nevertheless its beliefs depend on association with experience.

This experience is, indeed, the best and only guide available to us, as well as to the cat. The more weight of experience or evidence suggests a particular belief, the better justified we are in holding that belief. As the principle of scepticism suggests, no amount of experience will provide us with certainty, but as the principle of scepticism *also* implies, the lack of certainty does not justify denial. Applying the principle of incrementality instead, then, we conclude that the greater the weight of experience and evidence we have to go on, the more justified we are in the associated beliefs. Of course, there might also be further experiences that justify the opposite view, in which case we will need to *weigh up* the justification on each side, as discussed in 2.g. Weighing up is not a process of reasoning, matching the contents of one proposition to another, but rather one of integrating the confidence we have in one belief with the confidence we have in another – seeing each in a wider context formed by the other. Our judgements of weighing up are thus better justified by how much we take into account (i.e. by their *adequacy*), not by the precision with which we compare propositions for relationships of implication.

The skill of justification, then, depends on and develops that of all the principles of the Middle Way discussed in this book. We are justified in dependence on our experience, *as long as* our experience has not been hijacked to support absolute beliefs by rationalizing shortcuts. As long as you interpret your experience sceptically, provisionally, incrementally, agnostically, and integratively, your justification is likely to be as sound as you can manage to make it in the conditions you are operating in. None of the application of these principles depends on reasoning in any positive way, only as a negative check that we have not assumed that we have the whole story. Justification is what is often understood as 'knowledge' for embodied humans, the most valuable skill of critical thinking, but also interdependent with the others.

Recognizing context and adjusting for that context is another important skill of critical thinking. That's because justification does not occur in a vacuum, but is justification in a particular context for a particular purpose. Context is affected by features such as language, culture, disciplinary assumptions, cognitive models, metaphors, social groups and organizations, level of integrative development, gender, age, and goals (whether long- or short-term)

– that is far from a complete list. None of these features is enough for us to determine that a belief is *true* (and we need to avoid the relativist trap of believing in 'truth for me' or 'truth for us') but they do need to be taken into account as part of the judgement when we are practising critical thinking. The integration of a judgement is always integration *from a starting point* from which it becomes *more* integrated, so we cannot make progress in integrating our judgement until we are reasonably clear about what that starting point is. Indeed, universality is impossible without this particularity.

An obvious and uncontroversial example of this could be taken from the context of education. Education is always contextual, because it needs to begin with the student, her developmental needs and psychological states. Supposing a sixteen-year-old student is making a judgement about her course of study at sixth form or senior high school: she could obviously make better or worse judgements, and these will affect her future. Her parents and teachers may offer advice, but in the end she has to make the decision, and the effectiveness of that decision depends on who she is and how much she is capable of taking into account. Her parents might emphasize the importance of studying subjects that can help prepare for a remunerative occupation, but she may not fully appreciate the practical importance of that yet. One of her teachers may inspire her with the importance of helping the planet, but her judgement about this may not take her own capacities sufficiently into account – perhaps she might choose ecological science but fail at it. The adequacy of her decision cannot be judged according to any absolute criterion, for instance of what will lead to better consequences for everyone, or to her own happiness. Instead, we need to see how well she has responded to her own limitations, getting perspectives from others but also taking responsibility for her judgement. Without taking context into account she could not make a reasonably adequate judgement in the first place, nor could we have any basis to try to assess the adequacy of her judgement.

The same considerations apply to recognizing the contextuality of judgements that are often taken to be 'objective', such as those of a scientist about the relationship between theory and evidence. The 'objectivity' of such a judgement merely means that the standards we are likely to apply for its adequacy are higher, not that contextuality is not relevant. Given how much our judgement is affected by the states of our bodies – even by simple haptic factors like whether we are sitting on a hard chair or whether we have had lunch[4] – it would be extremely foolish to pretend that our judgement is absolutely 'objective' on any topic, without taking into account who we are and where we are coming from, along with every other aspect of the context.

Avoiding biases and fallacies follows from recognizing context. To ignore bias because the social context says we should be absolutely 'objective', is obviously to grossly undermine our actual degree of objectivity because of a failure of incrementality. Whilst bias is a psychological tendency to take easy absolutizing shortcuts in our judgement,[5] fallacy is the manifestation of that tendency in a pattern of argument. It is traditional, but mistaken, to think of fallacies as primarily technical faults in reasoning, but reasoning is usually irrelevant to them (one can make a good judgement that is formally fallacious or a bad one that is not). What logicians call 'informal fallacies' are the ones that actually matter, and these consist of arguments that cause further conflict rather than helping to make beliefs compatible.[6] For instance, an *ad hominem* argument is one where we irrelevantly claim that a person's status or other features invalidates their argument, even when the argument is largely independent of those features ('You're just a student: how could you know anything about that?'). It is not inconsistent with the assumptions of the accuser for someone's status to invalidate their argument, but it does make it impossible to integrate opposed positions by examining the justification of the actual claim they have put forward.

A fuller exploration of the ways that we can work with biases and fallacies will need to wait until volume V of this series. In brief, though, we should not underestimate the entrenchment of biases. The avoidance of biases and fallacies is not something that can be effectively pursued in isolation, but as part of critical thinking practice and of the Threefold Practice in general. It is our response to the bias that is important, once we have recognized it, rather than the mere fact of it. We overcome bias by contextualizing it, rather than either giving way to it or over-reacting to it. By contextualizing, using any of the other practices discussed in this section of the book, we cease to be biased, because we are no longer taking

---

4   Ackerman, Nocera, & Bargh (2010).
5   I.5.c.
6   Walton (1987).

our limited assumptions to be the whole story, even though we do not gain an absolutely 'objective' position. In addition, we can take certain more specific counter-measures in relation to specific biases: these will be discussed in volume V.

Interpretation is the critical thinking skill of helpfully contextualizing others' utterances (or in a few cases, our own in the past). This does not consist of finding one correct interpretation, but rather of ceasing to assume that the one we might first alight on is the only possible and correct one. Interpretation in critical thinking, then, consists of provisionality applied to our beliefs about the meaning of an utterance.

Given an embodied view of meaning, no interpretation can be entirely determined by the words used. Ambiguity and vagueness are unavoidable features of human communication. Additional indicators are offered by context in both speech and writing, and by tone, emphasis, and body language in speech. One aspect of contextual awareness in interpretation, then, is to make use of as many of these contextual clues as possible before reaching a judgement about how to interpret what has been said. For instance, we could consider whether an apparent inconsistency in an author's work is actually part of a larger consistent pattern, when we take into account the bigger picture offered by their other writings. There are of course practical limits to how much we can research such context before drawing a conclusion, and a balance has to be struck between fairness and effort.

A further aspect of interpretation practice applies, though, once we have done our best to interpret someone fairly, but ambiguity still remains, and thus ambiguity might make the difference between a positive or negative response. This is to apply the *principle of charity*. The principle of charity means assuming the best interpretation of an ambiguous utterance, all other things being equal. The justification for this principle is practical: if we assume the best of people, the result is more likely to be a mutually adjusting dialogue fuelled by goodwill, whereas if we assume the worst, a reinforcing feedback loop of reactions on both sides may ensue. The principle does not imply that we should always assume the best of people: obviously there are lots of situations where we have to make negative judgements about them to face up to the conditions they are creating. What it does imply is that we should assume the best of people when the evidence is sufficiently ambiguous to leave us hovering near the point of balance when we weigh it up (see 2.g). For instance, if someone in a crowded train carriage is annoying you by watching videos on their mobile phone, audibly without headphones, it's probably best to assume that it hasn't occurred to them that anyone else might have a problem with this, rather than that they are deliberately setting out to annoy you. A carefully-phrased polite request, drawing attention to the effect it has on you, might then resolve the situation and avoid a series of mutual reactions.

In some circumstances it is also worth mentioning here the possible importance of interpreting some utterances in terms of their meaning rather than only in terms of belief. This is particularly the case with statements of belief that might at first seem to be absolutizations. Before reacting to the absolutization, however, it is very helpful to also consider the possibility that the main value of what has been said is actually symbolic or archetypal, and that the person concerned may get inspiration from what has been said, but not have considered the possibility that it could be stated otherwise than in the form of absolute belief. This is particularly the case, for instance, with claims about God and his role in human life. We should not leap to a metaphysical interpretation without some wider awareness of the possible role of archetypes in what is being said.

Credibility assessment is the final element of critical thinking skills. This is needed for judgements on issues that we are unable to assess directly in our own experience, probably because they are remote or require expertise of some kind. It is effectively the extension of justification into a more indirect context, where we need to judge not only the justification of different possible beliefs, but also the justification of different possible sources that could give us information about the justification of different possible beliefs. Those different possible sources might include groups or organizations, media outlets, individuals, and books or other outlets. As in justification in general, it is crucial not to absolutize one source, just as it is crucial not to absolutize one belief. Instead, we may believe a particular source to a greater or lesser extent in awareness of possible alternative sources. This is the difference between absolute authority (where we do not consider alternatives) and provisional authority (where we do, but still give credibility to some sources over others based on experience).

The skills of credibility judgement are very much those of provisionality applied to issues of authority, and involve probabilizing and weighing up, as discussed in 2.f and 2.g. When we do not have any direct evidence or experience to decide an issue, then we need to judge how much credence to give to the sources available to us, deciding roughly how probable they are to be correct in comparison with each other, and weighing up the likelihood of the correctness of conflicting accounts. In doing this it can be helpful to work through a checklist of factors of credibility – that is, reasons we might have for trusting or not trusting a source. These can easily be recalled using the mnemonic RAVEN.[7]

1. *Reputation:* how far others tend to trust this source, particularly those others that we already trust for considered reasons – e.g. a scientific reputation indicates how far a scientist is trusted by other scientists
2. *Ability to observe:* how far the source had access to the information or experiences they would need to make adequate judgements about it – e.g. did they experience relevant events, see clearly, or have access to necessary documents
3. *Vested interest:* how far the source might benefit or suffer from communicating truthfully or deceptively – e.g. a salesperson on commission may have strong motives for exaggerating the virtues of her product
4. *Expertise:* how far relevant training and experience makes a source better able to understand and interpret information on a particular topic – e.g. we may trust a trained physicist more than an untrained person for information about the technicalities of physics
5. *Neutrality or bias:* how far a source's previous record is one of presenting issues with a reasonable degree of neutrality, or how far it has been unnecessarily biased – e.g. many media outlets, such as the *Daily Mail* or *Fox News*, have a record of intense bias, counting against the likely accuracy of their reporting

To apply these factors in credibility assessment, we need to consider each of them (as far as relevant and practicable) in relation to alternative possible sources and weigh them up. In practice, of

---

7   This device is used in critical thinking textbooks. I am not aware of its ultimate origin.

course, we come to rely on certain sources or types of sources on a regular basis, because we have made a judgement that they are generally reliable (or at least more reliable than the alternatives). It would involve an impractical amount of time and mental energy to weigh up all sources every time we believe a news report. What is important in practice is that our sources are assessed provisionally in relation to alternatives at points of particular disagreement where conflict is likely to develop. In this way, we can avoid not only the naïve absorption of unreliable or biased material, but also the unreflective negative dismissal of sources that challenge our assumptions.

***

These six skills of critical thinking can be developed either in the context of skills-based training using a variety of examples, or in the context of a content-focused discipline. The latter, however, carries the danger of a restricted context-dependency that makes it difficult for individuals to apply the skills beyond the context in which they originally applied them. There are many instances of the restricted application of critical thinking skills in a restricted sphere by a particular tradition or discipline that makes it taboo to apply them beyond that sphere. For instance, the Jesuits can apply critical thinking rigorously to everything except the examination of the assumptions in Catholic doctrine. If critical thinking skills are only learnt in the context of scientific training, there is likewise a danger that they will not be applied to the examination of the assumptions that frame that training.

Many other disciplines could thus also be described as integration of belief practices, except that they are only so to the extent that they develop these critical thinking skills and do not limit their application. Most education involves some version of some of these skills, but also to some extent constrains their application. For instance, the study of history lays a particular emphasis on credibility assessment skills when considering documents that give information about the past. It may, however, be constrained in its line of interpretation, by for instance interpreting the past only in terms of a particular ideological slant. The study of science in general can put a very helpful emphasis on provisionality, but can also be constrained by the belief that science gives us 'facts' entirely separable from values, and that these facts represent a deterministic world following 'natural laws'.

In an educational context, there is always a case that whatever the constraints of the teacher's viewpoint, the student is still learning just by understanding new possibilities, and that these can help him or her progress through the stages of psychological development. That case works best if a variety of views is reflected in the educational system, rather than it being seen more or less as a vehicle for religious or political indoctrination. However, absolutizations can start to become more prominent as academic research succeeds education, from postgraduate level onwards, because at that stage the discussion starts to become closed into ever smaller specialized groups. Accompanying economic pressures maintain those specializations, and incentivize specialists to ignore questions that lie beyond them.

The sad case of philosophy as a discipline reflects this pattern. Critical thinking skills have been maintained primarily by philosophers through the ages, and they can be rightly seen in some respects as philosophical skills, even though they can be applied to any area beyond the typically abstract concerns of philosophy. Philosophical education is rare enough in the population as a whole, and is thus one of the main ways that higher-level critical thinking skills can be developed. To the student, philosophy is an exciting enquiry constantly opening up new possibilities for meaning and belief. However, philosophical research in modern academia by contrast contributes very little to such enquiry, and instead does much to maintain absolutizations in society, because it is over-specialized (as discussed in 2.d), divided between analytic and continental schools, entrenched in dichotomous framing, and divided from psychology and other disciplines that could help develop its practical value. The very subject that is generally perceived as questioning underlying assumptions is often the last to question its own, and instead academic philosophers become skilled at rationalizing and defending absolutizing assumptions. If we are still stuck with the dogmatic frameworks of moral absolutism vs relativism, theism vs atheism, freewill vs determinism, realism vs idealism, mind vs brain, and so on, which still shape a great deal of discourse across society, it is largely due to philosophers, who have the skills to offer alternatives to them but have failed to do so.[8] The overwhelming majority of modern philosophy consists in the useless recycling of these assumptions in slightly varying forms. Thus philosophical education, whether as a teacher or a learner, can be highly recommended as an integrative practice, but philosophical research in modern academia cannot.

There is also a restricted therapeutic use of critical thinking in the form of Cognitive Behavioural Therapy (CBT). This particularly consists in a training in identifying and avoiding biases that have immediate negative effects on an individual's mental health. For example, a therapist may help a patient to identify 'catastrophizing' in their interpretation of negative events, effectively by putting them in a wider context of belief to prevent them being absolutized and contributing further to a reinforcing feedback loop of depression and negative interpretation. One study has found that CBT has a similar beneficial effect on the catastrophizing of pain as mindfulness-based stress reduction.[9] CBT has proved a highly effective therapy,[10] though obviously not suited to all cases. Clearly its limitation is its restricted focus – it does not question any assumption whatsoever, but only those judged to be psychotherapeutically damaging. Its medical framing also means that it is largely focused only on relieving those who are particularly suffering in the short term, rather than pursuing even the development of those people in the longer term, let alone helping those who are judged well or normal all along. Of course, some of the approaches and techniques of CBT can be adopted by individuals and used in their own practice, but these are not particularly distinguishable from critical thinking and bias awareness in general.

The use of reflective or contemplative practices in religious or spiritual traditions is a further restricted application of critical thinking skills. These may consist, for instance, in taking a religious doctrine (such as 'impermanence' in Buddhism) and exploring it in one's mind in a systematic way, constantly relating it to experience to make it more fully meaningful and thus also deepen one's beliefs about it.[11] This could be done in a way that is critical or uncritical, depending on whether one is prepared to fully consider the pos-

8   This point will be discussed in much more detail in volume VI.
9   Turner et al. (2017).
10 A wide range of studies, too numerous to list, have evidenced this in relation to a variety of disorders.
11 E.g. Ratnaguna (2010).

sibility that the doctrine one sets out to consider is false. If one's framing is only to confirm the doctrine, the effect of the reflection might only be to reinforce it as a dogma, but if one uses reflection in relation to experience to fully question and re-interpret it, then critical thinking skills can be developed and refined in the context of a reflection practice.

Some of my personal practice for developing Middle Way Philosophy has had some resemblance to this reflective tradition. Usually I do this in the context of solitary walking. I set out to work through the implications and connections that can be made with a particular belief, often by bringing it systematically into contact with other beliefs from other areas of my experience. A chain of new synthetic connections can thus be forged during the course of a walk, which I typically then go over several times, usually finding new connections each time. Analysis that critically examines my conclusions can also accompany this process, but it needs to be integrated into it rather than separated.

A final practice for integration of belief that applies critical thinking in a specific area is autobiography. Typically a practice for a reflective period of old age (but by no means restricted to that), autobiographical writing requires us to review and interpret our memories and the records of our individual life. To turn those memories into a written narrative, though, we will also need to examine different possible beliefs about our life, and resolve any conflicts between such beliefs. Where conflicts have not been resolved, we get self-deceptive autobiography – for instance, where a writer presents themselves in too one-sidedly positive or negative a light. There thus needs to be an awareness of autobiography as an integrative practice to make it successful, rather than a self-indulgent process of mere reminiscence. On a smaller scale, we also engage in autobiographical practice just by keeping a diary or by writing shorter autobiographical texts.

6.h. Socio-political Integration of Belief Practices

> *Summary*
>
> Socio-political integration of belief practice helps to create the conditions for individual integration of belief practice through communication. The media, education, politics, and academic activity provide obvious channels where critical dialogue can be created. However, the creation of genuine critical dialogue is always in tension with other social or economic priorities, so the cutting edge of the practice lies in finding the Middle Way, to enable that dialogue without destroying the conditions that allow it. I also see the development of Middle Way Philosophy itself as a socio-political integration of belief practice helping to support the conditions for integration through understanding.

At the socio-political level, integration of belief practice is focused on creating the conditions for the reconciliation of conflicting beliefs held by groups. Rather than only learning and applying the skills of critical thinking for oneself, it thus involves helping others to access them, or in any other way setting up the conditions for people to do so. It also clearly has a close relationship with integration of desire practice at the socio-political level (as discussed in 6.d), particularly with the mediation and political campaigning mentioned there. I described these practices as primarily focused on reconciling desires, but they cannot do this without changing beliefs as well. In popular language, both hearts and minds need to be won simultaneously.

The practices most directly focused on socio-political integration of belief, though, all involve a focus on communication that enables others to re-examine absolute beliefs by giving them a wider context. That communication could be in the context of ordinary discussion, through the media, through education, through politics, or through academic activity. Here we have to take for granted that anyone engaging in this level of practice is already practising integration of belief on an individual level through critical thinking, otherwise their wider communication is liable to make matters worse. Of course, individual practice always depends on the conditions created by socio-political events, but in attempting to influence those events we need to proceed cautiously, building socio-political practice on a foundation of individual practice. We need to ensure that we are communicating an increasingly integrated perspective, rather than spreading our own delusions and conflict so that they can then be reflected back at us and become even more entrenched.

It is critical dialogue that creates the conditions for integration of belief at socio-political level. There, individuals or groups with incompatible beliefs discuss those beliefs provisionally, recognizing and taking into account the others' beliefs. All the six skills of critical thinking need to be exerted to create and sustain such a dialogue: reasoning to recognize the assumptions behind one's own beliefs, justification to support those beliefs positively, recognizing context in both one's own and others' beliefs so as not to judge them in the wrong context, avoiding biases that will derail the whole discussion into a power-play, interpreting the other charitably, and using credibility assessments rather than absolutized appeals to authority to reach common ground on sources. In addition, though, the dialogue simply has to take place in the first instance. To support and encourage the context where such dialogues can take place is itself an integration of belief practice.

One cannot take such contexts for granted. They might happen in everyday conversation, but only if the participants stay in communication and commit themselves to the discussion to an unusual extent. They are more likely to happen in education, in the context of a classroom, seminar room, or debating society, but only if other goals do not supplant it, and the teacher or facilitator has sufficient commitment and skill to keep steering the discussion back into areas of fruitful dialogue. They might possibly happen in politics, but not if anxiety about political status with voters, one's party, or one's position takes precedence and interposes defensive shortcuts. In practice, critical dialogue in politics is rare, and a standoff in discussion between two fallacious shortcut arguments the norm. It might also happen in the media or journalism, but only if critical dialogue starts to take precedence over the need to constantly attract and maintain an audience with a short attention-span.

One can thus see the cutting edge of the practice of integration of belief at socio-political level to be maintaining a longer-term integrated motive in the face of short-term pressures to please the group or satisfy the group's authorities. The teacher or lecturer committed to integration of belief needs to care enough about stimulating critical thought in her students to give it priority in the face of pressure to get them through the exams, please their parents, or even meet the students' own expectations. The politician needs to care enough about engaging with his opponents' assumptions even in the face of the need to keep winning, and fulfilling his supporters' and party's expectations, to remain in political office. The journalist needs to care enough about stimulating her audience's critical thought even in the face of competition to keep her job in a popular newspaper or TV station. There is no magical way of overcoming all these absolutizing pressures whilst continuing to engage in critical dialogue: one just has to use the Middle Way at each turn to neither lose sight of all the practical conditions one is working with, nor lose sight of the wider value of integration. It may only take one wrong move to lose one's place in a slippery, competitive profession, but at the same time the value of being in that profession at all plummets if one cannot use it to serve long-term integration.

Beyond this, critical thinking skills also need a coherent framework to avoid their appropriation by absolutizations. Such absolutizations constrain the scope or application of critical thinking by creating absolute boundaries around the sphere in which it can be used, whether this is for instance only at work, only when questioning other people's assumptions, or only as critical ammunition against rival traditions. The belief that critical thinking is a type of 'logic' creates the absolutized assumption that reasoning coherently from your prior assumptions provides 'sound' beliefs, regardless of the assumptions with which you began, and thus enables those assumptions to continue unquestioned.

This need for a coherent framework is why Middle Way Philosophy is required – to provide a structure for critical thinking that links it to other practices, and maintains its experiential value. Of the five principles, we here return to our starting point with scepticism, as the most basic one shaping Middle Way Philosophy and maintaining its practice free of appropriation. The use of balanced scepticism, and the other principles following from this, is the practice of the Middle Way, but the development and communication of an intellectual structure to support that practice is the practice of Middle Way Philosophy. Obviously, I see this book as an exercise of that practice. A book is a public expression of an argument, in the most developed form that can be readily shared with others in the socio-political realm, to support its long-term integration. This book is, however, far from the only possible exercise of that practice, nor necessarily the best expression of the intellectual structure that is needed. So far, however, of the other sources I have examined, I have not found any that express Middle Way Philosophy with sufficient clarity and consistency.

This book needs no other conclusion than the structure of practice I have offered in the chapters of this section, which I commend to you, reader, for embodied engagement. That structure of practice in turn depends on the five principles developed in the body of this book, which in turn are interrelated with other volumes in this series wherever more detail is required in a particular area. May your path be fulfilling!

Appendix

Table 1. Multidisciplinary justification of the Five Principles.

Sources/disciplines	Scepticism	Provisionality	Incrementality	Agnosticism	Integration
Buddhism	Avoidance of metaphysical claims. Going forth from palace and forest.	The raft analogy: assumptions change in new context.	Ocean analogy: 'gradual training'. Implications of *anatta*.	Snake analogy: confident 'right grasp' through experience.	*Jhana* progression, wet piece of wood image.
Psychology	Avoidance of rigid biased positions recognized as maladaptive.	Flexibility and complexity in psychological development. Learning orientation.	Avoiding rigid framing and ambiguity aversion.	Avoiding an array of biases, each of which has an opposing over-reaction.	Dealing with conflict and repression in psychotherapy.
Neuroscience	Dominance of left prefrontal cortex (PFC) processes, but not whole story	Development of wider neural links to contextualize left PFC processes.	Gradual development or adjustment of neural links as a system.	Use of left PFC perspective to recognize its own limitations.	Long-term connection of previously isolated and conflicting systems of neural links.
Scientific method	Recognition of empirical limitations.	Openness to adjustment after negative results.	Use of probability and weight of evidence. Importance of measurement and statistical justification.	Argument against premature or pseudo-scientific acceptance or dismissal of theories.	Consensus of scientists overcoming divisions.
Embodiment	No 'knowing' because meaning not representational.	Bodily awareness and meaning as context for provisionality.	Gradual changes of body, avoiding absolutes of incorporeality.	Critical understanding of defects of representationalism.	Bodily sub-systems integrated in wider bodily system.
Systems theory	Recognition of uncertainty from observer being part of system.	Application of recognition that observer is part of system.	Gradual adjustment of systems (even if faster or slower) from mutual adjustment of sub-systems.	Avoidance of merely linear perspectives.	Uniting sub-systems that would be sub-optimizing if conflicting.

The Old and New Middle Way Philosophy Series

Although this book can stand alone as an account of the practice of the Middle Way, it is also the second of a planned series of at least nine books on Middle Way Philosophy, to be published by Equinox over the next few years. These books will together form a highly interconnected argument for the Middle Way as a practical philosophy. In the process they will synthesize various different sources of insight, and challenge various entrenched assumptions about human judgement, its justification and motivation. This series is in turn a substantial development, rewriting, and updating of an earlier series of four volumes.

While the new series is in the course of being written, I will need to refer the reader at a number of points to supporting and connecting arguments in both the old series and the new series. I suggest referring to the new series if possible, but using the old series if the required volume of the new series has not been published yet. To distinguish between them, I have used lower case Roman numerals (i, ii, iii, iv) in references to the books of the old series, and upper case Roman numerals (I, II, III, etc.) to refer to the planned books of the new series. Both series are listed below.

Old series (Robert M. Ellis, 2012–15)

This has been published both as four separate volumes and as an omnibus edition by Lulu, Raleigh. This series is referred to using lower case Roman numerals, followed by section and chapter numbers.

i. *Middle Way Philosophy 1: The Path of Objectivity* (2012)
ii. *Middle Way Philosophy 2: The Integration of Desire* (2013)
iii. *Middle Way Philosophy 3: The Integration of Meaning* (2013)
iv. *Middle Way Philosophy 4: The Integration of Belief* (2015)

Middle Way Philosophy: Omnibus Edition (2015)

New series (Robert M. Ellis, 2022 onwards)

This is the second book of this planned series to be published by Equinox. This series is referred to using upper case Roman numerals. Obviously, references to books that have not yet been written (at the time of writing this book) must be approximate. I have given an indicative section number, but otherwise you will need to use the contents and index of the relevant book in the new series to locate a reference.

   I. *Absolutization: The Source of Dogma, Repression, and Conflict*
   II. *The Five Principles of Middle Way Philosophy: Living Experientially in a World of Uncertainty*
   III. *A Systemic History of the Middle Way: The Biology, Psychological Development, and Cultural Change behind Integrative Practice*
   IV. *Embodied Meaning and Integration: Overcoming the Abstracted Grip on Meaning in Theory and Practice*
   V. *Bias and the Integration of Belief: The Psychology of Absolutized Judgement and the Middle Way*
   VI. *The Practice of Agnosticism: Overcoming False Dualities across Human Thought*
   VII. *Mindful Beauty: Aesthetics as Gathering Attention*
   VIII. *Middle Way Ethics: Stretching across the Gap between Relative and Absolute Values*
   IX. *The Middle Way Manifesto: Combining Radical Change with Political Effectiveness*

Bibliography

Ackerman, Joshua, Nocera, Christopher, & Bargh, John (2010) 'Incidental haptic sensations influence social judgments and decisions' *Science* 328:5986, pp. 1712–15. https://doi.org/10.1126/science.1189993
Al-Ghazali, trans. Mukhtar Holland (1980) *The Duties of Brotherhood in Islam*. The Islamic Foundation, Leicester.
Aristotle, trans. J.A.K. Thomson & Hugh Tredennick (1953, orig. c. 325 BCE) *Ethics*. Penguin, London.
Armson, Rosalind (2011) *Growing Wings on the Way: Systems Thinking for Messy Situations*. Triarchy Press, Charmouth Dorset.
Arthur-Cameselle, Jessyca (2016) 'Mindfulness, eating, body and performance' from Amy Baltzell, ed., *Mindfulness and Performance*. Cambridge University Press, Cambridge. https://doi.org/10.1017/CBO9781139871310.015
Asch, Solomon (1956) *Studies in Independence and Conformity: 1. A Minority of One against a Unanimous Majority*. Psychological Monographs. https://doi.org/10.1037/h0093718
Ault, James M. (2004) *Spirit and Flesh: Life in a Fundamentalist Baptist Church*. Vintage, New York.
Baer, Ruth, Crane, Catherine, Miller, Edward, & Kuyken, William (2019) 'Doing no harm in mindfulness-based programs: Conceptual issues and empirical findings' *Clinical Psychology Review* 77, pp. 101–14. https://doi.org/10.1016/j.cpr.2019.01.001
Batchelor, Stephen (2020) *The Art of Solitude*. Yale University Press, New Haven Conn.
Bateson, Gregory (1972) *Steps to an Ecology of Mind*. University of Chicago Press, Chicago.
Bekinschtein, Tristan, Davis, Matthew, Rodd, Jennifer, & Owen, Adrian (2011) 'Why clowns taste funny: The relationship between humor and semantic ambiguity' *The Journal of Neuroscience* 31:26, pp. 9665–71. https://doi.org/10.1523/JNEUROSCI.5058-10.2011
Berto, Rita (2014) 'The role of nature in coping with psycho-physiological stress: A literature review on restorativeness' *Behavioral Sciences* 4:4, pp. 394–409. https://doi.org/10.3390/bs4040394
Bialystok, Ellen (2009) 'Bilingualism: The good, the bad, and the indifferent' *Bilingualism: Language and Cognition* 12:1, pp. 3–11. https://doi.org/10.1017/S1366728908003477
Boag, Simon (2010) 'Repression, suppression and conscious awareness' *Psychoanalytic Psychology* 27:2, pp. 164–81. https://doi.org/10.1037/a0019416
Boulton, Jean, Allen, Peter, & Bowman, Cliff (2015) *Embracing Complexity: Strategic Perspectives for an Age of Turbulence*. Oxford University Press, Oxford. https://doi.org/10.1093/acprof:oso/9780199565252.001.0001

Burke, Edmund (1910, orig. 1790) *Reflections on the French Revolution and Other Essays*. Dent Dutton, London.

Burnyeat, Myles (1980) 'Can a sceptic live his scepticism?' from Malcolm Schofield, Myles Burnyeat, & Jonathan Barnes, eds., *Doubt and Dogmatism*. Oxford University Press, Oxford.

Cebolla, Ausias, Demarzo, Marcello, Martins, Patricia, Soler, Joaquim, & Garcia-Campayo, Javier (2017) 'Unwanted effects: Is there a negative side of meditation? A multicentre survey' *PLoS ONE* 12(9): e0183137. https://doi.org/10.1371/journal.pone.0183137

Chabris, Christopher & Simons, Daniel (2011) *The Invisible Gorilla*. HarperCollins, London.

Churchland, Paul M. (1984) *Matter and Consciousness*. MIT Press, Cambridge Mass.

Csikszentmihályi, Mihaly (1990) *Flow: The Psychology of Optimal Experience*. Harper & Row, London.

Damasio, Antonio (1996) 'The somatic marker hypothesis and the possible functions of the prefrontal cortex' *Transactions of the Royal Society* 351, pp. 1413-20. https://doi.org/10.1098/rstb.1996.0125

Danziger, Shai, Levav, Jonathan, & Avnaim-Pesso, Liora (2011) 'Extraneous factors in legal decisions' *Proceedings of the National Academy of Sciences* 108:17, pp. 6889-92. https://doi.org/10.1073/pnas.1018033108

Davidson, Donald (1967) 'Truth and meaning' *Synthese* 17:3, pp. 304-23. https://doi.org/10.1007/BF00485035

Dawkins, Richard (1995) *River out of Eden: A Darwinian View of Life*. Hachette, London.

Descartes, René, trans. F.E. Sutcliffe (1968) *Discourse on Method and the Meditations*. Penguin, London.

Dix, William Giles (1855) *The Unholy Alliance: An American View of the War in the East*. Norton, New York.

Dweck, Carol S. (2017) *Mindset: Changing the Way You Think to Fulfil Your Potential*. Robinson, London.

Ellis, Robert M. (1997) 'Revelation, wisdom, and learning from religion: A response to D.G. Attfield' *British Journal of Religious Education* 19:2. https://doi.org/10.1080/0141620970190206

Ellis, Robert M. (2001) *A Buddhist Theory of Moral Objectivity*. PhD thesis, Lancaster University. Published online by British Library.

Ellis, Robert M. (2011a) 'Taking the "meta" out of physics' *Journal of Consciousness Exploration and Research* 2:8.

Ellis, Robert M. (2011b) *A New Buddhist Ethics*. Lulu, Raleigh.

Ellis, Robert M. (2016) *Parables of the Middle Way*. Lulu, Raleigh.

Ellis, Robert M. (2017) 'Reason is not objectivity: A response to Julian Baggini's narrowly rational criteria for objectivity' https://www.researchgate.net/publication/313696637_Reason_is_not_objectivity_A_response_to_Julian_Baggini%27s_narrowly_rational_criteria_for_objectivity

Ellis, Robert M. (2019) *The Buddha's Middle Way: Experiential Judgement in His Life and Teaching*. Equinox, Sheffield.

Ellis, Robert M. (2020a) *The Thought of Sangharakshita: A Critical Assessment*. Equinox, Sheffield. https://doi.org/10.1558/isbn.9781781799284

Ellis, Robert M. (2020b) *Red Book, Middle Way: How Jung Parallels the Buddha's Method for Human Integration.* Equinox, Sheffield. https://doi.org/10.1558/isbn.9781800500082

Ellis, Robert M. (2022) *Archetypes in Religion and Beyond: A Practical Theory of Human Integration and Inspiration.* Equinox, Sheffield.

Erasmus, Desiderius (1974 onwards) *Collected Works.* University of Toronto Press, Toronto.

Facione, Peter (1990) 'Critical thinking: A statement of expert consensus for purposes of educational assessment and instruction' American Philosophical Association.

Fujita, Frank & Diener, Ed (2005) 'Life satisfaction set point: Stability and change' *Journal of Personality and Social Psychology* 88:1, pp. 158–64. https://doi.org/10.1037/0022-3514.88.1.158

Fuller, C.J. (1976) 'Kerala Christians and the caste system' *Man* 11:1, pp. 53–70. https://doi.org/10.2307/2800388

Garvey, Brian (2010) 'Absence of evidence, evidence of absence, and the atheist's teapot' *Ars Disputandi* 10:1, pp. 9–22. https://doi.org/10.1080/15665399.2010.10820011

Gendlin, Eugene (2003) *Focusing.* Rider, London.

Gendlin, Eugene (2018) *A Process Model.* Northwestern University Press, Evanston Illinois.

Gettier, Edmund (1963) 'Is justified true belief knowledge?' *Analysis* 23, pp. 121–3. https://doi.org/10.1093/analys/23.6.121

Gladwell, Malcolm (2000) *The Tipping Point: How Little Things Can Make a Big Difference.* Abacus, London.

Guilbeault, Douglas, Woolley, Samuel, & Becker, Joshua (2021) 'Probabilistic social learning improves the public's judgments of news veracity' *PLoS ONE* 16:3, e0247487. https://doi.org/10.1371/journal.pone.0247487

Haidt, Jonathan (2012) *The Righteous Mind: Why Good People are Divided by Politics and Religion.* Pantheon Books, New York.

Harries, Richard (1990) *Shalom and Pax: Christian Concepts of Peace.* Oxford Project for Peace Studies, Oxford.

Hofmann, Stefan, Sawyer, Alice, Witt, Ashley, & Oh, Diana (2010) 'The effect of mindfulness-based therapy on anxiety and depression: A meta-analytic review' *Journal of Consulting and Clinical Psychology* 78:2, pp. 269–83. https://doi.org/10.1037/a0018555

Hume, David (1975) *Enquiries Concerning Human Understanding and Concerning the Principles of Morals.* Oxford University Press, Oxford. https://doi.org/10.1093/actrade/9780198245353.book.1

Hume, David (1978) *A Treatise of Human Nature.* Oxford University Press, Oxford.

Ikemoto, Satoshi & Panksepp, Jaak (1999) 'The role of nucleus accumbens dopamine in motivated behavior: A unifying interpretation with special reference to reward-seeking' *Brain Research Reviews* 31:1, pp. 6–41. https://doi.org/10.1016/S0165-0173(99)00023-5

Ireland, John D. (1990) *The Udana: Inspired Utterances of the Buddha.* Buddhist Publications Society, Kandy.

Janis, Irving L. (1982) *Groupthink: Psychological Studies of Policy Decisions and Fiascos*. Houghton Mifflin, Boston.
Johnson, Mark (2007) *The Meaning of the Body: Aesthetics of Human Understanding*. University of Chicago Press, Chicago. https://doi.org/10.7208/chicago/9780226026992.001.0001
Johnson, Mark (2017) *Embodied Mind, Meaning and Reason: How Our Bodies Give Rise to Understanding*. University of Chicago Press, Chicago. https://doi.org/10.7208/chicago/9780226500393.001.0001
Jung, Carl, trans. R.F.C. Hull (1960) *The Structure and Dynamics of the Psyche* (Collected Works Vol. 8). Routledge, London.
Jung, Carl, trans. Sonu Shamdasani et al. (2009) *The Red Book*. Norton, New York.
Kahneman, Daniel (2011) *Thinking, Fast and Slow*. Penguin, London.
Kegan, Robert (1982) *The Evolving Self: Problem and Process in Human Development*. Harvard University Press, Cambridge Mass. https://doi.org/10.4159/9780674039414
Kegan, Robert (1994) *In Over Our Heads: The Mental Demands of Modern Life*. Harvard University Press, Cambridge Mass.
Kelly, Kevin (2007) 'Ockham's Razor, empirical complexity, and truth-finding efficiency' *Theoretical Computer Science* 383, pp. 270-87. https://doi.org/10.1016/j.tcs.2007.04.009
Kenny, Anthony (1973) *Wittgenstein*. Penguin, London.
Kinsbourne, Marcel & Bemporad, Brenda (1984) 'Lateralization of emotion: A model and the evidence', from Nathan A. Fox & Richard J. Davidson, eds., *The Psychobiology of Affective Development*. Psychology Press, London.
Korzybski, Alfred (1993) *Science and Sanity: An Introduction to Non-Aristotelian Systems and General Semantics*. Institute of General Semantics, New York.
Lakoff, George (1987) *Women, Fire and Dangerous Things: What Categories Reveal about the Mind*. University of Chicago Press, Chicago. https://doi.org/10.7208/chicago/9780226471013.001.0001
Lakoff, George (2014) *Don't Think of an Elephant! Know Your Values and Frame the Debate*. Chelsea Green Publishing, White River Junction Vermont.
Lakoff, George & Johnson, Mark (1980) *Metaphors We Live By*. University of Chicago Press, Chicago.
Lakoff, George & Nuñez, Rafael (2000) *Where Mathematics Comes From: How the Embodied Mind Brings Mathematics into Being*. Basic Books, New York.
Lambdin, Charles (2006) 'Fallacy' (The Fallacy of the Golden Mean) *Skeptic* 12:4.
Lamberson, P.J. & Page, Scott (2012) 'Tipping Points' Sante Fe Institute Working Paper. https://citeseerx.ist.psu.edu/viewdoc/download?doi=10.1.1.664.4625
Langer, Ellen (1997) *The Power of Mindful Learning*. Da Capo Press, Boston.
Langer, Ellen (2014) *Mindfulness*. Da Capo Press, Boston.
Le Poidevin, Robin (2010) *Agnosticism: A Very Short Introduction*. Oxford University Press, Oxford. https://doi.org/10.1093/actrade/9780199575268.001.0001
Locke, John (1824) *An Essay Concerning Human Understanding*. Rivington, London.

Looser, Christine & Wheatley, Thalia (2010) 'The tipping point of animacy: How, when and where we perceive life in a face' *Psychological Science* 21:12, pp. 1854–62. https://doi.org/10.1177/0956797610388044

MacIntyre, Alasdair (1981) *After Virtue*. Duckworth, London.

Marinoff, Lou (2007) *The Middle Way: Finding Happiness in a World of Extremes*. Sterling Publishing, New York.

Matthews, Cynthia & Salazar, Carmen (2013) 'Second-generation adult former cult group members' recovery experiences: Implications for counseling' *International Journal for the Advancement of Counselling* 35:4. https://doi.org/10.1007/s10447-013-9201-0

McGilchrist, Iain (2009) *The Master and His Emissary: The Divided Brain and the Making of the Western World*. Yale University Press, New Haven.

McGilchrist, Iain (2021) *The Matter with Things; Our Brains, Our Delusions, and the Unmaking of the World*. Perspectiva Press, London.

Michalski, Joseph (2016) 'Ritualistic rape in sociological perspective' *Cross-Cultural Research* 50:1, pp. 3–33. https://doi.org/10.1177/1069397115609025

Moore, G.E. (1962) 'Proof of an external world' from *Philosophical Papers*. Collier Books, New York.

Murphy, Paul Austin (2020) 'Rumsfeld's logic of known knowns, known unknowns and unknown unknowns' https://medium.com/the-philosophers-stone/rumsfelds-logic-of-known-knowns-known-unknowns-and-unknown-unknowns-f506db31ac74 (accessed 2022).

Murray, Charles (2021) *Facing Reality: Two Truths about Race in America*. Encounter Books, New York.

Ñanamoli, Bhikkhu & Bodhi, Bhikkhu (1995) *The Middle Length Discourses of the Buddha: A New Translation of the Majjhima Nikaya*. Wisdom Publications, Boston.

Oppy, Graham (2006) *Arguing about Gods*. Cambridge University Press, Cambridge. https://doi.org/10.1017/CBO9780511498978

Otis, Leon (1984) 'Adverse effects of transcendental meditation', from D. Shapiro & R. Walsh, eds., *Meditation: Classic and Contemporary Perspectives*. Aldine, New York.

Paradiso, Sergio & 5 others (2020) 'Integration between cerebral hemispheres contributes to defense mechanisms' *Frontiers in Psychology* 11. https://doi.org/10.3389/fpsyg.2020.01534

Paxton, Joseph, Ungar, Leo, & Greene, Joshua (2011) 'Reflection and reasoning in moral judgment' *Cognitive Science* 36:1, pp. 163–77. https://doi.org/10.1111/j.1551-6709.2011.01210.x

Pesala, Bhikkhu (2013) Quotation from translation of commentary on the *Dighanakha Sutta* (*Majjhima Nikaya* 74) at https://dhammawheel.com/viewtopic.php?t=16541

Pinker, Steven (2011) *The Better Angels of Our Nature: A History of Violence and Humanity*. Penguin, London.

Poloma, Margaret & Pendleton, Brian (1991) 'The effects of prayer and prayer experiences on measures of general well-being' *Journal of Psychology and Theology* 19:1, pp. 71–83. https://doi.org/10.1177/009164719101900107

Popper, Karl (1940) 'What is Dialectic?' *Mind* 49:196, pp. 403–26. https://doi.org/10.1093/mind/XLIX.194.403

Quine, Willard van Orman (1960) *Word and Object*. MIT Press, Cambridge Mass.
Ratnaguna (2010) *The Art of Reflection*. Windhorse, Cambridge.
Roberts, Geoffrey K. (1989) *The Unholy Alliance: Stalin's Pact with Hitler*. Indiana University Press, Bloomington.
Rosenberg, Marshall (2002) *Non-violent Communication: A Language of Compassion*. Puddledancer Press, Encinitas, California.
Ross, Lee, Greene, David, & House, Pamela (1977) 'The false consensus effect: An egocentric bias in social perception and attribution processes' *Journal of Experimental Social Psychology* 13:3, pp. 279–301. https://doi.org/10.1016/0022-1031(77)90049-X
Sangharakshita (1988) *The Religion of Art*. Windhorse, Glasgow.
Schwartz, Richard & Sweezy, Martha (2020 – 2nd Edn) *Internal Family Systems Therapy*. Guilford Press, New York.
Sextus Empiricus, trans. Benson Mates (1996) *The Skeptic Way: Sextus Empiricus's Outlines of Pyrrhonism*. Oxford University Press, New York.
Stolstorff, Melanie, Vartanian, Oshin, & Goel, Vinod (2012) 'Levels of conflict in reasoning modulate right lateral prefrontal cortex' *Brain Research* 1428, pp. 24–32. https://doi.org/10.1016/j.brainres.2011.05.045
Stroud, Barry (1984) *The Significance of Philosophical Scepticism*. Oxford University Press, Oxford. https://doi.org/10.1093/0198247613.001.0001
Taleb, Nassim Nicholas (2012) *Antifragile: Things that Gain from Disorder*. Penguin, London.
Taylor, Donald & Doria, Janet (1981) 'Self-serving and group-serving bias in attribution' *Journal of Social Psychology* 113:2, pp. 201–11. https://doi.org/10.1080/00224545.1981.9924371
Taylor, J.B. (1975) 'Law school stress and the *deformation professionelle*' *Journal of Legal Education* 27:3, pp. 251 ff.
Teramae, Jun-nosuke, Tsubo, Yasuhiro, & Fukai, Tomoki (2012) 'Optimal spike-based communication in excitable networks with strong-sparse and weak-dense links' *Scientific Reports* 2:485. https://doi.org/10.1038/srep00485
Turner, Judith & 5 others (2017) 'Mindfulness-based stress reduction and cognitive-behavioral therapy for chronic low back pain: Similar effects on mindfulness, catastrophizing, self-efficacy, and acceptance in a randomized controlled trial' *Pain* 157:11, pp. 2434–44. https://doi.org/10.1097/j.pain.0000000000000635
Vaillant, George E. (1993) *The Wisdom of the Ego*. Harvard University Press, Cambridge Mass.
Walton, Douglas (1987) *Informal Fallacies: Towards a Theory of Argument Criticisms*. John Benjamins, Amsterdam.
Williams, Patricia (2021) 'They, the People', review of Charles Murray's book *Facing Reality*, in *Times Literary Supplement* 6175 (6 August).
Williamson, Timothy (1994) *Vagueness*. Routledge, London.
Wittgenstein, Ludwig, trans. G.E.M. Anscombe (1967) *Philosophical Investigations*. Blackwell, Oxford.
Wittgenstein, Ludwig, trans. Denis Paul & G.E.M. Anscombe (1969) *On Certainty*. Blackwell, Oxford.
Woodruff, C. Chad (2018) 'Reflections of others and of self: The mirror neuron system's relationship to empathy', ch. 6 from Larry Stevens & Christopher

Woodruff, eds., *The Neuroscience of Empathy, Compassion and Self-Compassion*. Academic Press, Cambridge Mass. https://doi.org/10.1016/B978-0-12-809837-0.00006-4

Woźniak, P.A. & Gorzelańczyk, E.J. (1994) 'Optimization of repetition spacing in the practice of learning' *Acta Neurobiologiae Experimentalis* 54:1, pp. 59–62.

Young, Adrian Valdez (2009) 'Honorary Whiteness' *Asian Ethnicity* 10:2, pp. 177–85. https://doi.org/10.1080/14631360902906862

Index

a priori beliefs, 18, 23, 90, 123, 195
Abhaya, Prince, 249-50
ability to observe (credibility criterion), 265
abortion, 113, 115, 182
absoluteness, 14, 18, 131, 137
absolutism, 130, 132, 155, 267
absolutization, *passim*. Introduced **1-4**
Absolutization (book), 1-4, 6, 10, 14, 24, 30, 33, 45, 47, 55, 57, 66, 69, 81, 90, 94, 98, 117, 131, 135, 138, 148, 155, 170-1, 276
abstention, 221
academic study, 9, 78, 256
acting out, 83
active learning, 253
ad hoc argument, 18, 49
ad hominem argument, 228, 262
Adam Bede (novel character), 242
adaptability, 64
adaptiveness, 56-8
addiction, 140-1, 158, 221-2, 256
adequacy, 55, 69, 89, 92, 94, 104, 249, 260-1. See also *adaptiveness, objectivity*
adultery, 54
aesthetic context (for conflict), 182-4, 187
aesthetics, 53, 68, 90, 181, 183-4, 187-8, 198, 237, 239, 252. See also *beauty*
After Virtue, 207, 281
aggression, 230
agnosticism, 4, 7-8, 11, 22-8, 34, 41, 82, 95, 97, 115-16, 120, 129, **130-67**, 191, 203, 219, 228-9, 232, 251, 253

Al Qaida, 114
alcohol, 91, 205, 221
Al-Ghazali, 233, 277
alienation, 220, 222, 235, 250-1
altruism, 81, 83-5
ambiguity, 110, 123, 145-6, 237, 245, 263
Anaesidimus, 16
analysis, 62, 73, **77**, 78, 94, 160, 185, 193, 196, 215
analytic philosophy, 14, 44, 79, 94, 173
anima/animus (archetype), 234
animals, 16, 54, 57, 73, 110, 116, 252, 259
anthropology, 78
anticipation, 83
antifragility, 64, 66
antithesis, 74-5
anxiety, 171, 182, 200, 207, 213, 271
appeal to ignorance, 22-3
appeal to moderation, 137
appropriation, 26, 79, 130, 136, **144-9**, 150-1, 153, 257, 272
~ by application, 146
~ by composition, 147
~ by definition, 146
~ by division, 148
~ by substitution, 148
Aquinas, St Thomas 26, 144
archetypal art, 240
archetypes, 43, 48, 91, 212, 214, 224, 233-4, 237, 239-41, 250, 264
Archetypes in Religion and Beyond, 203, 214, 279
argument, 3-6, 14, 16-20, 22-5, 29-33, 35-7, 40, 42-3, 46, 48-9, 52-3, 86, 136, 138, 153, 156, 256,

Index

258, 262, 272. See also *reasoning, critical thinking*
Aristotle, 137, 153, 206, 233, 277
arithmetic, 90
art, 74, 84, 184, **240–2**, 244, 252
arts, 8–9, 73–4, 78, 84, 124, 174, 183, 185, 190, 209, 213, 218–19, 237–8, **239–42**, 247, 252, 254
asceticism, 147, 151, 186
assessment, (educational) 213, 253; (of credibility) 208, 255, 258, **264–6**, 271
association, **19**, 25, 37, 46–7, 50, 70, 124, 165, 185, 188–9, 214, 237, 240, 243. See also *embodied meaning*
asymmetrical integration, 168, **205–11**, 238
asymptotes, 18–19, 52, 86, **89–90**, 107, 138
atheism, 23, 26, 132, 138, 151, 156, 267
Ault, James, 130, 277
authenticity, 160
authority, 13, 42, 67, 78, 107, 126, 128–9, 136, 154–5, 205, **208**, 213, 218, 232, 249, 264–5, 271
autobiography, 255, 269
awareness, 2, **8–9**, 13, 17, 25, 31, 35–6, 39–41, 45, 59, 60, 62, 65, 68, 72, 79, 81–2, 84, 94–5, 97, 100, 118–25, 128–9, 131, 134–5, 141, 143, 146, 150–2, 171–2, 175, 177, 179–82, 186–8, 191, 195, 201–3, 207, 222–4, 232, 240, 243, 252, 256, 258, 263–4, 268–9

balancing feedback loop, 84, 169, 177
Batchelor, Stephen, 218, 277
Bateson, Gregory, 175, 277
Bayesian probability, 88
beauty, 182, **237–40**. See also *aesthetics*
Belarus, 114
belief, *passim*. See especially **12–21**, **255–73**

bias, 3, 42, 45, **69**, 96, 117, 120, 136, 139, 148, 151–3, 163–4, 206, 219, 232, 255, **262–3**, 268, 271
Bible, 136, 154
Big Five Personality Traits, 210
bilingualism, 244
black swans, 67
Boag, Simon, 81–2, 277
bodily context (in conflict), 182
bodily disciplines: see *bodywork*
body, 7–8, **35–41**, 57, 68, 70, 115, 119, 132, 138–9, 141, 169, 183, 187, 194–5, 199, 218, 220, 223–4, 273. See also *embodiment, embodied meaning*
body language, 263
bodywork, 9, 223, 225. See also *yoga, tai chi*
borders: see *boundaries*
bottom-up universality, 1
boundaries, 19, 45, 50, 60, 101, 107, 111, 113, 115–16, **122–5**, 127, 184, 206, 245, 272
brain, 10, 19, 29–30, 36, 37, 59, 71, 78, 93, 116–17, 119, 171, 177, 186, 229, 267
brain hemispheres, 10, 116–17. See also *left hemisphere* and *right hemisphere*
brain in a vat, 29–30
Broca's area, 19
Buddha (Gautama), 36, 43, 127, 132, 136, 151, 164, 186, 214–15, 224, 249–50
Buddhism, 3–4, 43–4, 67, 76, 94, 101–2, 113, 115, 119, 127, 130, 132, 136–7, 148, 152, 173, 177, 199–200, 204, 214, 217–18, 238, 242–3, 256, 268
Burnyeat, Miles, 31, 278

Calvin, Jean, 155
capitalism, 145, 149
care, 10, 221, 226, **232–3**, 234–6, 271–2
catastrophizing, 268

categorization, 16, 94, 113–14, 116, 215
Catholicism, 26, 43, 136, 144, 266
causality, 123
causation, 143
centrist politics, 27
character, 113, 164–5, 168, 205, **206–7**, 209, 217, 241–2
Christ, 214–15
Christian Middle Way, The, 26
Christianity, 19, 24, 26, 43, 107, 124, 150, 152, 155, 157, 196–7, 224
church government, 155
clear and distinct perceptions (Descartes), 42
climate change, 58, 65, 103–4, 179, 191
Cognitive Behavioural Therapy, 255, 268
cognitive dissonance, 8
cognitive linguistics, 20. See *embodied meaning*
comedy, 245
communicability, 48, 50
communication, 47, 51–2, 210, 227, 233, **247–50**, 251–2, 263, 270, 272
complexity, 6, 62, **64–7**, 68, 78, 87–8, 97, 107, 110, 113, 145, 156, 165, 173, 180–1, 191, 194–5, 206, 228, 230, 238, 241, 247, 249
conceptual art, 240
conceptual boundaries, 122
conceptual models, 122
conceptual space, 98, 123–4
conditionality, 15, 87. See also *provisionality*
confidence, 17, 19, 29, **30**, 32–3, 35, 37, 40–1, 58, 161, 202–3, 210, 256, 259–60
confirmation bias, 42, 45, 95, 125, 171. See also *bias*
conflict, 3, 6–9, 24, 27–9, 33–4, 54–5, 57, 73–4, 76, 79, 81, 94, 97, 100, 114–15, 126–7, 133, 136, 143, 147, 155, 162, **168–74**, 175–6, 178–9, **180–4**, 185–7, 189–91, 194–7, 199–200, 203–5, 209–10, 213, 217–22, 226–31, 233, 238–9, 250, 254–5, 262, 266, 271
connectivity, 58
conspiracy theory, 31
constitutions, 230
contemplative practices, 268
context, *passim*. See also *contextualization*
contextualization, 9, 35, 124, 128, 147, **181–4**, 198, 224, 227, 255, 258
continuity, 37, **98–102**, 103–29, 141, 163, 166. See also *incrementality*
~ of persons, 100, **113–16**, 119
~ of space, 101, **122–5**
~ of time, 101, **117–21**, 122
~ of training, 102, **126–9**, 163
conventional morality, 173
corpus callosum, 168, 171
cosmic justice, 132
courage, 7, 207
craving, 35–6, 39, 141, 171
credibility, 208, 255, 258, **264–6**, 271
credibility assessment, 255, **264–6**
Crimean War, 157
critical dialogue, 270–1
critical thinking, 4, 8–9, 125, 149, 174, 183, 185, 199, 208–9, 213, 229, **255–66**, 267–70, 272
cross-modal perception, 39
culture, 37, 79, 100, 153, 159, 165–6, 245, 252, 260
Czikszentmihalyi, Mihaly, 200, 278

Damasio, Antonio, 25, 223, 278
Dawkins, Richard, 115, 278
death, 41, 48, 85, 106, 170
decisiveness, 56, 112, 140, 142
deduction, 1, 55, 93–5, 144, 175, 211, 218, 259
deformation professionelle, 206, 282
democracy, 158, 165, 198, 229, 238, 251, 254
denialism, 22, 34, **151–5**
Descartes, René, 17, 22, 29, 36, 42, 55, 278

desire, 8-9, 33, 52-3, 56-8, 62-3, 75-6, 81-2, 86, 91, 93, 105, 117-19, 123, 149, 155, 157-8, 163, 168-9, 185, **186-7**, 188-90, 192, 194, 197, 200-1, 203, 212, 215, 219, **221-36**, 237-8, 240, 255, 270
detachment, 31
determinism, 43, 132, 138-9, 142, 156, 176, 259, 267
developmental psychology, 127
dialectics, 73, **74-5**, 76, 137
dialogue, 242, 263, 270-2. See also *dialectics, discussion, communication*
diary, 49, 242, 269
dichotomy, 11, 26, 35-6, 110
discipline, 4, 44-5, 127, 255-6, 266-7
discontinuity, 6, 14, 20, 37, 86, 98, **99**, 100, 103, 105, **109-12**, 114-17, 120, 123, 129, 140-2, 191, 213, 217-18
discussion, 4, 40, 48, 53, 66, 74, 79, 90, 100, 111, 116, 120, 136, 142, 149, 175-6, 198, 219, 226, **227-8**, 230-1, 237, 239, 243, 247, 251, 267, 271. See also *dialogue, communication*
disembodiment, 12, 37, 41, 51, 174
diversity, 64
Dix, William, 157, 278
dogma, 55, 253, 269
dogmatism, 79
Don't Think of an Elephant!, **25**, 29, 280
dopamine, 119, 171
double-blind testing, 6
doubt, 15, 40, 43, 48-9, 90, 96, 181, 208. See also *scepticism*
dream argument, 17
dualisms: see *dichotomy*
dukkha, 76, 177
Dweck, Carol, 128, 278

echo chambers, 243
education, 10, 20, 71, 77-8, 190, 229, 238, 245, 247, **252-4**, 261, 266-8, 270-1

effectiveness, 3, 29, 33-4, 66, 88
ego depletion, 70
Eightfold Path (Buddhist), 214, 217-18
elephant, blind men and (parable), 78
eliminativism, 37
embodied meaning, 20, 44, 218, 250
embodiment, 3, 4, 20, 33, 35, 37, 40, 53, 98, 109, 111, 141, 247. See also *embodied meaning*
empathy, 54
empirical justification, 12, 218
Enlightenment, 210
epistemology, 44, 172
Erasmus, Desiderius, 42, 279
error focus, 3, 10, 77
error, 1, 3, 10, **17**, 23, 44, 77, 88, 90, 175, **178**
esotericism, 162
essentialism, 113
eternalism (Buddhism), 132, **136-7**, 148
ethical practice, 217
ethics, 11, 33, 55, 91, 109, 111, 116, 138, 151, 172, 207, 221, 225
even-handedness, 3, 20, 42, 46, 132, **135-9**
evolution, 58
excluded middle, 110, 153
exercise, 8, 139, 192, 219-20, 222, 242, 272
experiential context (of conflict), 182
expertise, 34, 128-9, 208, 264-5
extroversion, 210

facts, 13, 52, 54, 252, 266, 267
factual claims, 52, 54, 90, 92
fact-value distinction, 20, 33
fallacies, 120, 255, 258, 262
fallacy of composition, 106
fallacy of moderation, 159
fallacy of the single cause, 106
false consensus, 152
false dichotomy, 19, 23, 26, 35, 52, 259. See also *restricting the options*

false speech, 249
falsehood, 12, 22–3, 49, 52, 89, 153, 219, 228
falsifiability, 60
families, 250
fast thinking, **69–72**, 83
fissiparousness, 151, **154–5**
Five Principles of Middle Way Philosophy *passim*. Introduced **1–11**
fixed mindset, 128
flips, 64, 118, **151–2**, 154–6, 172
flow, 200
fluctuation, 64
focusing (practice), 38, 237, 242
foreign languages, 189, 237–8, **244–5**, 256
Forest (in Buddha's life), 136, 151, 164
foundations, 42
fragility, 30, 33, 45, 55, 171, 174
fragmentation of meaning, 218–19, 237–8
framing, 6–8, 25, 27, 45, 65, **75–7**, 86, 99, 107, 122, 133, 136, 138, 142, 154, 157, **175–9**, 181, 197, 213, 228, 249, 267–9
freedom, 132, 138, 142–3
freewill, 59, 104, 126, 132, 139, 142–3, 155, 176, 259, 267
Freud, Sigmund, 81
friendship, 10, 58, 161, 226, 232, **233–4**, 235–6
frustration, 73, 76, 119, 175, **176–8**, 180, 187
fundamentalism, 95, 130, 196

Gandalf (fiction character), 242
Gandhi, Mahatma, 106, 181
gender, 260
Gendlin, Eugene, 38, 242, 279
geometry, 90
Germany, 158, 181
gestalt, 106, 116
Gettier, Edmund, 13, 279
Gladwell, Malcolm, 105, 279

goals, 10, 17, 38, 52, 65–6, 70, 77, 112, 114, 117–18, 124, 167–71, 185–6, 189–90, 195–6, 200, 202, 227–8, 233, 250, 260, 271
God, 3, 7, 23–4, 26, 45, 48, 54, 95, 131–3, 135, 138, 140–3, 149, 151, 172, 184, 203, 224, 234, 264
God archetype, 214, 234
God's eye view, 36, 44
Golden Mean (Aristotle), 137, 280
gossip, 249
Greece, 78
green environments, 222
group binding, 20, 174, 196
group identity, 77, 85, 107
group conformity, 33
groups, 1, 27, 33, 54, 100, 130–1, 136, 152, 155, 164, 168, 172, 178, 180, **194–8**, 203, 209–11, 213, 219, 226, 229, 232, 236, 246, 250, 260, 264, 267, 270–1
Groupthink, 152, 280
growth mindset, 126, 128
guru, 205, 208, 213, 234
guru trap, 205, 208

Hamlet (drama character), 123
haptic factors, 261
harsh speech, 249–50
hatred, 83–4, 195, 230
hedonic treadmill, 204
Hegel, Georg, 74, 79
Hegelianism, 79
Heidegger, Martin, 120
hero, 234
hierarchization, 162
hierarchy, 58, 137, 162, 164–5, 199
hindrance, 212
Hinduism, 155
history, 20, 74, 103, 115, 133, 154, 194, 257, 266
humanities, 87, 238
Hume, David, 4, 29, 31, 43, 44, 279
humour, 81, 83, **84–5**, 237, **245–6**
Huxley, Thomas, 131
hypocrisy, 43, 157

idealism, 37, 66, 132, 138, 149, 214, 267
idealization, 91, 210
ideals, 1, 3, 214, 251
ideology, 142, 145, 151–2, 230
Ikemoto, Satoshi, 171, 279
imagination, 8, 25–6, 30, 47, 56, 62, **74**, 124, 177, 190, 192, 209, 243, 259
immature defences, 83
impatience, 117–21
impermanence, 101, 119, 268
impracticality, 5, 20, 29, 33–4, 42, 48, 59, 266
In Over Our Heads, 127, 162, 280
incrementality, 4, 6–7, 46, 53–4, 63, 66, 81, 86, 96–7, **98–129**, 138, 141, 153, 158–9, 173, 191, 199, 203, 208, 213, 217–19, 232, 247–8, 253, 260, 262
incrementalization, 125
indecisiveness, 93, 158–9
indefeasibility, 49
India, 106, 181
indoctrination, 267
infinite regression, 12, 18
inflation of logic, 94
inflation of metaphysics, 15, 18, 48
informal fallacies, 262. See also *fallacies*
ingroup language, 248
ingroup-outgroup bias, 152
insight, 104, 123, 275
inspiration, 47–8, **203**, 214, 224, 234, 240, 264
integration, 1, 4, 8–9, 22, 28, 31, 39, 54, 58, 67, 76, 83–4, 91, 97, 150, **168–211**, 212–73
integration of belief, 9, 150, 185, 187, **190–3**, 201, 237, **255–73**
integration of desire, 9, **185–7,** 189, 191, 200–1, 203, **221–36**, 237–8
integration of meaning, 9, **188–90**, 200–2, 226, 235, **237–54**
internal family systems therapy, 224
interoception, 39, 223–4

interpretation, 29, 31–2, 43, 47, 86, 95, 112–13, 141, 144–5, 147, 154, 156, 177, 183, 201, 203, 213, 241, 250, 254–5, 258, **263–4**, 266, 268
intoxicants, 221
intractability, 136, 139, **180–4**, 196
introversion, 210
investment, 202
IQ, 146
Islam, 155, 157, 196

jargon, 248
Jesuits, 266
jhana, 36, 76, 199, 204, 213, 230
Johnson, Mark, 38–9, 50, 65, 122, 244, 248, 280
journalism, 271–2
Judaism, 155, 184
judgement, 1–2, 4, 8, **10**, 23, 27, 30, 33, 45–6, 52–4, 56, 58–9, 61–3, 65–9, 73–4, 76, 80, 83, 85, 87–8, 90–7, 100, 109–12, 114–15, 127, 130, 141, 147, 149, 154, 156, 159–60, 164–5, 167, 172–3, 175, 180–1, 186, 191, 195–6, 199, 202, 205–6, 209, 215, 217, 228, 231, 234, 261–3, 265–6, 275
judgement focus, 3, **10**
Jung, Carl, 4, 161, 163–4, 279–80
justice, 55, 132, 138
justification, 5, 12, 14–18, 20, 22, 26, 30–1, 33, 44, 52–4, 86, 88, 90, 92–3, **95–6**, 125, 141, 154–5, 160, 172–3, 176, 214, 227, 255, 258–9, 260, 262–4, 271, 275

Kahneman, Daniel, 69, 70, 71, 88–9, 148, 163, 280
Kegan, Robert, 126–7, 162–7, 178, 209, 280
kidneys, 57
killing, 54, 92, 114, 230
knowledge, 1, 3, **12–21**, 35, 37, 40, 42–4, 49, 55, 127, 140–2, 188, 190, 238, 245, 253, 260
knowledge by acquaintance, 13

known unknowns, 12
Korzybski, Alfred, 52, 280

labour, 235
Lakoff, George, 25, 38, 50, 65, 90, 122, 244, 280
Langer, Ellen, 68-9, 252, 280
language, 15-16, **19**, 39, 48, 51, 57, 79, 88, 94, 105, 112, 227, 242, 244, 248, 260, 270
language game, 48, 50-1
lateralization of brain: see *brain hemispheres*
law, 37, 90, **109-10**, 112, 115, 136, 153, 230, 267
Le Poidevin, Robin, 140, 280
learning, 34, 38, 102, 104-5, **126-9**, 178, 180, 190, **237-45**, 252-3, 257, 267, 270
left hemisphere (of brain), 36, 40, 82, 98-9, 116-17, 170-1
left pre-frontal cortex, 36, 170-1. See also *left hemisphere, pre-frontal cortex*
limbic system, 171
line of ancestors (Dawkins), 115-16
linguistics, 19-20, 44, 49, 51-2, 76, 78, 142, 239-40, 247-8. See also *language*
listening, 226, 235, 242, 252
liturgy, 251
logic, 7, 18, 74, 90, 94, 258-9, 272. See also *reasoning*
logical positivism, 135
loving-kindness, 238, 242-3
Lukashenko, Alexander, 114
lumping, 7, 26, 130, 136, **144-50**, 158
Luther, Martin, 136, 154-5

MacIntyre, Alasdair, 207, 281
macro level agnosticism, 162, 165, 167
malicious speech, 249
margin of error, 88
Marinoff, Lou, 137, 281
marriage, 61, 251

Martin, John, 241
Marx, Karl, 74, 222
Marxism, 94, 148, 194
Maslow's Hierarchy of Needs, 58
materialism, 37, 138, 155
mathematics, 18, 90, 176
Matrix, The, 31
Maturana, Humberto, 20
McCarthy, Joseph, 153
McGilchrist, Iain, 65, 82, 94, 116-17, 258, 281
meaning, 8-9, 12, **19-20**, 22, 25, 27, 29, 31, 37-40, 44-51, 59, 65, 70, 73-4, 76-7, 79, 86, 90, 102, 104-5, 111, 123, 141, 149, 168, 177, 184-5, 188-90, 192, 194, 200-4, 212-13, 215, 217-18, 224, 226, 235-55, 258-9, 263-4, 267. See also *embodied meaning, integration of meaning*
meaningful education, 247, 252
media, 13, 228, 254, 264-5, 270-1
mediation, 197-8, **226-7**, 270
meditation, 17, 147, 174, 182-3, 187, 199-200, 202, 204, 209, 213, 217, **223-4**, 235, 237-8, 240, 242-3. See also *mindfulness*
metaphor, 1, 50, 59, 70, 73, 93, 102, 125, 175-8, 190, 241, 244, 260
metaphysics, 1, 3, 7, 9, 11, 23, 25, 37, 44, 48, 54, 66, 79, 101, 113, 115, 131, **135-6**, 138, 142-3, 147, 149, 172-3, 175-6, 231, 251, 264
metonymy, 50
metta-bhavana, 238, 242
micro level agnosticism, 162, 165-6
Middle Way, Middle Way Philosophy, *passim*. Introduced 1-11
mind, 2, 8, 27, 35-7, 57, 62, 74, 78, 82, 101, 109, 113, 123, 132-3, 138-9, 147, 170, 172, 177, 218, 226, 229, 234, 243, 247, 267, 268. See also *brain, mind-brain*
mind-body system, 8, 170
mind-brain, 37, 78, 218, 247

mindfulness, 8-9, 35-6, 39-41, 50, 67-8, 124, 147, 185, 187, 212, 217, 221, **223-5**, 240
misunderstandings, 4, 19, 131-2
'mitigated' scepticism, 43-4
models (cognitive), 7, 39, 54, 59-60, 67, 74, 90, 94, 97, 122, 136, 143, 161, 163, 166, 172, 176-9, 209-10, 217-18, 221, 244-5, 253, 259-60
moderation, 137, 140, 158-9
modernity, 77
Molotov-Ribbentrop Pact, 157
monism, 37
Montaigne, Michel de, 43
Moore, G.E., 32, 281
moral context (of conflict), 182
Mr Micawber (fictional character), 242
multi-scalar complexity, 64
Murray, Charles, 146, 281
music, 152, 188, 240, 252
Myers-Briggs Index, 210

natural law, 137
naturalism, 44, 94, 147
naturalized epistemology, 44
nature, 4, 17, 37, 43, 48, 54, 100, 103, 111, 172, 203, 208, 214. See also *green environments*
negation, 5, **22-8**, 50-1, 56, 65, 118
negativity, 5, 34
neomania, 118, 120
nervous system, 25, 70, 186. See also *neural networks*
neural networks, 56, 58-9, 229
neuroscience, 3, 78-9
neutrality or bias (credibility criterion), 265
nihilism, 3, 33, 132, 136-7, 148, 156
Nixon, Richard, 25
'no self', 113, 173
non-violent communication, 227. See also *mediation*
novel, 238, 240-2, 247, 252
Nuñez, Rafael, 90, 280

objectivity, 52-3, 261-3
obsessiveness, 9
Ockham's Razor, 22-3, 280
one-sidedness, 135
ontology, 64, 109-10, 151, 153. See also *metaphysics*
Oppy, Graham, 140, 281
optionality, 1-2, 15, 23, 26-7, 48, **56-64**, 65-70, 73-4, 82, 85, 87, 93-4, 95, 97, 99, 122-4, 137, 145, 155, 174-5, 228, 233, 235, 239-40, 244
ordinary language, 32
organic life, 7, 186
Ottoman Empire, 157
over-confidence, 30, 115
over-specialization, 73, 245, 267

pacifism, 231
Palace (in Buddha's life), 136, 151, 164
Palestinian- Israeli conflict, 180-1
Pali Canon, 4, 43
Panksepp, Jaak, 171, 279
paradox, 42, 46, 204
particularity, 52-5, 261
passive aggression, 83
patience, 61, 117, 178, 207
Pavlov, Ivan, 259
pax, 194-6
peace, 54, 161, 194-8
peer review, 6
persons (personal identity), 19, 100, **113-16**, 119, 126, 164, 170, 189, 210, 224, 231-2, 242-3
perspective, 4, 22, **35-7**, 44, 64, 79, 101, 112, 140-1, 172-3, 176-82, 189, 219, 235, 248, 270
philosophy, 3, 13, 15, 37, 40, 42, **44-5**, 70, 74, **78-80**, 94, 112-13, 155, 173, 175, 206, **267-8**
philosophy of mind, 37
philosophy of religion, 4
philosophy of science, 4
physicalism, 35, 37

physics, 66, 257, 265
Piaget, Jean, 126, 163
piano, 71
Pinker, Steven, 238, 281
Plato, 74, 195
pleasure, 42, 199, 203-4, 222
political activity, 252
political campaigning, 10, 226, **228-30**, 270
politician, 271
politics, 42, 45, 228-30, 247, 254, 270-1
popes, 136, 154
Popper, Karl 74, 281
postmodernism, 135
power, 107, 132, 146, 154, 162, 164-5, **180-1**, 204, 208, 229, 234, 248-9, 251, 271
practical discontinuity, 109-12
practicality, 3, 10, 32-3, 212
practice, *passim*. See especially 212-73
Practice of Agnosticism, The, 156
practices, 8-10, 21, 40, 46, 95, 124-6, 151, 180, 184, 187, 193, 197-8, 202, 208, **212-73**
Pratasevich, Roman, 114
prayer, 224
pre-frontal cortex, 171, 186. See also *brain*
principle of charity, 263
private language argument, 49
probability, 19, 23-4, 30, 52, 61, 69, 70-1, **86-92**, 96, 138, 153. See also *probabilizing*
probabilizing, **86-92**, 97, 227
procrastination, 118, 120
professions, 245
projection, 3, 9, 48, 171, 203, 234
proliferation, 9, 171, 200. See also *reinforcing feedback loops, rumination*
propositional knowledge, 13. See also *knowledge*
Protestantism, 136, 154

prototype, 65
provisional belief, 47. See also *provisionality*
provisionality, 4-6, 22, 26, 28, 30, 36, 46, 48, **56-97**, 113, 130-1, 137-8, 147, 165, 176, 184, 189, 191, 202, 215, 219, 227, 229, 232, 246, 249, 263, 266
provisionality markers, 227
psychoanalysis, 81
psychological integration, 168, 198, 226. See also *integration*
psychology, 3, 24, 44, 45, 69, 78-9, 81, 83, 106, 120, 152, 163, 178, 204, 206, 267
psychotherapy, 1, 4, 9, 224-5
Pyrrhonism, 16, 22, 282

Quakers, 75
qualitative research, 87
quantitative research, 87
quantum physics, 66, 78
Quine, Willem, 44, 282

rationalism, 42-4
RAVEN (credibility mnemonic), 265
reaction formation, 84
realism, 132, 214-15, 267
reality, **12-21**, 31, 37, 40, 47-8, 86, 90, 113, 141, 142, 153, 160, 203, 218, 245, 249. See also *truth, knowledge*
reasoning, 16, 70, 71, 93-5, 255-7, **258-9**, 260, 262, 271-2
recognizing contexts (critical thinking skill), 258
recreation, 9, 221, **222**
Red Book (Jung), 161, 279, 280
reflection, 5, 23, 30, 54, 65, 69, 74, 89, 98, 100, 103, 209, 223, 231, 233, 255, 258, **268-9**
Reformation, 154
reforms, 151, 154, 254
reframing, 25, 27, 169, **175-9**, 180-2, 196, 229, 255, 256

reinforcing feedback loops, 3, 36, 76, 103, 154, 158, 169–70, 177, 182, 204, 222, 263, 268
relativism, 3, **33**, 132, 138, 151, 155, 261, 267
religion, 4, 45, 78, 91, 110, 197, 214, 278
religious education, 155
religious experience, 47, 182, **184**
representationalism, 14, 16, **19–20**, 36–7, 40, 42, 46–7, 86, 90, 111, 141, 145, 218, 247–8, 250
repression, 31, 63, 74, 81–3, 85, 97, 104, 132, **171**, 204, 222, 224, 232, 235
reputation (credibility criterion), 265
resilience, 64, 66
responsibility, 3, 29, **33**, 55, 106, 124, 127, 143, 208, 248, 261
restricting the options, 9, 56. See also *false dichotomy*
revelation, 26, 54, 140
revolution, 104, 151, 154
right hemisphere (of brain), 65, 82, 99, 117, 258
ritual, 10, 219, 247, **250–1**, 254
romanticism, 234
rules, 91, 93, 95, **109–10**, 112, 184, 221, 231
rumination, 223–4. See also *proliferation, reinforcing feedback loops*
Russell, Bertrand, 22–4
Russell's Teapot, 22–4
Russia, 157

salvation, 155
Samaritans, 235
Sangharakshita, 76, 130, 218, 278, 282
Sanjaya Bellatthaputta, 43
satori, 218
sceptical slippage, 26, 134, **151–6**
scepticism, 4, 5, **12–55**, 56, 59, 64, 70, 79, 82, 90, 92, 97, 131, 151, 184, 202, 219, 245, 253, 260, 272
schemas, 176

school, 173, 222, 261. See also *education*
science, 4, 6, 20, 44, 55, **60**, 238, 261, 266
scientific method, 4, 60, 147, 215
selective scepticism, **42–6**, 79
self-confidence, 115. See also *confidence*
self-organization, 65
senses, **16–18**, 35, 39, 42, 44, 107, 122, 185
sensual art, 239–40
sequencing, 98–9, 101, 117
sex, 85
Sextus Empiricus, 4, 16, 282
sexual abuse, 181
sexual transgression, 231
Shakespeare, William, 123
shalom, 194, 196–7
signs, 90, 199, 206
Skinner, Burrhus, 259
slow thinking, 68–72, 97
slowness, 62, 68–72
social context (of conflict), 182
social morality, 109
social proof, 152
social psychology, 194
social rules, 107, 109, 112
sociology, 78, 194
socio-political integration, 168, **194–8**, 226–36, 247–54, 270–3
socio-political level, 8–9, 165, 168, 170, 173–4, 179, 180, 194–8, 212, 215, 219, 226–36, 238, 247–54, 270–3
solidarity, 230–2
solitary walking, 269
somatic marker hypothesis, 223
Sorites Paradox, 111
soul, 132
space, 23, 35, 50, 98, 101, **122–5**, 176, 183
spatial context (in conflict), 182
specialism, 77–9
specialization, 45, 73, **77–9**, 245

sport, 219-20
St Augustine (of Hippo), 120
stage theory, 164. See also *Kegan*
stochastic resonance, 59
straw man, 158-60
stream entry, 218
stretch, 31, 33, 48, 55, 91, 183
striatum, 186
strong agnosticism, **140-3**
study (as practice), 182-3, 202, 212, 238, 245, 256, 258, 261, 266
subjectivism, 26
subjectivity, 52-3
sublimation, 81, 83, **84**, 85
substitution, 27, 45, 146, 148-9, 171
sunk cost fallacy, 120, 148
superficiality, 157
supernaturalism, 26, 214
supervenience, 194
suppression, 63, **81-5**, 97, 171, 246
survivorship bias, 120
symbolic art, 240
symbolism, 212, 214, 242
symbols, 1, 3, 9, 36, 38-9, 48-50, 70, 73, 90-1, 100, 124, 185, 188-90, 197, 210, 214-15, 219, 224, 226, **237-9**, 240-3, 245, 247-8, 252-3, 255
synergy, 64
synthesis, 5, 38, 62, **73-80**, 85, 94
systems, 4, 18, 20, 44, 55, **64-7**, 69, 76, 78, 97-100, 103-5, 124, 127, 142, 165, 170, 194-5, 204, 210, 218, 238, 247
systems theory, 4, 78. See also *systems*

tai chi, 9, 187, 223
Taleb, Nassim, 66, 282
teacher, 81, 107, 127, 151, 190, 209, 234-5, 253, 261, 267-8, 271
teaching of the arts, 252
teetotalism, 221
teleology, 169
temporal biases, 120
temporal context (in conflict), 182

temporal fallacies, 120
temporary integration, 168, **199-204**
theft, 231
theism, 132, 138, 149, 267
theology, 42, 45, 124
thesis, 74-5. See also *dialectics*
Threefold Path, The (Buddhist), 217-18
Threefold Practice, 9, 212, **216-20**, 221-73
time, 26, 33, 49-50, 53-4, 57, 61-2, 65-6, 68-72, 76, 83-5, 91, 98-108, 113-15, **117-21**, 122, 127-8, 148, 151, 160-65, 170-3, 176, 186-7, 195, 197, 200, 202, 218, 221, 224, 232-3, 240, 249, 266, 269
time-framing, 56
tipping points, 65, 76, 100, **103-8**, 126, 163
tolerance, 83
top-down universality, 1, 10, 172
totalitarian regimes, 74
training, 77, 102, 125, **126-9**, 142, 159, 163, 234, 265-6, 268, 274. See also *education, learning*
transition, 127, 165-6
travel, 92, 243-4, 237
tribalism, 220
truth, 2-3, 10, **12-21**, 22-3, 27, 42, 47-8, 111, 112, 115, 119, 120, 137, 153, 172-3, 203, 228, 248, **249-50**, 261, 265
truth-conditional theory of meaning, 19
truthfulness, **249-50**, 265
two mules, 75-6, 176-7, 183

Udana, 127, 279
UK, 27, 235, 250, 254
uncertainty, 1, 5, **12-55**, 64, 66, 86, 88, 106, 131, 141, 151, 153, 191, 202, 207, 213
unconscious, 57, 81-3, 170-1
unholy alliances, 8, 26-7, 130, 134, **157-61**
unity of the virtues, 207

universal aspiration, 3, 10
universal morality, 55
universality, 10, 54, 209, 227, 239, 261
unknown unknowns, 12, 30, 89–90
utilitarianism, 155

vaccines, 15, 88
vagueness, 4, 19, 50-1, 54, 88, 107, 111, 263
Vaillant, George, 83-4, 282
values, 3, 9, 19–20, 24, 33, 44–5, 48, 50, **52–5**, 77, 86, 90–2, 111–12, 116, 123, 128, 138, 151–2, 155, **163–6**, 172–3, 177, 250. See also *ethics*
Varela, Francisco, 20
variation, 64, 114, 218, 222
vested interest (credibility criterion), 265
violence, 114, 226, **230–1**, 238–9
virtue ethics, 206
virtues, 112, 205, 207, 265

visual arts, 240
vitality affects, 39
volunteering, 226, **235**, 236
voting system, 27

war, 12, 54, 75, 76, 180, 209, 227
wariness of serpents, 27, 150, 161
weak agnosticism, 136, **140–3**
weak links (neural), 56, 59–61
weighing up, 63, **93–7**, 148, 227, 260, 265
Western Buddhism, 67, 130, 218
Western philosophy: see *philosophy*
Wilber, Ken, 79
wisdom, 128–30, 217
Wittgenstein, Ludwig, 22, 32, **47–51**, 247, 280, 282
Wittgensteinianism, 247

yoga, 9, 182, 187, 201, 223

Zwingli, Ulrich, 155

www.ingramcontent.com/pod-product-compliance
Lightning Source LLC
Chambersburg PA
CBHW061244230426
43662CB00020B/2416